How To Triple Your Money Every Year
With Stock Index Futures

How To Triple Your Money Every Year With Stock Index Futures

An Insider's Strategy to Tap the Riches of Wall Street

By George Angell

WINDSOR BOOKS, BRIGHTWATERS, N.Y.

Published by Windsor Books
P. O. Box 280
Brightwaters, N.Y. 11718

Manufactured in the United States of America

ISBN 0-930233-03-4

CAVEAT: It should be noted that all commodity trades, patterns, charts, systems, etc., discussed in this book are for illustrative purposes only and are not to be construed as specific advisory recommendations. Further note that no method of trading or investing is foolproof or without difficulty, and past performance is no guarantee of future performance. All ideas and material presented are entirely those of the author and do not necessarily reflect those of the publisher or bookseller.

For My Mother and Father

Acknowledgements

While I am alone responsible for its contents, this book is the result of the many helpful insights and observations of friends in the trading community. Among those to whom I owe gratitude for sharing their thoughts are Barry Haigh, a member of the Chicago Mercantile Exchange's IMM and IOM divisions, for his insightful comments on the art of floor trading; Joe English, a stock index specialist with Prudential-Bache Securities in Newport Beach, California, who first recognized the promise and potential of the LSS 3-Day Cycle Method; and fellow-trader Jeff Gordon of Los Angeles who so thoughtfully shared his observations on the futures markets. I would also like to thank Earl Hadady and Susan C. Yonai, of the Professional Chart Service division of Hadady Publications in Pasadena, California, for providing their charts and Joel Optholt of Chicago for his services in preparing the art work. Without their patient co-operation, my task would have been much more difficult.

G. A.

Table of Contents

Will the System Self-Destruct?…Time and Price…The Timing Dilemma
…Putting the LSS System To Work For You…Testing the Waters…
When Everything Goes Right—Or Wrong!…How the Momentum
Trend Indicator Works…Money Management…The Most Frequently-
Asked Questions About LSS…Beware the Psychological Pitfalls

APPENDICES

Figures

Tables

Preface

The futures markets have changed significantly since I published my first book, *Winning in the Commodities Market*, in May, 1979. What was once primarily an agricultural market, designed to transfer risk from the nation's growers and processors of grains, livestock, and other food and fiber products to a small group of highly-specialized commodity speculators, has suddenly grown into an international arena of sophisticated financial instrument trading. Foreign currency dealers in Zurich, precious metals arbitrageurs in London, livestock breeders in Nebraska—all transmit orders to buy and sell in today's commodity pits. In recent years, they've been joined by the Wall Street crowd who, according to one market sage, "wouldn't know a soybean from a jellybean." Nor, for that matter, would they much care to know the difference since their primary area of interest is financial futures—Treasury bonds and bills, Certificates of Deposit, Eurodollars, and the like. In just over a half-dozen years, this segment of the futures market has grown from just 3.9 million contracts traded in 1976 to over 42 million last year. And, given the explosion in financial futures trading in recent months, the end is nowhere in sight. *Business Week* recently heralded the arrival of the new stock index futures by frontpaging the headline *"A Hot New World"* across its cover. To deal with the surge in trading, the Chicago Mercantile Exchange, home of the booming Standard & Poor's 500 futures contract, recently abandoned its quarters on Chicago's Jackson Boulevard for a new trading facility across the river. The old "Merc" was merely the size of a football field; the new "Merc" can accommodate two Super Bowls. Exchange officials credit the growth to the spectacularly successful S&P 500 contract—the fastest-growing new contract ever introduced on a futures exchange.

This change in character in the commodities market, from farm futures to financial futures, is not surprising. Recent economic events have made what *Forbes* Magazine calls the "fastest-growing market in America" the center of high-stakes financial action. "Futures markets thrive on economic uncertainty, high interest rates and violent price swings,'' former Chicago Mercantile Exchange chairman Jack Sandner explained a couple of years ago. ''And despite the growth of recent years, the market is still in its infancy.'' At the time, the high-flying interest-rate futures market was setting volume records. But today, due to a lessening in high interest rates, the action has shifted from interest-rate futures to the newest wrinkle in the booming financial futures market, stock index futures. Almost three years old at this writing, stock index futures have taken over as the ''hot new act'' in the futures game, according to a recent article in the *New York Times*. ''No new investment instruments have attracted so many investors in so short a time,'' writes the newspaper's columnist, H. J. Maidenberg. ''Nor have so many market analysts, brokers, professional and ordinary investors struggled so hard to understand their use.'' Apparently, along with investor enthusiasm has grown a need for up-to-the-minute information, explaining the intricacies of this new, fast-paced market.

The boom in the index market is evident among small investors and large institutions alike. The major wire houses, long content to emphasize the equity side of their retail brokerage business, have found the new index futures accounting for a growing share of their customer business. Not to miss out on a potentially lucrative opportunity, the large institutions, which include pension funds, banks, insurance firms, even universities and the like, have joined the fray in the stock index pits. The large institutions, it should be noted, use the index markets to protect—or hedge—their holdings. The individual speculator, on the other hand, is apt to be playing the wiggles in the market, trying to outguess the averages—a favorite game of investors for years. But now it is really possible. Although their goals may differ, it is a testament to the versatility of the index markets that both small and large investors alike find these highly-leveraged new financial products suitable for their individual needs. To meet the growing need, the nation's exchanges are introducing new index products at a rapid pace—so rapid, in fact, that the Securities & Exchange Commission has called for a moratorium on new index products until the brokerage community has an opportunity to educate its employees on the current crop of financial instruments. The Commodity Futures Trading Commission, whose job it is to regulate the futures industry, has slapped a $10,000 filing fee on any exchange attempting to introduce any new futures contract—yet still the newspapers announce new ideas almost daily for financial index trading. During the several months' of writing this book, more than half a dozen new stock index products commenced trading. Such is the feverish growth.

WHAT'S BEHIND ALL THE EXCITEMENT?

Obviously, the main attraction of the new stock index futures market is the opportunity to reap sizable profits—or, at least from an institution's standpoint, hedge risks that might otherwise result in portfolio losses. Fueled by a soaring stock market that roared to life over a year ago, the new index contracts, which are leveraged with as little as five percent of the total contract's value down, have outpaced, on occasion, even the total value of all the stocks traded on the New York Stock Exchange. In an atmosphere that caused one broker to quip, "If you jumped out the window right now, you'd probably go up," it isn't surprising that these new financial instruments have caught on with a vengeance. What's surprising is that market analysts fully expect the daily volume to double and even triple in the months ahead.

Nevertheless, the success of the new markets comes as a surprise to some industry insiders. Many new contracts enjoy a brief stellar performance prior to a retreat into the doldrums once the novelty wears off. Witness the near dormant markets in broilers, eggs, plywood, and potatoes—all commodities that once enjoyed considerable trading success. Not so stock index futures. From the very first, they enjoyed wide support among the financial community. More significantly, contrary to the expectations of many, the new index contracts have thrived on three separate futures exchanges, not to mention the proliferating number of options on indexes which are traded in New York and Chicago in higher numbers every day. Here again, stock index futures proved the exception to the generally accepted notion that when the same futures contract is traded on more than one exchange only one survives.

One reason cited for the boom in stock index futures trading is high volatility. Pegged as they are to the major stock averages, the new index futures have soared along with the averages. "When the contracts were originated," explains one broker, "I don't think anyone ever dreamed they would be this volatile." Highly leveraged, the stock index futures magnify profits—and losses—when the market rises or falls.

Just how dramatically this leverage can translate into substantial profits and losses is sometimes hard to envision. "You can easily lose $100,000 a day down here," one S&P floor trader told me. "That isn't a lot of money in this market." For the uninformed, the potential bonanza can easily turn into a financial nightmare—as it did, tragically, last year for the president of the New York Cotton Exchange, who committed suicide after a series of losses in index futures just as the big bull market was beginning.

Despite the high risks involved, these new markets have found acceptance among the professional floor traders, which is perhaps the most promising sign that they are here to stay. Quick to size up a contract's prospects, the professionals are drawn to the liquidity, volatility, and economic viability of index futures—all measures of a new contract's acceptance by the investment public. By these standards, the new stock index futures have made a good showing so far. Legendary trader Harry "the hat" Lowrance, who, in his dozen years on the floor of the Chicago Mercantile Exchange has earned himself a fortune in the frenzy of the Merc's trading pits, calls index futures the greatest roller-coaster of them all.

"I've been in all the markets from cattle to T-bills," says Lowrance, "and S&P is the Coney Island of the Mercantile Exchange."

The metaphor is apt. To a casual observer of the Merc's jammed S&P stock index trading pit, the unrestrained exuberance and seeming mayhem that rises and falls in response to price changes as arms swing and voices shout, resembles nothing so much as a wild roller-coaster ride—duplicated, no doubt, in the emotions of thousands of speculators sitting in front of cathode ray price screens across the land. Called the "quintessential commodity," much to the chagrin of seasoned stock traders whose time-honored trading techniques are often ineffective in such a fast-paced market, stock index futures indeed share more in common with their agricultural cousins in the grain and livestock pits than with common stocks traded on the nation's security exchanges. Here, where one dollar may control twenty times as many, money changes hands in micro seconds and fortunes are made and lost in an afternoon. These "pin-striped pork bellies," which are anything but staid, are the very epitome of the plunger's dream.

Before you grab your checkbook and head for the nearest brokerage house, however, a few caveats are in order. First and foremost, you must remember that stock index futures trading is a zero sum game. This means that the pie doesn't get any bigger; for every dollar made, there is a dollar

16

lost. And, since there are many more losers than winners in the market, the many provide the profits for a few. Estimates range as high as 90 percent of all participants in the futures markets become victims of the razor-thin margins. This zero sum game aspect of futures trading is in sharp contrast to the stock market, where virtually everyone gains when prices rise. Second, the index markets, like the futures markets in general, are a highly-specialized undertaking where precise timing is vital. Whether you buy or sell a stock on Monday or Tuesday usually isn't critical. In the index markets, minutes and even seconds can spell the difference between thousands of dollars won or lost. Third, if you haven't got the money to lose, you haven't got the money to win in the index markets. Risk capital is vital—and knowing how to use it even more vital. Even the best traders have setbacks; unless you have a cushion behind you, your early mistakes may be your last. "To make a small fortune in the futures markets," goes one popular saying "start with a large one."

Risks aside, the new index products are undeniably popular, a factor that has not been overlooked by the brokerage community. In just the past year, the initial introduction of index futures trading was followed by the introduction of *options* on index futures, a wrinkle on the idea that allows an investor to limit risk. "Despite the increasing clutter of index products, some of which may not survive, they are here to stay because they have become vital to both the professional portfolio manager and the small investor," says an analyst with the Wall Street brokerage firm of Goldman, Sachs. There is even talk of introducing futures on subindexes—industrials, transportation, and the like. With the anticipated advent of futures on subindexes, the sophisticated investor will be able to construct a hedge "tailor-made" to his stock portfolio.

Finding themselves in the thick of the battle over the new index products are the major futures and security exchanges, each vying for its share of the hundreds of millions of dollars in business the new futures and options will bring. At this writing, the new stock index futures are currently traded on three exchanges: the New York Futures Exchange, a subsidiary of the prestigious New York Stock Exchange, offers an index on the New York Stock Exchange Composite Average; the Chicago Mercantile Exchange's newly created Index and Option Market (IOM) offers the Standard & Poor's 500 and 100 stock index contracts on the S&P average; and the Kansas City Board of Trade, which originated the idea of index futures, offers the Value Line Index. To put it mildly, the rivalry among these, and other, exchanges vying for the index business is hot. When the Merc first introduced its S&P index contract in April, 1982, two months after the first index future traded in Kansas City, members were encouraged to build volume in the fledging S&P pit by signs proclaiming, "Fifteen minutes please." This was to encourage members to spend at least 15 minutes trading the new stock index contracts. The Merc ultimately won the volume sweepstakes and today holds a commanding lead among the three. But the volatility of the new contract is best summarized by one floor trader who commented that the sign should have read, "Fifteen hundred dollars please."

When the Merc introduced options on its S&P index last year, its cross-town rival, the Chicago Board Options Exchange, which had pioneered the idea of listed stock options in the early seventies, felt its role was being usurped. Not to be outdone, the CBOE launched its own "home-made" index, the CBOE 100, in early March, 1983. Geared up to take orders from security brokers (in contrast to futures brokers who handle orders on the futures exchanges), the new index made the biggest splash yet in the marketplace, trading over one million contracts in its first two months. To make matters more confusing, the Chicago Mercantile Exchange made a deal with the Chicago Board Options Exchange in which the CBOE 100 (pronounced "cee-bow") would become the S&P 100 and be traded on the floor of the CBOE. Not to be outdone, the Chicago Board of Trade, which had failed to introduce an index based on the Dow-Jones averages, agreed to become the marketplace for Value Line Index options. Although the Value Line options became one of the first casualties of the index game—the Chicago Board of Trade stopped trading them after several weeks of dwindling volume—the cooperation of rival exchanges clearly shows the future trend of both the futures and the securities industry. More and more, as the so-called "shadow" market expands, one can expect cooperating agreements among erstwhile competitors.

Clearly, the exchanges recognize the potential of stock index futures and options. And this is drawing them closer together in mutually agreeable ventures. In brief, Wall Street has been in pursuit of a hedge for years now, but had nowhere to go. Now, with the introduction of index products, the more than $1.4 trillion held in securities has a hedge in the index markets. Why shouldn't the Wall Street community want to make the most of this lucrative new source of income?

The fact is, index futures and options can be an amazingly versatile tool in the hands of a skillful investor. Certainly, the use of index futures and options as a hedge still has some distance to go since there really hasn't been a sharp break in the market since their introduction, and, as a result, they haven't really been tested. But, clearly, the promise is there. Right now, the newness of the product and the lack of experience among hedgers and speculators alike has been a negative factor for some. A great many investors, institutional investors among them, are put off by the fast-paced action of the index markets. Clearly, some traders are attracted by high volatility, others less so. "The shooters like the volatility," says Chicago Mercantile Exchange vice president Michael Asay. "But there is a whole group of people who have been turned off by the volatility of stock index futures, particularly our contract. Institutions are scared by the fact that futures vary all over the map. They ask, 'How can this be a good hedge to a portfolio when it doesn't even always move in the same direction as the cash'?"

Such concerns suggest that an important learning curve must be mastered before many stock investors will feel comfortable with the new index futures. Long used to making judgments based on so-called fundamental factors, stock investors are often put off by the importance of psychological factors in the determination of index prices. "The problem with the fundamentals," says one floor trader in Chicago, "is that they seem to change when the price changes. With the market lower, a whole new set of supply and demand factors now seem more relevant." Indeed, if the reasoned supply and demand approach (used in traditional stock analysis) is inadequate in analyzing index trends, what does work? The answer is simple: knowing how to trade. "If the price is going up, I buy it," says one floor trader who does what are called "big numbers" in the pits. "And if it is going down, I sell short." Unfortunately, knowing precisely what to do under what circumstances is not all that easy, and a number of traders, this one included, rely on a sort of instinctual sense of timing in their trades—hardly an easily taught skill.

But much, aside from instinct, can be taught. Learning how to trade and developing winning strategies is what this book is about. Part of the problem for most traders is becoming a victim of their own psychological temperament—being too opinionated, overstaying the market, refusing to take a loss, and so on. The winners are neither too confident nor overly cautious. They know when to plunge and when to walk away from a losing trade. Learning how to emulate them is the difficult part. But that will come in time. First, we have to acquaint ourselves with the basics, then we'll talk strategy. Let's get started.

Part I

STOCKS WITHOUT SHARES

New Ways To Invest In The Stock Market

Chapter One

STOCK INDEX FUTURES—
The Newest Game
On Wall Street

Until a few years ago, if you wanted to make money on Wall Street you played the stock market. So-called conservative investors, widows, orphans, trust departments and the like, confined their activities to the bluest of the blue-chips, while the speculative-minded played the new issues market, and, later, the takeover game. If you were wealthy enough, you may have clipped coupons in the bond market. And if you were truly daring, you may have even taken a flier in the commodities market, buying soybean or cotton futures, but this was considered by many on the Street to be just a step above gambling—the sort of thing best engaged in at the green-felt crap tables of Las Vegas and Atlantic City, hardly appropriate for investors.

Looking back, it all made a lot of sense back then. During the late sixties, the stock market provided enough thrills and cash to keep just about everyone happy—brokers, mutual fund salesmen, even investors. But the stock market soon fell apart and the hopes and dreams of investors were shattered. The once fashionable stock funds of the sixties, the so-called "go-go" funds, fell victim to the market decline. Investors had to look elsewhere for profits. In time, ever-rising inflation became the game to beat and real estate, among other inflation hedges, became popular. But the advent of high interest rates made even real estate a chancy investment at best and investors turned to money market funds, the latest rage to sweep Wall Street. Now that interest rates have retreated, the stock market has again regained its prominence. And the trend has come full cycle.

This time, however, the stock investor has a host of new financial products available—a number of which didn't exist several years ago. Using one or more of the new index futures or options on index futures, today's investor can lock-in stock market profits, hedge a stock position, or magnify leverage ten-or twenty-fold on speculative funds by using a number of new innovative market strategies. On Wall Street, the new products provide genuine maneuverability—the ability to move in and out of the stock market with remarkable ease. The change reflects an adaptation to a new economic reality—one where risk and safety must be successfully mastered if today's investor is to survive. Consider, for example, the new supermarket approach to Wall Street investments being promoted by a number of the full-service houses. Using one of these firms, an investor can purchase stocks, bonds, options, mutual funds, money market funds, even insurance. So-called switch funds enable you to move your money from, say, a stock fund to a bond fund to a money market fund with a toll-free phone call. The number of investment decisions and the increased complexity of those decisions has also never been greater.

Despite the growing proliferation of new investment products, how do you decide which one's for you? Chances are, you already own some stocks and you want an investment vehicle to enhance the value of your portfolio or, at least, protect the value of your portfolio. In that case, you may find the hedging aspect of the new index futures suitable. You may, however, feel a bit more adventurous and may be attracted to the speculative potential of the index futures game. In either case, stock index futures can be a versatile and profitable addition to your portfolio.

A MARKETBASKET OF STOCKS

The newest innovation in the booming financial futures market, stock index futures combine the volatility and high stakes of the commodities market with the popularity of the stock market. Rather than buying or selling actual shares, the stock index trader purchases or sells a futures contract pegged to a leading market average such as the New York Stock Exchange Composite Index of the S&P 500 stock average. Immediately successful since their introduction in the late winter and early spring of 1982, stock index futures enable an investor for the first time to buy and sell a marketbasket of stocks, to buy and sell the averages. Moreover, for the first time, they provide a reliable investment hedge for stock market investors and large institutional portfolio managers who are now able to *hedge* large quantities of stock. Investors seeking to magnify their leverage in a booming stock market will find the new index futures ideal for the fast track approach to the market, capable of producing enormous profits on invested capital. Significantly, in the hot commodity futures field, where substantial profits and losses are commonplace, stock index futures are among the leaders in volume and volatility.

Neither a stock nor a commodity, stock index futures are a hybrid of the two. They are composed of a group of stocks, usually a major market average for statistical purposes, although no such contract actually exists. In fact, a stock index is just a legal fiction, and nothing else. Incapable of being delivered, they are unlike a traditional futures contract of corn, cattle, or gold. If you do indeed hold an index futures to maturity, you'll receive only cash, not stock. This cash delivery aspect of the new market makes it unique in the world of futures trading. And it adds to the contract's liquidity and usefulness.

MARGIN

Index futures are purchased and sold on *margin*—usually just five to ten percent of the value of the contract. The significance of this low margin is that a relatively small amount of money controls an asset—namely, an index futures contract—worth many times as much. As a result, a small percentage move in the value of the stock index futures contract can translate into a much larger percentage gain—or loss—in the value of the invested margin. This magnifying power of a small margin deposit controlling an asset worth many times as much is known as leverage.

Unlike in the stock market, where margin refers to funds deposited as a down payment on securities, in the futures market, since ownership of the underlying product is not actually transferred, the margin is not a down payment; it is essentially a good-faith deposit to protect against the non-performance of the contract. No money is borrowed and hence no interest is paid on margin on a futures position. In general, margin will vary depending on which index contract you trade, from approximately $3,500 to $6,500 per contract. For index options, where margins are required by writers of the options, the requirements may be even lower.

How can this low margin work for you in the stock index futures market? Well, if you purchase a stock index futures contract with a value of, let us say, $65,000 on a margin of just 10 percent as much, each dollar you deposit controls ten times as many. Should the contract then *increase* in value by just 10 percent, the profit on invested margin will be 100 percent! Now for the bad news. If you are wrong in your judgment of the direction of stock market prices, and the value of the stock index futures contract *decreases* by 10 percent, the $6,500 in margin is wiped out and you have sustained a 100 percent loss. Leverage is a double-edged sword.

WHAT ARE THE ADVANTAGES OF STOCK INDEX TRADING?

Stock index futures are not for everyone. No question about it. But they do offer a number of advantages that investors will find inviting and useful. First, is the ability to turn a modest amount of money into a substantial amount. Traders with even modest positions can make several thousands of dollars a day if they are skillful in the stock index futures market. In the short time that index futures have been trading, fortunes have been made in this volatile, high-stakes market. Second, index futures provide a viable hedge or protection for investors holding a portfolio of stock. While few portfolio holdings will move dollar for dollar with the leading averages, the correlation is close enough to protect a diversified portfolio from substantial loss. Third, index futures enable you to "buy the market." Never before could an investor buy a market average—only a stock. Now, for the first time, you can profit by going "long" index futures prior to a market rise or, conversely, by going "short" an index future prior to a market decline. Fourth, index futures provide you with an easy means to speculate on price rises or declines. Futures are easily sold short; there is no borrowing of stock or waiting for an uptick to sell short. Fifth, stock index futures are extremely liquid, meaning you can easily enter and exit the market (indeed, many index speculators are day-traders who initiate and close out their positions prior to the close daily). Moreover, all accounts are marked to the market following each day's close. Winners are paid following the close, by having their accounts credited with the day's winnings, and losers have funds deducted from their accounts on a daily basis. Unlike in the stock market, you are free to withdraw any paper profits, over and above required margin, at any time. Sixth, and most important, you are assured of being in a fair game. All participants in the futures market have an equal opportunity to buy and sell as they see fit. There are no specialists in futures trading. All trades are consummated by open-outcry, providing everyone an equal opportunity to trade.

If you have traded futures in the past, you probably have a good grasp on how the stock index market works. If you have traded stocks but not futures, however, you may be in for a surprise when you see the speed with which profits and losses can accumulate. Since the stock market is a good jumping off place for novice traders, let's compare the differences between the two markets.

FUTURES CONTRACTS
VERSUS ROUND LOTS

The standardized unit of exchange in the futures market is the futures contract. Because every futures contract of a given commodity or financial instrument is identical, the contract serves the same purpose as does the round lot in the stock market—namely, standardization. A stock index trader knows that every contract is identical and that to liquidate or offset a position in the index contract he need only buy or sell an identical contract. For example, a buyer of June S&P futures need only sell June S&P futures to take profits or liquidate the position at a loss in the event that prices have moved against him. Because every contract is identical, liquidity in the market is assured.

Stock shares differ from stock index futures contracts, however, in what they represent. When you purchase shares of DuPont, IBM, or General Motors, you actually become part owner of one of these companies. Traded in round lots consisting of 100 shares, stocks are purchased for cash or on "margin," in which case the buyer borrows up to 50 percent of the value of the stock. When stock is purchased on margin, however, the buyer must pay interest on the funds he borrows from his broker. In the futures market, on the other hand, margin merely refers to a good-faith deposit, as we've discussed, that the buyer or seller will fulfill his obligations on the performance of the contract. Additional margin may be required should the stock index futures position move against you.

Now contrast the purchase of stocks with the purchase of a stock index futures contract. The buyer of a futures contract doesn't actually buy shares but rather makes a legally binding agreement to purchase a statistical average at the agreed upon price. The average represents the current market price of the particular stock index contract. For example, let's say you purchase one New York Stock Exchange Composite futures index at a price of 100.00 on a margin of just $3,500. Since the index contract is worth *500 times the quoted price,* the value of the contract is $50,000. As a buyer or seller of a futures contract, you stand to profit—or lose—on the entire value of the contract, however. Thus, if the contract should move up in price to, let us say, 110.00, the contract will now be worth $55,000 (110.00 times $500 = $55,000), and you will have a $5,000 profit. There will be a commission fee subtracted from this profit of approximately $20 to $100, depending upon your broker. But the initial margin of $3,500 will be returned to you in full.

Unlike in the stock market, where you actually purchase shares, the futures market only provides you with the *promise* to purchase the underlying index at the agreed upon purchase price. You don't actually own anything. Rather, you stand to profit from a price rise if you are a buyer, and, conversely, stand to profit from a price decline if you are a short seller. The order in which you buy or sell stock index futures is unimportant. That is, you can just as easily initiate a position by buying or going ''long'' a stock index futures contract or selling or going ''short'' a stock index futures contract. Buyers must subsequently sell, of course; and sellers must subsequently buy, or ''cover'' their short positions. Those who do not liquidate their positions, but rather hold them until the contract matures, will have their accounts credited or debited by the difference between where they originally bought or sold and the final settlement of the *actual index* on the last day of trading.

Index futures are traded in what are known as *contract months*. There are four key trading months: March, June, September, and December. As a rule, the closest month in time, known as the *nearby month*, will have the greatest *open interest*, or number of contracts outstanding. Open interest measures the number of contracts that have yet to be offset, or closed out. For instance, when you initiate a new position in the market, the open interest will increase by one. When you close out the position, the open interest will decrease by one.

HEDGERS AND SPECULATORS

the reason for the existence of the futures market is to transfer risk from users of the cash product, known as *hedgers,* to *speculators,* who are willing to assume risk in pursuit of profit. In the stock index futures markets, a hedger may be an individual investor who seeks to limit risk on his stock portfolio or a large institution seeking the same protection. By definition, a hedge involves taking an *opposite* position in the futures market to that held in the cash market. Thus, a hedger who is long cash stocks would sell index futures. Should the market then decline, the loss on the stock portfolio would be offset by a comparable gain on the short index position.

Let's look at an example of hedging using a bank that seeks to lock-in costs by hedging in the Treasury bond futures market. A bank, we'll call it Amalgamated Trust, engaged in providing loans at, say, 11 percent might be satisfied with a 2 point profit if it can secure funds at a cost of 9 percent. Yet, given the recent volatility in interest rates, Amalgamated bank officers might be concerned lest interest rates rise, thus increasing their costs and threatening their profits. As a result, Amalgamated Trust might attempt to lock-in loan costs at 9 percent by hedging its exposure in the Treasury bond futures market. Essentially, the strategy is to offset losses in one market by earning comparable gains in another market. In this instance, should the cost of money rise in the form of higher interest rates, the hedged bond futures will return the bank's losses by providing profits. Should rates stay stable or decline, the gains in the cash market will be offset by losses in the futures. But because the bank realized at the outset that it could live with the locked-in "hedged" cost of 9 percent, the risk has been eliminated.

What about the speculator on the other side of the futures equation? He agrees to assume the risks that the hedger wants to avoid. In return for his assumption of the risk, he stands to make a profit. But only if his market judgment proves correct. If his judgment is wrong, of course, the speculator must pay for his error in the form of a market loss.

This transference of risk, from hedger to speculator, has worked successfully on organized futures exchanges in this country since 1848, when the Chicago Board of Trade first opened for business. At first primarily a market for the grain trade, the futures market has grown tremendously in recent years. Today, the futures market still provides this risk transference mechanism for the grain trade. But the number of products it now covers has expanded from agricultural products that can be stored, such as grains, to non-storable commodities such as livestock, and even non-agricultural products such as gasoline and heating oil, foreign currencies, metals, and financial instruments. The futures market provides the centralized marketplace where hedgers and speculators can meet and transfer risks while protecting themselves and often profiting from the vagaries of price fluctuations.

CASH DELIVERY

When stock index futures were first introduced in early 1982, a new twist was introduced along with the new contracts. For the first time, a futures contract would have *cash delivery*. This meant that instead of actually receiving one share of each of the 500 stocks that comprise the Standard & Poor's 500, an expiring contract would be marked to the cash index on the last day of trading, and the profits or losses paid as a cash amount determined by where the cash index settled. This is a departure from the traditional means of settling futures by having the sellers give delivery to the buyers. It also avoided the very real problem of determining *how* to take delivery of a stock index futures contract—an impossibility in practical terms. Cash delivery, however, is a concept that is catching on. The Commodity Futures Trading Commission, the regulatory body for the futures industry, recently approved a contract on potatoes calling for cash delivery. Other cash settlement contracts are before the CFTC for approval.

Although speculators, who offset positions prior to expiration, were never much concerned with delivery, the economic justification of a futures contract rests with delivery. After all, you must realize that the processors and producers of traditional "commodities," whether they be in the cotton, grain, or livestock business, actually *used* or *produced* those commodities. As a result, buyers would accept delivery at the maturity date of the contract. But where stocks are concerned, the delivery of the actual shares isn't important; in fact, delivery would result in great inconvenience were it physically possible. Nevertheless, stock index futures provide a viable means of hedging portfolio exposure. With the advent of stock index futures trading, investors and institutions with a cash position in the equities market, for the first time, could hedge their risks. Having the new contracts at their disposal, hedgers could protect themselves against so-called *systematic risk*, or risk associated with a stock moving in concert with the major averages.

WIDE APPEAL

What accounts for the popularity of the new indexes among small speculators? Apart from the high leverage involved in futures trading, index futures are attractive because they can be traded with small resources. Using the new mini-contracts, an investor can get started for about $1,500. Given the high leverage effect, even modest price moves can enable a skilled speculator to earn many times his initial margin investment. Even a shoestring investment can be parlayed into a substantial amount of money given the high leverage. But to achieve a worthwhile investment goal, the speculator must have the know-how to avoid the many pitfalls and a sound knowledge of how futures contracts are traded. That's what this book is intended to provide.

How risky is stock index futures trading? As a general rule, risk is commensurate with reward. If you want to make the big money, you have to withstand a lot of risk, and vice versa. But risk can be controlled, moderated, hedged, and even dispensed with entirely by using specific trading strategies. The information contained in the pages that follow will help you learn to control risk. This book is going to give you the information know-how to trade the index markets like the professionals. Here's what you'll learn:

- What index futures can do for you as a speculator or hedger.
- Why the market fools most of the traders most of the time.
- How orders are filled on the floor—and how you can avoid the most common mistakes in placing orders.
- How not to fall victim to the market's psychological trap.
- How to limit losses.
- The best way to select the direction of the market.
- When to have the courage to plunge—and why you must be aggressive to win.

You will also learn a strategy for knowing when to trade counter to the trend. This will enable you to place orders near major reversal points, provide safe executions, and help you decide when best to nail down profits or cut short losses. Hopefully, you'll gain insight into why you must be a short-term trader—contrary to accepted opinion—in order to win in this volatile and exciting market.

This book is the result of actual experience trading stock index futures contracts—all of it hard-won in the fight to survive in a difficult investment medium. It is amazing how, in the heat of a battle so to speak, so many of the theories prove less than helpful—and only the pragmatic, no-nonsense approach counts. So often in the market, you'll be puzzled about the meaning of a move, the significance of this or that event. After finishing this book, you'll understand that there are market forces at work that make successful speculation about as easy as walking across a minefield. Don't be discouraged. The losses of the many provide the profits of the few—the few who make *all* the money. The key to profits is *knowing how to trade*. This cannot be stressed enough. Once you know what to look for, you'll be much better prepared *not* to make the careless mistakes that prove ruinous to so many new traders. You must remember that the winners are no different than you—only more knowledgeable.

The task, then, is to learn the rules, *the real rules* of trading. And I don't mean the kind of advice you are apt to receive from your broker about where to place the stop, and that sort of thing. Most of the conventional wisdom about the futures market is worthless. In fact, the professional floor traders routinely "fade," or trade against, the public precisely because the traditional rules don't work. And they often grow rich in the process. Simply put, if you are going to make it in the stock index futures market, you have to know exactly what you are doing—and then have the courage to follow your plan. There is nothing magical about it. Just common sense. If I had to list three traits for success, I'd say: money, brains, and nerve. Given a modicum of each you have a fighting chance to win the gold ring.

In order to win, you'd better acquaint yourself with the pitfalls early on—why, for instance, the popular fundamental approach is almost useless in this fast-paced game where the direction of prices changes a half dozen times daily. Futures trading has always been a specialty in the investment world, and it has just gotten more specialized with the advent of index trading. But this needn't be a deterrent to your success. As a member of the informed minority, you'll be competing with some of the best traders in the world—and, hopefully, earning some of the most impressive profits.

THE FAST TRACK

Right now, the stock index futures market is booming and is today's hottest "money magnet." Fueled by a roaring bull market for stocks, the averages immediately skyrocketed, soaring into new high ground almost daily. While not unique (we've had bull markets before), this phenomenon is not an everyday occurrence. And it does mark the first time that fortunes have been made in the new index futures.

Just how profitable can stock index trading be? In the first nine months of the 1982-83 bull market, a single stock index futures contract, purchased at the August 1982 low, increased in value by more than $25,000. That's a 50 point gain, or a profit of about 384 percent on the initial margin of $6,500. Given the magic of leverage arrived at by *pyramiding*—a strategy in which you use your paper profits to acquire additional contracts—a similar position would have grown to about $75,000!

In actual practice, traders tend to buy and sell on a frequent basis and take multiple positions in the index contracts. By concentrating on high-quality buy and sell situations, a short term trader can turn even a small amount of money into real megabucks in the stock index futures market.

To see just how profitable index trading can be, consider the volatility of a contract on an *average* day: about $1,000 from the high to the low. Occasionally, the index will vary in price by about $2,000 to $2,500 per day per contract. To understand the amount of money changing hands, you have to realize that many traders buy and sell not one or two contracts but twenty or thirty. If you can learn to predict the direction of prices for only a short period of time, the profits can be enormous. The percent probability of catching a small move, moreover, is far, far greater than trying to outguess the market over a period of time. In addition, you lower your risk exposure considerably if you can earn quick profits on a very short-term basis.

Stocks, on the other hand, are mild by comparison. Let's assume you start with just $6,500 in capital. For that amount of money, you could buy 100 shares of a security selling for $65 a share, transaction costs aside. Or you could post margin for one stock index futures. How many $65 stocks move more than two or three points in a day? Very few. But the average range of a stock index futures contract is $1,000—comparable to a $10 per share move in the stock. Again, the reason the stock index contract may *appear* more volatile is due to the high leverage. The stock index futures contract, unlike the $65 stock, isn't worth just $6,500 but possibly ten times as much, or more! As a result, the gain or loss on the stock index contract will be magnified in terms of the initial margin.

With the possibility of substantial profits or losses in the stock index futures market, you need a guiding hand to help you master the challenge in trading. In short, you need a system.

Systems abound in the futures market. There are systems based on a number of technical indicators—moving averages, contrary opinion sentiment, relative strength, on-balance volume, even astrology. Without going into the merits or drawbacks of individual systems, it is sufficient to mention that most suffer from the same drawback: inflexibility. When the market changes, the systems do not. Ask yourself: since the market is apt to change over time, why shouldn't a trading system do likewise?

THE KEY TO TRADING PROFITS

A good trading system isn't the last word in securing consistent profits. Rather, it is the first; a departure point that provides a point of view on the market—one that, significantly, can be modified, updated, and improved to smooth the path to profits. Such a system is the LSS 3-day Cycle Method. Based on the legendary "Book Method" created more than 30 years ago by George Douglas Taylor, a Chicago Board of Trade grain speculator, the LSS system is short-term in approach and the epitome of flexibility. Sometimes the very best advice is the simplest. Using the LSS 3-day Cycle Method, you will have initial entry and exit points. But these objectives may change once the trading day begins. Such flexibility is notably absent from most trading systems. But it is at the heart of the LSS 3-day system. If the professional floor traders find it profitable to switch positions at a moment's notice, doesn't it make sense that the trading public can learn from the professional's activities?

What's surprising is how ill-informed the majority of all speculators are, considering the sophistication of today's computer-tracked markets. Unfortunately, those who are in a position to influence public thinking—namely, the leading commission houses and their armies of commission-hungry brokers—are as tied to conventional wisdom of the past as anyone. "Why rock the boat?," they say. The problem is that they find no shortage of eager customers with dollar signs in their eyes. That the customers will soon be parted from their money is of little consequence to the commission house. There's quite a bit of wisdom in the old Wall Street joke:

"Well, the broker made money and the firm made money—and two out of three isn't bad." The problem is you-know-who is expected to lose.

George Douglas Taylor made quite a contribution to the literature of Wall Street when he commented that the markets are "engineered from within." For indeed this is precisely what happens. Markets frequently appear to be moving this way or that only to react and surprise the unwary. A sort of bandwagon effect is created by the market professionals who do their buying long before the unsuspecting public moves in; then, naturally, the public supplies the profits at the top. You don't have to put the market under a microscope for long to see how consistent and predictable this pattern is; nor do you have to be a genius to see how this "false" buying creates a misleading impression. Such buying inevitably contains the seeds of its own destruction; in short order, the buying subsides and the market reverses.

You don't have to experience this whipsawing action often in order to see the pattern involved. In time, one wants to throw up one's hands in frustration. Just when the market *looked* so bullish. What could have gone wrong? And that's just the point. The market is made to look so one-sided that only a fool would consider taking the other side—that's real market "engineering" at work. As it says in the McDonald's commercial, "Why not give yourself a break today?" Why not give yourself a chance to win? You can be sure your brokerage house and broker *know* that they are going to win. They're in the commission business. But what about you?

"YOU'RE THINKING TOO HARD"

One of the most valuable pieces of information I ever received about the futures market, came over lunch one afternoon in a restaurant in the Chicago Loop. I'd had a particularly difficult day trading gold and was explaining my frustration at getting badly whipsawed to a fellow trader.

"Look, you're thinking too hard," he told me. "It's not all that complicated." He explained a very simple rule that he'd used to earn a tidy income. Essentially, it involved doubling up and going the other way when he found himself on the wrong side of the market. It sounded deceptively simple.

"But what about the money?" I asked, realizing how one might easily find oneself throwing good money after bad.

"Don't think about the money," he assured me. "Just do it."

35

Although this is the kind of advice that investors usually scoff at, I later learned it was invaluable—probably the single most valuable piece of advice I'd ever learned. But hearing it and experiencing it prove quite different. It wasn't long after this converation took place that I took what, in the jargon of the floor, is called a "hit"—a loss which can be debilitating. Undaunted, I immediately plunged on the other side and emerged a winner. That single piece of advice has stood me in good stead ever since.

If you are going to profit from the information in this book, you are going to have to do likewise, and experience some of the ups and downs of the market first-hand. This is the only way you can gain the confidence needed to dismiss the misleading messages that abound in the market and "just do it"—put your money on the line and take the plunge. But before you risk a dime, I suggest you first read the pages that follow.

While there is no way of knowing with certainty how much money you'll make in the stock index futures market, it is almost certain that if you speculate without knowledge of what is really taking place, you will surely lose. Recent history has shown how treacherous the index markets can be to the uninitiated. Perhaps an apt illustration is provided by the seasoned professionals on the New York Stock Exchange who moved over to the exchange's subsidiary, The New York Futures Exchange, to show the locals how the new index markets should be traded. They soon retreated to what is known as the "other side," completely out-maneuvered by the fast-paced futures game. After all, these guys *knew* the stock market. They just hadn't learned that futures trading is a completely different game.

Stock index futures can be very profitable. But you have to know how to use them correctly in order to profit from them. Many new investors in the stock index markets, familiar with the stock market, take a long-term investment approach, which is inappropriate in these highly-leveraged contracts. Short-term trading can both magnify profits and minimize risk. With the help of a sound, no-nonsense trading system that capitalizes on readily predictable day-to-day market patterns, the profits can be earned consistently as well. And by confining your activities to day trading, you can obtain even higher leverage by taking on positions that aren't backed by additional upfront margin. I'll explain this in more detail later.

You'll benefit if you *understand* that human nature encourages traders to make mistakes in the market. "It's funny what emotions do to people," one S&P trader told me. Finding themselves caught on the wrong side of the market, many traders frequently panic. But one man's loss in the index markets is another man's profit. Not only does familiar market action result in losses for the panic-stricken, but those who understand the market frequently set the stampede in motion. "I'd like to see what's up there," one Merc floor trader told me. "So I'll often high-ball the market in hopes of hitting the stops. If I'm right, a flurry of buy orders will hit the market all at once—like dominoes—and my profit is assured."

If you've ever been on the receiving end of what floor traders call "search and destroy missions," you'll know what he's talking about. If you are confused, the tactics will be explained in the chapters that follow. The point is, there's a rhyme and reason behind price movements in the index futures market. In order to compete, you'd better know what's going on. Which is not to imply that you can't join the informed speculators; far from it, given a sound understanding in what *really* goes on, you'll be in a better position to profit accordingly.

"The S&P pit is the most cut-throat pit there is," the same Merc trader told me. "Guys doing one and two lots will bid up the price on those doing 30 and 40." Translated into English, this means in order to get out of the market by paying another $25 or $50, traders may cost paper losses amounting to thousands for others. Put another way, a trader explains, "Once the bell rings, you don't have any friends down here." For the public speculator who trades from the "outside," placing his orders through brokerage houses, the machinations of the floor are particularly important to understand. Remember, everyone is operating in *their* self-interest; to the floor, public orders exist to provide *them* with a steady flow of funds, so certain are they of emerging winners. But even the sophisticated floor traders occasionally lose, so it's best to disabuse yourself of the notion that they have a sure-thing situation. They don't. Still, the game is conducted in a fair manner and everyone has a fair chance of winning—again, *if* they know what they are doing.

A WINNING STRATEGY

I tend to be suspicious of people who have all of the answers but haven't bothered to ask the proper questions, which is one reason why I distrust the typical broker who calls you on the phone. His job is to make sales, not profitably trade the market. Fortunately, you don't have to rely on anyone but yourself. But to be successful, you first have to ask the right questions.

It's well worth learning to ask them before you take a trade—and not after you've lost money.

If you've been around the markets for any period of time, you already know that the world is filled with people willing to give you free advice to risk *your* money. If you emerge from a reading of this book with only one single piece of information, it is to run as fast as you can from such advice. However well-meaning, it can't take the responsibility off your shoulders to make the decision to buy or sell. To do this, you need a way to process the information which the market provides. All the trading signals are in the market itself; you simply have to know how to read them.

There are people who can tell you how they took a profitable trade, but it is worthless information to you unless you share their risk temperament. Everyone's attitude toward risk is different. In every trade, you are caught between the twin dangers of fear and greed. On the one hand, assuming you are ahead, you are fearful the market is going to take away your profits; assuming you are behind, you are naturally concerned whether you're going to recoup or not. On the other, the greed factor becomes a hindrance as it blinds you to the reality of a situation. When is enough? I've included some advice on letting the market decide when you get out, because if you overstay the market, the market may take back all your profits—and then some. You have to be careful at all times; you can never grow over-confident. After reading this book, you'll know when it is best to run, even if you have to leave a few chips on the table. After all, when you're trading stock index futures, the very first rule is to insure your own financial survival. You can't very well make the big money if you've been cleaned out. But that requires one steadfast prejudice: to be right. Why else risk your hard-won money?

Chapter Two

THE NEW INDEX MARKETS— What You Need To Know To Get Started

If you are new to futures trading, you'll want to acquaint yourself with a few basic terms and strategies before you take your first trade. Futures, whether you trade stock indexes, metals, or grains, all pretty much share a common nomenclature. So if you are familiar with the market jargon you'll have that much less to worry about. Once acquainted, the vocabulary becomes second nature and you can engage in this verbal shorthand with your broker to communicate your trading decisions quickly and simply.

WHAT'S A FUTURES CONTRACT?

A futures contract, which is a legally binding agreement between buyer and seller established on the floor of a designated futures exchange, is created when buyer and seller agree to trade at a given price. The price is established in the *pit* or *ring* of the futures exchange by an *open outcry* method. Buyers *bid* prices by yelling them out in the pit and sellers *offer* or *ask* prices by the same open outcry method. Open outcry enables every trader to hear the respective bids and offers at the same time. Thus, no trader is favored and all have an opportunity to obtain the best possible price. For a trade to be consummated, both buyer and seller must agree on a *single* price. That is, the seller must agree to sell at the buyer's bid or the buyer must agree to buy at the seller's offer. A futures pit is the essence of a free marketplace with no one forced to trade at a price he doesn't hear and agree to in advance.

To *offset* or *liquidate* a position, the buyer must sell his position and the seller must *cover* or buy back his position. In the futures market it does not matter whether you buy or sell first. An investor anticipating higher prices purchases index contracts; an investor anticipating lower prices sells short index contracts. As we've mentioned, a contract held to maturity is settled in cash after the final day of trading by having the contract marked-to-the-market of the cash index. Prior to maturity, contracts are marked-to-the-market daily using the futures settlement price. Cash settlement upon maturity of the contract is a unique feature of stock index futures and doesn't apply to traditional futures contracts where the buyers must stand for delivery upon maturity and sellers must give delivery. It is an important provision that circumvents the problem of delivery of a statistical average of a large number of stocks.

LONG AND SHORT

There are two parties to every futures contract—a buyer and a seller. The buyer, who expects prices to rise, is said to have a *long* position, or be *long* the market; the seller, who expects prices to fall, is said to have a *short* position, or be *short* the market. There is a buyer for every seller. But a market need not be characterized by buyers and sellers in a one-to-one ratio, since one well-capitalized buyer may hold all the long contracts and a multitude of sellers may hold the short contracts. Sellers of futures contracts, also known as *short sellers*, profit when the market declines; conversely, buyers profit when the market rises. The interaction between buyers and sellers is what makes prices rise and fall.

BROAD STATISTICAL AVERAGE

Stock index futures permit traders to participate in the up and down price movements of a broad statistical average of stocks. Assuming it is

Monday morning and you are bullish on stock prices, you might decide to purchase stock index futures on the New York Futures Exchange. We'll assume you purchase the contract at a price of 87.00 (representing a value of $43,500 since the contract is worth $500 times the quoted price). By the following Thursday morning, the price of the New York Stock Exchange Composite Index futures has risen to 94.00 and you instruct your broker to sell one contract at the market. The transaction would appear as follows:

A Long Position

Monday:	Buy one NYSE Composite Index future at 87.00
Thursday:	Sell one NYSE Composite Index future at 94.00
Gain:	7.00 X $500 = $3,500

Sellers of index futures would profit by taking a short position in a market that is about decline. For example: Assume that it is Monday morning and the market looks weak. You instruct your broker to sell a NYSE Composite Index contract at the prevailing market price which is about 95.00. He does so, and you are now short the market. By Thursday morning, NYSE Composite Index futures are trading at 86.00 and you have a nine point profit. You instruct your broker to cover your short position and you are out of the market with a $4,500 profit. The transaction would appear as follows:

A Short Position

Monday:	Sell one NYSE Composite Index future at 95.00
Thursday:	Buy one NYSE Composite Index future at 86.00
Gain:	9.00 X $500 = $4,500

Stock index traders can profit from both market declines and market rallies. But one's market judgment must be correct. In the two illustrations above, had either trader's judgment been wrong, the realized gains of $3,500 and $4,500, respectively, would have been realized losses.

HOW FUTURES EXCHANGES TRANSFER RISK

Futures exchanges serve as risk transference centers for our national economy. Contrary to the widespread popular belief that futures trading in general, and stock index trading in particular, is nothing more than gambling, the exchanges, in fact, serve a vital economic function. Their purpose is to lower the cost of doing business in any one of the many agricultural or financial areas covered by the futures markets. In the case of stock index futures, the economic function is particularly important. As a result of the introduction of stock index futures, the owners of securities (including the millions of investors whose future livelihood is dependent upon the prudent handling of the billions of dollars in institutional accounts) can now hedge their equity exposure. Thus, the new index products serve two functions: one, they make the ownership of securities safer; and two, they offer an unprecedented speculative opportunity for investors with risk capital.

THE MAJOR STOCK INDEX CONTRACTS

There are two different types of index contracts. There are index *futures* and index *options*. The two are fundamentally different. Both, however, may play a role in your portfolio.

An index *futures contract* is a *commitment to buy or sell a standardized representative statistical stock market average for a specific futures settlement date at a currently agreed upon price.* An *index option*, on the other hand, *represents an opportunity to buy or sell a given index—which may or may not be an underlying futures contract—at a given price, known as a strike price.* There are two types of options—*puts* and *calls.* The *call* option gives the buyer the right to *purchase* the index at the established strike price; the *put* option gives the buyer the right to *sell* the index at the strike price. The price one pays to purchase an option is known as the *premium,* or *premium price.* The key difference between a futures and an option is one of risk. The buyer of a futures contract has unlimited risk, whereas the put or call buyer has a very limited risk, the option premium. The index option is known as a unilateral instrument in legal circles, which means that the holder of the option is not obligated to *exercise* his option. Should it not prove profitable, the option buyer can simply let the option expire and he can walk away without further obligation. The writer or seller of a futures contract, however, must guarantee the performance of his contractual obligations as long as he holds the position.

There are three major stock index futures contracts currently trading on futures exchanges, although more will eventually be introduced in the months and years ahead. They are:

1. **The New York Stock Exchange Composite Index.** Traded on the Big Board's subsidiary, the New York Futures Exchange, the NYSE Composite Index futures contract is comprised of 1,505 common stocks. It is a weighted index that reflects the market value of individual stocks and is quite popular with small speculators because the contract is about half the size of the larger S&P 500 and Value Line contracts traded in Chicago and Kansas City, respectively. The underlying NYSE Composite Index is a widely disseminated average which is updated continuously and readily available in major newspapers and mass media. On its first day of trading, the NYSE Composite Index futures set a record for the number of contracts traded on the opening day of any exchange. Like the other major index futures contracts, the NYSE Composite Index futures contract is quoted at a dollar figure which is 1/500th the size of the underlying contract. In terms of volume, the New York Composite Index futures trade about half as many as the leading Standard & Poor's 500 contract.

2. **The Value Line Composite Stock Index.** Traded on the Kansas City Board of Trade, the Value Line contract is an equally-weighted average of 1,683 common shares, most of which are traded on the New York Stock Exchange. Because every share is weighted equally and because the Value Line Index is comprised of some highly volatile issues, the index is more volatile than other index contracts. The Kansas City Board of Trade also offers a job-lot contract, or "mini" contract, on its Value Line Index. This smaller-sized contract, which is one-fifth the size of its larger counterpart, is especially appealing to the smaller investor due to its reduced margin requirements. The Value Line contract is based on a proprietary index, which is published and maintained by Arnold Bernhard & Co., Inc., a leading stock market advisory service. The index is based on a value of 100 which was established as of June 30, 1961. It is the only average that uses a so-called geometric measurement in which all stocks are weighted equally. Although it was the first stock index contract to be traded, the Value Line contract has since been outpaced in volume and popularity by the New York Stock Exchange Composite Index and the Standard & Poor's 100 and 500 indexes.

43

3. **The Standard & Poor's 500 Stock Index.** The leading index futures contract, the Standard & Poor's 500 commenced trading on the Chicago Mercantile Exchange's new Index and Options Market (IOM) during April, 1982. A weighted average to reflect market value of the stocks that comprise the S&P 500, the index is calculated by multiplying the shares outstanding of each of the 500 stocks by its market price. These amounts are then totalled and compared to a 1941-43 base period. The S&P Stock Price Index was originally introduced in 1917 as a weekly index. But it wasn't until 40 years later, in 1957, that the S&P 500 was first introduced. The S&P 500 futures contract is valued at $500 times its quoted price. As a market-value-weighted index, the S&P 500 is useful for institutional hedging, since many of the stocks comprising the index are held by large portfolio managers. Speculators likewise enjoy the wide participation in the S&P contract and find it ideal for day trading. The IOM recently introduced a futures contract on the S&P 100. This contract is two-fifths the size of the S&P 500, with each tick worth just $10 as compared to $25 for the larger contract. The S&P index is currently among the 12 leading economic indicators followed by the U.S. Commerce Department and represents approximately 80 percent of all issues traded on the New York Stock Exchange. It is comprised of 400 industrial, 40 public utilities, 20 transportation and 40 financial companies.

OPTIONS ON INDEXES

Put and call options on indexes come in two varieties. One type of option is based on an underlying futures contract, such as the S&P 500 options traded on the Chicago Mercantile Exchange; the other type of option, such as the American Stock Exchange's Major Market Index option, has no underlying futures contract and is strictly a "home-made" option.* The "home-made" options are similar in every respect to listed stock options but one: they are settled for cash. Hence, no delivery of stock occurs. This is significant since these new options cannot, therefore, be written as hedged positions—a strategy known as "covered writing." In addition, the new options that are not based on underlying futures have proved popular because investors, often more familiar with the securities

---

* As of this writing, the Chicago Board of Trade has announced plans to introduce a futures contract based on the Major Market Index, but trading has not commenced.

markets, can trade them in their stock accounts through their securities broker; options on futures require the opening of a futures account with a futures broker.

A sampling of the leading options currently trading are:

1. **Major Market Index.** Traded on the American Stock Exchange, the Major Market Index is based on the stock performance of 20 leading blue-chip companies. The MMI, which is *not* traded in connection with a futures contract, has been proven to show a high degree of correlation with the widely accepted broad market averages, including the Dow Jones Industrial Averages and the Standard & Poor's 500. The index is *not* market weighted; that is, the total market value of a component stock is *not* a factor in determining that stock's effect on the index as a whole. Instead, a given change in an individual stock will have the identical effect on the index. The quoted price of the Major Market Index is 1/100th of the total value of the option. Hence, a quote of 1¼ would correspond to a value of $125. The 20 companies that comprise the MMI include a broad spectrum of industries, such as chemicals, pharmaceuticals, manufacturing, merchandising, computer technology, and consumer products.

2. **Market Value Index.** The Market Value Index option, which commenced trading on the American Stock Exchange in July, 1983, is based on the collective performance of over 800 issues traded on the Amex. The index, which was split just prior to the introduction of options trading, was originally introduced at a base level of 100 in September, 1973. One unique feature of the index design is that cash dividends paid by the component stocks are treated as if "reinvested" and therefore reflected in the index, which measures the total return of its component stocks. Like the MMI, the Market Value Index does *not* have an underlying futures contract. As a result, it can be traded by investors who already have options accounts with their securities brokers without the necessity of opening a futures account. Like the other key indexes, the Market Value Index is updated continuously and disseminated approximately once per minute. The index is market weighted, which means that the total value of the shares outstanding is taken into account in calculating the average. This is in contrast to the Major Market Index, which is price weighted. The quoted price of the Market Value Index is 1/100th the size of the contract.

4. **Standard & Poor's 500 and 100.** The S&P 100, which was once known as the CBOE (pronounced "Cee-Bow") 100, is traded on the Chicago Board Options Exchange. Perhaps the most successful index option ever introduced, the S&P 100 is traded at the Chicago Board Options Exchange due to a deal worked out between the Chicago Mercantile Exchange, which had obtained the proprietary use of the Standard & Poor's name, and Standard & Poor's. The S&P 100 is valued at 100 times the quoted price; a larger version of the S&P 100 is the S&P 500, which is valued at 500 times the quoted price. Standard & Poor's 500 index options are also traded at the Chicago Mercantile Exchange. A new futures contract, corresponding to the smaller S&P 100 option, is also now trading at the Chicago Mercantile Exchange.

4. **New York Stock Exchange Composite Index.** Traded on the New York Futures Exchange, a subsidiary of the New York Stock Exchange, this option on the underlying NYSE Composite Index futures has identical terms of the futures contract. Like the NYSE Composite futures, the option is quoted in points and is valued at $500 times the quoted premium. A quote of, say, 7.70 for a December 92 call, therefore, would have a value of $3,850. As with other options having a futures contract as the underlying security, the buyer of a call receives a long futures contract when exercising, whereas the seller will receive a short futures at the designated strike price. In the case of a put option, the buyer will receive a short position in the underlying NYSE Composite Index and the seller of the put will receive a long position at the designated strike price. Quotations on the NYSE Composite Index options are available from most quotation services, as well as being published daily in the "Futures Options" column on the Futures page of *The Wall Street Journal*. A second NYSE Composite Index option was recently introduced by the New York Stock Exchange. This "home-made" option, while based on the same average as the above, has *no* underlying futures (settlement is in cash) and a multiplier of 100. The quotes, like those of listed stock options, are in sixteenths, eighths, and quarters. Unlike the options on futures, that have a March-June-September-December trading cycle, the new NYSE Composite Index options have a monthly cycle to provide sufficient liquidity and depth. The NYSE Index covers the 1,505 common stocks traded on the Big Board. The average is weighted according to the number of shares outstanding and the strike prices are set 5 points apart with new strikes added as the index rises or falls. Since the NYSE Index includes *every* common stock

traded on the Big Board, it is not a *sampling* of NYSE stocks but the actual market. For this reason, it is expected to attract a broad segment of the option business.

SPECIALTY INDUSTRY INDEXES

The newest wrinkle on the stock index option idea is the option tied to a representative sampling of securities in one industry. Like the broad-based indexes that enable investors to hedge or speculate in options based on the market as a whole, the specialty indexes enable an investor to do the same with one industry, such as oil and gas or computer technology. At the time of this writing, the following indexes are trading, but more can be expected in the future.*

1. **The Amex Computer Technology Index.** Introduced on August 26, 1983, this first narrow industry index is currently the most popular new specialty index. Traded on the American Stock Exchange, which is fast becoming the most innovative exchange for new option ideas, the index is composed of 30 leading U.S. corporations involved in various phases of the computer industry. The index shares the cash settlement provisions of the other broader-based Amex indexes such as the Market Value Index and the Major Market Index, and the contract size is similar. The index number represents one-hundredth the value of the entire contract. Thus, a premium of, let us say, 7½, would cost the investor $750 plus commissions to purchase.

2. **The Amex Oil and Gas Index.** This narrow-based specialty option designed to represent the oil and gas industry was introduced by the Amex in early September, 1983. The oil and gas index is based on 30 of the largest firms in the two industries, including Exxon—which represents 17 percent of the index—and Indiana Standard, Socal, Sohio, the Sun Company, Mobil and Atlantic Richfield, among others. Like the other specialty index options, the multiplier is 100.

---

* On December 19, 1983, the Philadelphia Stock Exchange entered the stock index option market with two new entries—a Gold/Silver index composed of seven mining stocks and a Gaming/Hotel index composed of nine casino and lodging stocks. But this is only the beginning. With the lifting of the moratorium on new narrow-based index options by the SEC, more than 10 new products are scheduled for the future, including a NYSE index based on 20 over-the-counter stocks.

THE ARITHMETIC OF
STOCK INDEX FUTURES TRADING

Understanding the meaning of the quoted prices of stock index futures is easy once you understand the value of the contract. Each of the major stock index futures contracts is valued at $500 times the level of the index.* As a result, each one point move in the value of the index translates into a $500 profit or loss to the index investor. For instance, if you purchase one March S&P 500 stock index futures contract for a price of 162.00 and later sell the contract for 163.00, your profit is one point or $500—minus transaction costs.

Stock index futures are quoted in minimum *tick* increments of 5/100ths of a point. Thus, the next higher tick after, say, 164.55, will be 164.60, and so on. This is in contrast to the actual cash indexes, which are quoted in increments of 1/100ths of a point. Thus, when the cash S&P 500 Index is trading at, say, 168.81, the nearby futures, assuming a discount of about one point, might be trading at about 167.80. Since 5/100ths of a point valued at $500 equals $25, this is the amount an investor gains or loses when the market moves by one tick. Unlike traditional futures contracts on tangible commodities, stock index contracts do not have daily trading limits. As a result, there is virtually no limit on what you might make or lose in a single trading session. However, two points is about the average range from high to low during a typical day, although some indexes have moved as far as five to six points in a single trading session.

On the following page I have listed the settlement prices for the first three nearby contracts of the New York Stock Exchange Composite Index futures as it appeared in *The Wall Street Journal.*

---

* The exception is the S&P 100 futures contract and the Value Line mini-contract. The S&P 100 is valued at $200 times the level of the contract. The Value Line mini-contract is valued at $100 times the quoted price. At recent price levels, the S&P 100 contract was worth about $34,000 and the Value Line mini-contract was worth about $20,000.

Table 1

NYSE COMPOSITE FUTURES (NYFE)

500 Times Index

	Open	High	Low	Settle	Change	Lifetime High	Lifetime Low	Open Interest
Sept	97.70	97.85	96.25	96.30	− 1.55	100.75	59.65	7,091
Dec	98.45	98.50	96.95	97.00	− 1.55	101.45	60.85	1,011
Mar 84	98.30	98.30	97.65	97.70	− 1.55	101.65	79.25	817

Est vol 13,001; vol Mon 11,457; open int 9,406, − 46

NYSE COMPOSITE STOCK INDEX

| 97.44 | 97.44 | 96.03 | 96.04 | − 1.40 |

This listing, which appeared in the Wednesday, July 13, 1983 edition of *The Wall Street Journal's* "Futures Prices" column, contains all the pertinent information of the previous day's trading action in the NYSE Composite Stock Index. Since the session occurred in July, the bulk of the trading is currently taking place in the September futures contract, or closest futures contract, also known as the *nearby* contract. The number of open contracts—contracts which have yet to be offset by liquidation—is largest by far in the September contract, a total of 7,091. If you have any doubts about which contract to trade, the open interest column will provide the necessary clue. As a rule, you always want to trade the nearby contract, where the open interest is greatest. The only exception to this rule will occur during the maturing month, when the nearby contract will still be trading but the bulk of the action will be in the following contract. Open interest measures the participation in a futures contract and pinpoints where the most trading is taking place.

Reading horizontally across from the September designation, you can see

49

that the NYSE Composite Index futures for September maturity opened at 97.70, traded as high as 97.85, prior to falling to 96.25, prior to closing at 96.30. Often you can't tell whether the high or low is made first in the trading session, but in this instance it is pretty certain that the high of the day occurred just after the open and the low of the day just prior to the close. This type of information can prove quite useful when it comes to working out a trading plan, as we shall see in a subsequent chapter. Returning to the list of prices, we can also see that the *range* of the day—the difference between the high and the low—was 1.60 points. This information is also useful to know. If you look under the "Change" column, you'll see that a minus 1.55 appears. This is the difference between this day's close and the prior day's close, which must have been 1.55 points higher, or 97.85. The lifetime high and low refers to the contract's high and low during the time it has been trading, probably about a year.

At the bottom of the list of prices appears the estimated volume for the previous day, followed by actual volume for the day two days prior. The open interest at the bottom refers to the total open interest for all the open contracts. The 9,406 open contracts quoted is larger than the sum of the three months listed because a couple of the more distant trading months were left off. It is significant to note, however, that more than 7,000 contracts of the 9,406 open contracts are in the September contract—the month you'll want to trade during mid-July and throughout the summer months once the June contract expires.

Assuming that you had the good fortune to sell one contract at the opening price of 97.70 and later covered the short position at the close at 96.30, how would you have fared? Disregarding transaction costs, the profit would have been 1.40 points, or $700. Remember, the value of the contract is $500 times the quoted price. Since you *sold* one contract at 97.70, the value of the contract would be: 97.70 X $500 = $48,850. You later bought back the contract for a price of 96.30 when the value was only $48,150. The difference between where you originally sold and later purchased the contract constitutes your profit of $700.

In the example above, had you purchased one September NYSE Composite Index futures at 97.70 and later sold at 96.30, the $700 difference in the value of the contract at those prices would constitute your loss. Because the initial margin relative to the overall value of the contract is small, the potential for sizable *percentage* gains is considerable. For instance, in the example above, the initial margin was just $3,500. Since you earned $700 on the $3,500 margin, the gain was a respectable 20 percent on margin in a single day!

SPECULATING IN INDEX FUTURES— AN EXAMPLE

Suppose that you are bullish on the major stock market averages and you decide to purchase one contract of September S&P 500 index futures at a price of 175.15. To take the trade, you are required to post a margin deposit of $6,500. At the end of the first day of trading, September S&P futures have gained one point, closing at 176.15. Your profit, which you can then withdraw from your account, would amount to $500, and your account would look as follows:

Day One

	Equity	September S&P Price	Net Gain/Loss (points)
Initial Margin	$6,500	175.15	
Gain/Loss	+ $ 500	176.15	+ 1.00

You continue to hold the position in anticipation of higher prices. On the second day of trading, you begin with an equity of $7,000. This is the sum of your initial margin plus the $500 in profits you earned on day one. We will ignore transaction costs in the interest of simplicity. Once again prices rise, and the gain on the day is 1.60 points. The September S&P index closes at 177.75. Your account would now look as follows:

Day Two

	Equity	September S&P Price	Net Gain/Loss (points)
Initial Margin	$6,500	177.75	+ 2.60
Gain/Loss	+ $1,300		

On the following day, prices rise once again to 179.75 and you decide to take profits, since you are anticipating a setback in the market. The contract which you originally purchased for 175.15, or a value of $87,575 (175.15 X $500 = $87,575), now has a value of $89,875 when the index is quoted at 179.75 (179.75 X $500 = $89,875). Your profit is the difference between the buying and selling price value, or $2,300. Your equity has risen by that amount to $8,800, minus transaction costs when you close out your position. Your account would appear as follows:

Day Three

	Equity	September S&P Price	Net Gain/Loss (points)
Initial Margin	$6,500	179.75	4.60
Gain/Loss	+ $2,300		

Selling short works in reverse fashion. If, as an opening transaction, you are a seller, you must subsequently buy back or "cover" your short position. In order to profit, of course, you must be able to purchase the futures at a *lower* price than you initially sold them; should the market rise when you are short, you will sustain a loss on the trade.

The speculator's goal is to make a profit by correctly judging the direction of prices. He does not need to own securities to trade index futures, nor does he even have to have an interest in a particular stock. His sole interest is forecasting the market averages and profiting by his abilities.

HEDGING IN INDEX FUTURES— AN EXAMPLE

The hedger approaches the index market with the thought of protection in mind. The hedger wants to minimize his market risk—usually the risk of holding securities. Suppose a hedger holds a portfolio of stock valued at approximately $80,000. His risk is that a market decline will result in a paper loss in the stock. Forecasting a temporary market decline, the hedger, of course, has the opportunity to sell his stock. But he may not want to do this because of the tax considerations or due to the high transaction costs involved. Moreover, he is only a temporary bear on the market, let us say. He anticipates substantially higher prices six months down the road, but the near-term prospect has him worried. He might consider *selling* index futures as a hedge against a market decline that would adversely impact his portfolio. Because he holds $80,000 in stock, he wants his hedge to mirror this value. With the New York Stock Exchange Composite Index futures trading at, let us say, 90 (value: $45,000), the Standard & Poor's at 125.00 (value: $62,500), and the Value Line Index at 160.00 (value: $80,000), he may decide that the Value Line Index is the best one to use as a hedge. He deposits $6,500 in margin and instructs his broker to *sell* one Value Line Index at a price of 160.00. Assuming the market remains unchanged, his stock portfolio and index hedge should appear as follows on day one:

Day One

Futures	Stock Portfolio
Sells one Value Line Index futures at 160.00 (value: $80,000)	Holds stock valued at $80,000
Net equity: $6,500 (margin)	

After more than six weeks, the stock market may have declined to a point where the value of the $80,000 portfolio is now only, let us say, $70,000. As a result of overall market weakness, the same stocks are worth $10,000 less than they were valued at forty-five days earlier. But because you are still bullish on the long-term prospects of the market, you decide to continue holding the stocks. In the meantime, the index hedge has been working in your favor. We'll assume that K.C. Value Line futures, reflecting the market decline, fall to 145.00 (value: $72,500), and you cover your short position at a profit of $7,500. Instead of losing $10,000, therefore, a gain of $7,500 on the futures position has minimized the paper loss to just $2,500. Day forty-five would appear as follows:

Day Forty-five

Futures	Stock Portfolio
Buys one Value Line Index futures at 145.00 (value: $72,500) for a profit of $7,500. Net Equity: $14,000 (margin & profit)	Holds stock valued at $70,000 (paper loss: $10,000)

Net Loss: $2,500

53

There are many other types of hedges. But this simplified version is sufficient to illustrate the concept involved. Hedging will never work in a dollar-for-dollar fashion unless your portfolio is identical with one of the averages upon which an index is based.* Nevertheless, you can readily see the advantages of hedging. In the above example, had your judgment been incorrect, a rise in the market would have resulted in losses on the index futures hedge; however, this loss would have been offset, in part if not entirely, by a corresponding rise in the value of the stock portfolio. Another important consideration involves margin. Had the index price risen, the mounting losses on the short futures position would have necessitated posting additional margin.

HOW CASH SETTLEMENT WORKS

Cash settlement of futures contracts is presently a unique feature of the stock index market, which is expected to be expanded to other markets. Already, the concept has been suggested for futures contracts on such traditional commodities as soybeans, potatoes, and live hogs. And the CFTC has other proposals for cash settlement contracts on leading economic indexes under study. The cash settlement idea is an important one because it allows buyers and sellers of intangible items, for the first time, to come together and establish prices and transfer risk. When you think about it, the idea makes good economic sense.

For example, why shouldn't a portfolio manager who manages millions of dollars in assets have the same opportunity to hedge his risks as, say, a soybean farmer? No one would deny that a portfolio manager is subject to risk. Yet, until the advent of stock index futures trading, the precise form of risk that most portfolio managers encountered wasn't hedgable. They could hedge individual stocks in the options market, but not the entire portfolio. Now all that is changed. Stock index futures trading allows the same opportunity to cut losses in the stock market as commodities trading offers the cattle rancher or the wheat farmer in the futures market. Moreover, you don't have to be a large investment portfolio manager to benefit. With the new mini-contracts, such as those offered on the Value Line contract and the new S&P 100 futures, an investor with as little as $15,000 in stock can avail himself of the hedging opportunities in the index markets.

---

* Even if you could construct a portfolio identical to the average you are trading, due to basis risk, the hedge might prove somewhat less than perfect.

Traditional futures contracts are settled by delivery. The buyer takes delivery and the seller gives delivery. Naturally, since the number of speculators far exceeds the number of hedgers in any market, the ranks of those traders who held contracts to maturity has been very small. As few as two or three percent of the participants in the futures markets stand for delivery. Nevertheless, delivery is a viable and desirable method of settlement when you are dealing in standardized contracts of grain, precious metals, or even financial instruments. But how do you deliver one share of each of the 500 shares that comprise the S&P index? You don't.

To get around the difficulty of the traditional means of settlement in the futures market, the idea of cash settlement was devised. Put simply, the concept means that following the final day of trading of a stock index contract, the expiring futures is settled at the price of the *cash index*. Until the final day of trading, of course, the futures contract is *marked-to-the-market* based on the settlement price. This means that all winners are paid daily following the close of trading, and all losers have funds deducted from their accounts based on the settlement price of the futures. The implication of having the cash settlement pegged to the cash index—at least just prior to expiration—is that the futures will closely track the cash index. Anyone who has followed the index market recently, however, knows that the nearby futures and the cash index are often far apart. At times, notably when the futures market has been bullish on the averages, the futures have maintained a *premium*; at other times, the futures have gone to a *discount* under the cash. Having the futures become the cash index following expiration has another vital significance: no one will ever try to corner the stock index futures market. The only way such a market could be successfully manipulated would be for someone to manipulate the entire stock market and influence the prices of all or most of the shares trading on the New York Stock Exchange. Obviously, this won't happen. Any large trader who tried to take the index futures out of line with the underlying averages upon which they are based would find a huge number of opposing speculators trying to capitalize on the situation by bringing the market back in line with the underlying averages.

Most traders offset their positions prior to the maturity of the contract. But if you do hold a stock index futures contract to maturity, you will pay or receive the difference (depending upon whether your particular trade is profitable or not) between the price at which you initiated the position and the cash index price on the settlement day. Prior to the last day of trading, your open contract is marked-to-the-market daily to the *futures settlement price.* On the last day of trading, all positions are marked-to-the-market based on the *cash index settlement price.*

Assuming a NYSE Composite Index futures contract settles at 95.45 on the day prior to the last trading day and the contract is held to maturity, the final settlement will be based on the actual cash index on the last day of trading. We'll assume the cash index on the last trading day settles at 93.41. Remember, all other gains or losses prior to this time will have been credited or debited based on the daily mark-to-the-market procedure. The calculations would appear as follows:

Settlement Value of Contract on Next to Last Trading Day	95.45
Value of Actual Index on Last Trading Day	93.41
Change In Contract	– 2.04
Dollar Value of Difference ($500 X 2.04)	$1,020
Amount Debited to Long Account	($1,020)
Amount Credited to Short Account	$1,020

HOW LEVERAGE MAGNIFIES PROFITS— AND LOSSES

The high leverage inherent in futures trading is the key to the high profit—and loss—potential. Leverage means to use a relatively small amount of money to control an asset worth many times as much. Because the investor stands to benefit from the entire move in the underlying asset—in this case, a stock index futures contract—the rewards can be considerable.

The initial margin deposit you place with your broker is only a "good-faith" deposit to insure the performance of your side of the contract. Should you have paper losses as the market moves against your position, you'll be asked to deposit additional margin money—or risk having the position liquidated at a loss.

In general, the margin deposit is about 10 percent of the value of the underlying stock index contract, but it can be higher or lower. The exchanges set minimum margin requirements that all brokerage houses must abide by, but the individual firms may set the margin requirements higher, and often do. Naturally, the purpose of setting the higher margins is to protect the brokerage firms, who are ultimately responsible to the clearing house (a non-profit organization that is a party to all trades) for the performance of all contracts held by their customers. Brokerage firms also increase margin requirements in order to curb excess speculation among their customers. When the market becomes overly volatile, the exchanges might raise the minimum margin as well. This serves to prevent speculation among those thinly-financed traders who can't meet the higher requirements and causes others to decrease the number of positions they hold. You should also know that there are two different types of margin: called *initial margin* and *maintenance margin.* The initial margin is that amount which you need to enter a position; the maintenance margin is that amount that you must maintain once the trade is taken. Thus, the initial margin might be $3,500 per contract, but the maintenance might be just $1,500. Once your funds are impaired to the extent that you are under the maintenance level, you will receive a *margin call* and be required to bring your level of margin back up to the initial margin requirement.

Leverage, obviously, is a double-edged sword. To the speculator who is earning profits, leverage is a welcome means of rapid capital gain; but to those speculators on the losing end of the trade, high leverage can spell ruin. Let's consider an example of how leverage can work to your advantage or disadvantage.

Suppose that you purchase an index futures contract at a price of 166.00. Since the value of the contract is $500 times the index, the total value is $83,000 (166.00 X $500 = $83,000). Now assume that the price of the contract declines two points to 164.00. The value of the contract will fall by $1,000 (2.00 X $500 = $1,000) and the index futures will only be worth $82,000. If we assume that the maintenance margin on this contract is $4,000, this would provide a trader with five points of adversity before additional funds would be required. ($6,500 initial margin - $4,000 maintenance margin = $2,500; $2,500 divided by $500 = 5 points). In the table below, we've tracked the impact on equity to either long or short at the initial entry price of 166.00.

Table 2

	Long	Short
Initial Margin	$6,500	$6,500
Mark-to-Market Change		
Day One	− $1,000	+ $1,000
Current Equity	$5,500	$7,500
Excess Equity Withdrawal	—	—
Equity Loss	($1,000)	—
Margin Call	No	—

Note that the short seller has a profit of $1,000 in his account. He can withdraw these and any other profits in excess of his initial margin at any time.

Now assume that a week later the market is trading at 160.00, down 6 points from the original entry price. This 6 points translates into $3,000 in losses for the long position and $3,000 in profits for the short position. The long trader's original equity of $6,500 has declined to $3,500, which is below the maintenance level margin, and the long trader is asked to deposit additional margin or have his position liquidated. The accounts would appear as follows:

Table 3

	Long	Short
Initial Margin	$6,500	$6,500
Change Since Entry	− $3,000	+ $3,000
Current Equity	$3,500	$9,500
Excess Equity Withdrawal	—	$3,000
Equity Loss	($3,000)	—
Margin Call	($3,000)	—

At the price of 160.00, the long trader has lost almost one-half of his initial equity. But this small decline in price represents just a 3.6 percent decline in the overall value of the index contract. Conversely, from the short seller's standpoint, the same 3.6 percent decline represents almost a 50 percent profit on initial equity that was deposited in the form of margin.

In actual practice, the buyer would be wise to cut his losses long before this hypothetical level were reached. But the example does show the impact on equity of even a modest price move.

WHY YOU MUST AVOID
HIGH COMMISSION COSTS

Initial margin is the sum of money you'll need to get started in the stock index futures game, but it isn't really a cost since your margin is returned to you if your trading is profitable. Commission costs, however, will eat into your capital and it is vital to shop around to get the best service at the lowest cost possible. A number of myths persist concerning commission costs and it is important that you understand what you are paying for.

Essentially, there are just two types of commission houses—the full-service firms and the discounters. Among the full-service houses, you will find so-called "wire" houses who deal in stocks as well as futures, and perhaps many more financial services. In addition, there are full-service houses that deal in futures exclusively. Among the former are Merrill Lynch, Prudential-Bache, E. F. Hutton, Shearson, and Dean Witter Reynolds. The commodity houses include, among others, Conti Commodities, Peavey, Stotler, Anspacher, Clayton, and Rouse Woodstock. In recent years, commissions have become negotiable and the discount business has grown rapidly. Leading discounters include Lind-Waldock, Chicago Commodities, the Futures Discount Group, Jack Carl, Eastern Capital, 3-1-2 Futures, and Macro Source. All of these houses offer similar service at comparable rates.

But this is not to say each will be successful in meeting your unique trading needs. When the traditional wire houses got into the futures business, it was primarily to accommodate commercial clients who were apt to require hedging services and relied on their research departments for statistical studies and other advice. As for the typical investor, his interest was primarily the stock market—and that's where the major wire houses placed most of their resources. Stock commissions were major moneymakers for the old-line Wall Street houses. Futures trading, as recently as the late sixties, was considered just a side-line for the wire houses—and not a major source of revenue.

All that is changed now. Commissions generated in the futures markets now account for a substantial amount of the business of the wire houses and they have huge staffs to service and promote their futures business. Indeed, Merrill Lynch even created its own division, Merrill Lynch Futures, to deal with the lucrative futures market.

But which house is right for you?

There are many reasons why an investor selects one brokerage house over another, but two key reasons should be service and cost. Granted, the types of services available from the large commission houses cannot be duplicated by the lower-cost discounters; but then again, the costs aren't comparable either. To make an intelligent decision, you should consider precisely what a brokerage firm can do for you and how well it meets your needs.

The brokerage house, known within the futures industry as a *futures commission merchant*, serves as a middle-man between the public investor and the trading floor. Members alone are entitled to execute trades on the futures exchanges and stock exchanges. Thus, if your brokerage firm owns a membership on a given exchange, it can execute an order directly; otherwise, it must hire a member firm to handle orders that it solicits from the public. To keep costs low, most brokerage houses maintain multiple memberships on the leading futures exchanges. As exchange members, they are permitted to trade for their clients without paying commissions.

Many firms maintain their own cadre of floor brokers whose sole function is to execute orders on the floor; in addition, they may hire free-lance floor brokers, who own their own memberships, in order to handle orders in "fast" markets and at other times, such as the opening and close, when activity is high. Every broker who fills orders for the public must be registered with the CFTC, or, in the case of the new index options, the SEC. For every floor broker, there is a small army of floor personnel to back him up; men and women to handle the phones and telex machines, runners to carry orders into the pits, trade-checkers to see that orders are transmitted correctly, and floor managers to oversee the whole operation. All are vital to the efficient running of a floor operation, and, understandably, all must be paid out of commission revenues.

But floor expenses are only part of a major brokerage house's expenses. Off-the-floor expenses for the typical wire house are even larger. The account executive, or customer's man, who is often referred to as a broker, receives anywhere from a quarter to a third of all his clients' commissions. The in-house research departments, which are maintained by the major firms competing for the full-service business, likewise take a substantial bite out of the commission dollar. And, of course, there is the cost of maintaining offices in the major cities, advertising, and so on. The bottom line is that the major wire house has to charge the commission fees which will support such operations.

The discounter, by contrast, operates with a much lower overhead which it can pass along to its clients in the form of lower commissions. By cutting research, eliminating brokers in favor of phone order clerks, dispensing with ground-level, expensive office space, and paring down its operations to the sheer necessities, a discounter can maintain a much leaner brokerage service. In short, the discounter can provide what a trader really needs, namely fast executions at competitive low rates.

If this suggests a bias in favor of the discounter, it should. As a member of a futures exchange, I've had an opportunity to see first-hand that the order of the big brokerage firm isn't treated any differently than the order of the small discounter. In fact, often-times the *same brokers execute the orders for both types of firms.* The only difference is that client A is paying probably $25 and client B $100—for, essentially, the identical service.

This is not to say that different floor brokers won't possess greater or lesser skills in executing orders. They will. But, in general, to the floor, an order is just an order and the commission fee one is paying for that order won't insure better treatment in the pit.

To the floor broker, who is either on salary or being paid a flat fee of, say, $2 an order, the challenge is to fill as many orders without mistakes in the fastest manner possible. He may only spend five or ten seconds with each order, long enough to yell out an offer or a bid, and find a willing floor trader to take the other side. He does this with caution, however, because in the event of an error, he will be held responsible. In volatile markets, and even some not-so-volatile ones, a simple momentary lapse in concentration can cost a floor broker thousands of dollars if he thinks he's buying, say, when he's really selling, or if he reads an order wrong and trades a 100-lot instead of a 10-lot. In the frenzy and bedlam that passes for an orderly trading situation, an order filler may find himself "out" on a half-dozen or more trades—all of which must be reconciled prior to the next day's resumption of trading, and perhaps at substantial cost.

While an exchange member trading for his own account—frequently known on the floor as a "local"—may pay only a one dollar transaction fee (or even less if he is a clearing member) per round-trip, the public investor enjoys no such luxury. His cost will likely range from $15 to $100 or more per round-turn. The point should be obvious by now. Commission costs add up. If you trade with one eye on the commission fee, chances are you are going to stay in some situations you shouldn't be in and miss out on others for fear of churning out another commission. While a $60 or $70 commission on an asset worth $85,000 or more seems modest, it really isn't when you take into account the speed with which stock index futures are traded. Even a small trader may complete four or five round-turn trips per day. Unless the profits warrant paying those high commissions, the only one profiting from the trading will be the broker.

Then trade less often, you say. Perhaps this is one solution. But you'll find the buy-and-hold strategy is just too risky in the stock index futures market. You really want to get in there and make your money and get out—quick. Like the professionals do. To try to hold a position in such a highly-leveraged asset such as a futures contract only invites failure. Stock index futures trading is a fast-paced, exciting game to play. But you can't very well buy or sell a futures contract and disappear for six months, as you can in the stock market, and expect good things to happen. For one, although you only post a margin equivalent of 5 to 10 percent of the value of the contract, you are responsible for the full value of any position you hold. As a result, you may only put up $6,500 in margin, but if you aren't attentive, you may end up *owing* ten times as much. Futures contracts are meant to be traded; make sure you use them that way—and don't let commission costs be a factor in your decision to buy or sell.

Then what should you pay?

That depends on your financial resources and the frequency with which you intend to trade. Since we live in an age of negotiated commissions, you can pretty much write your own commission ticket if you have the wherewithal to convince a brokerage firm you will generate a lot of trades or will simply leave a lot of cash in your account. On the other hand, if you approach a brokerage house with just five or ten thousand dollars and plan to trade only five or six times a month, you will be paying the going rate—whatever it is for that particular house. The brokerage houses don't set different fees just to be perverse. They know they can earn income on even segregated funds by purchasing T-bills with your margin money and letting the interest income accrue in their name. This is known as the "float" to a brokerage house and it is an important source of income.

Then, too, even if you are a small trader, you can obtain favorable commissions by shopping around. Recently, the competition among the discounters has been particularly intense, and the public has been the chief beneficiary. To generate new business, discounter A might offer a special commission of, say, $12 per round-turn in S&P futures for the month of August while discounter B might be offering free use of a video quote machine for two months' time if you generate a given level of commissions. In addition, there is no rule that you can have only one brokerage account. Why not open two or three accounts with different firms and trade the account where the commissions are most favorable this month? The way things are going, next month you may want to be with another house offering a special rate on the contract you trade.

Once you decide on a house, make sure you understand their Treasury bill policy. A low commission structure may entice you in, but you may learn to your regret that the firm insists on cash only in its trading accounts—in which case you can count on them investing the money in T-bills and keeping the interest for themselves. But remember, it's your money. Why shouldn't you be the one to derive income from margin funds just sitting in your account?

WILL YOUR FUNDS BE SAFE?

One understandable reluctance that many investors have about discount brokerage firms relates to safety. In the past, some small firms have engaged in illegal practices and disappeared with their investors' money. This is regrettable. And there's no guarantee that it won't happen again. But there are a few guidelines you can follow which will insure that the house you select is legitimate. First and foremost, ask around and see if you can come up with any adverse publicity about a firm. Fly-by-nighters rapidly achieve a degree of notoriety on the Street, by word of mouth if not official investigation, and illegal practices are rarely permitted for long in a business where integrity is so important to everyone's livelihood. If it is a discounter you are considering, find out if they are clearing members—and, if not, who do they clear through? Every firm must deal with a clearing member, either their own or someone else's. Clearing members must meet rigorous financial standards and are routinely audited on a regular basis. They have far, far too much at stake to engage in illegal practices. If the firm doesn't clear its own trades, make sure the firm it does say it clears through agrees to that statement. Only a phone call is necessary to find this out. Since futures transactions are all marked-to-the-market daily, any sign of insufficient margin or any other irregularity would be found out long before a serious problem could occur. Secondly, make sure a discounter has a toll-free number and plenty of incoming lines. Given the need for fast executions, you shouldn't have to tolerate busy signals when the market is running and you want to get a trade off. Since the telephone service is vital to your ability to trade through the firm, you really want to know if the discounter is equipped to do the job. This will be an important clue. Thirdly, how long has the firm been in business? Obviously, the longer a firm has been in business, the greater the likelihood it has created a niche for itself in the industry, one it wouldn't want to jeopardize by any financial impropriety. Lastly, if you are in the town where the discounter is headquartered, ask them if you can come by. Don't expect fancy offices, but do expect the office to be equipped with quote machines and order takers all going about their business taking orders on the phone and transmitting them to the floor. If there is any reluctance on this last point, you are probably better off going elsewhere.

DISCOUNT BROKERAGE FIRMS

More than a half-dozen firms specialize in discount brokerage services in the futures market—and more are likely to join this growing field in the future. So fast has the business grown that discounters, who didn't even exist a few years ago when commissions were regulated, today account for 20 percent of all the public orders on the futures exchanges; in the past year alone, the discount business has doubled in volume. As we've mentioned, a number of firms offer special incentives for opening new accounts—often in the popular index contracts. To find a discounter, you might turn to the "Futures Column" page of the *Wall Street Journal*. A list of some of the more popular firms includes:

Eastern Capital
545 Boylston St.
Boston, Massachusetts 02116
(617) 262-4400

Macro Source Commodities
111 Broadway
New York, New York 1006
(212) 285-8741

Futures Discount Group
c/o Filler, Zaner & Associates
600 West Jackson Blvd.
Chicago, Illinois 60606
(312) 444-1155
(800) 621-1414

Jack Carl
222 South Riverside Plaza
Chicago, Illinois 60606
(312) 454-5301
(800) 621-0270

Chicago Commodities, Inc.
330 South Wells Street
Chicago, Illinois 60606
(312) 341-2550
(800) 621-4094

Lind-Waldock
222 South Riverside Plaza
Chicago, Illinois 60606
(312) 648-1400
(800) 621-0762

Taking the discount rate is a meaningful way to cut down on your trading costs. And, at the same time, it will force you to formulate your own trading plan and keep you free from the influence of a futures account executive who may not have your interests at heart.

By following the information contained in this book, plus whatever knowledge you may have already gained on the stock index futures market, you should be in a position to make intelligent decisions regarding your trading account. A discount brokerage firm will follow your advice to the letter and do precisely what you instruct. This is the role of a good discount firm. By calling your own shots, you at once become the master of your own fate and you avoid the propensity of so many investors of relying on a broker's advice. In many instances, your broker may know less than you do about the market. For one, a broker is primarily a salesman who profits from generating commissions—not customer profits. For another, the futures market is so highly specialized that few brokers are truly knowledgeable about the many contracts available today. Don't expect a grain expert to know anything about the stock index futures market. Instead, become an expert yourself and use the brokerage firm solely as a conduit for orders. You'll be glad you did.

TRADING ORDERS

Once you decide on a brokerage house, deposit the necessary margin funds, sign the appropriate account forms, and read the compulsory CFTC "Risk Disclosure" statement, you'll be ready to place your first trade. Typically, the brokerage firm will supply you with information concerning the exact procedure they'll want you to follow in placing an order—account number, number of contracts, buy or sell, etc. But they won't go into depth on the relative advantages or disadvantages of different types of market orders, or how and why you should prefer one over another. By the way, virtually every brokerage firm, discount or otherwise, will supply you with a special toll-free number direct to their order desk. If you happen to live outside of New York or Chicago, therefore, your phone expenses won't increase as a result of dealing with a firm situated in one of those cities.

To insure the best possible executions, it is important that you communicate as clearly as possible with the brokerage firm. The brokerage firm will insist on repeating orders back to you before they are placed and the entire conversation will be taped should subsequent disagreements arise. Because enormous amounts of money are riding on brief 30-second conversations, you might make it a practice to record your conversations from your end as well. Unfortunately, there have been mixups in which a client lost money and the brokerage house and broker insisted the order was never communicated. Should you ever find yourself in this situation, a tape recording of the conversation can be valuable indeed.

There are many different types of orders you can use in the futures market. But I subscribe to the theory that the simplest is often the best—a system that a friend of mine calls "KISS," the acronym standing for "keep it simple, stupid." For this reason, I often rely on the so-called *market order* in the stock index market. Put simply, the market order calls for executing the order at the best possible price at the instant the order hits the floor. Trading over the phone using this type of order, I've been able to get an order filled in less than 30 seconds from the time I picked up the phone—often, by the way, at a very favorable price. With a direct line to the floor, the order is conveyed by hard signal to the pit and is often filled within seconds.

To understand how a market order is filled, you have to visualize the action in the pit. At any given moment, there will be both a *bid* and *asked* price. The bid, by definition, is the *highest* price at which buyers are willing to buy at that instant. The highest bid constitutes the market, and any bid which is lower is considered to be "off the market" and inappropriate. All subsequent bids, in that immediate time frame, must be the same as the last bid or higher; in the event that the latest bid is higher, all traders bidding lower must cease bidding or raise their bid to match the new bid. On the sell side, the sellers are *asking* or *offering* to sell index futures. The asked price is the *lowest price* at which sellers are willing to sell. No one, therefore, can offer to sell at a higher price—again, during the immediate time frame—lest he be considered "off the market."

When you call your brokerage firm and get a quote, you might be told the last price and the current bid and asked. Although March S&P futures might have traded a minute ago at, say, 162.25, there is no guarantee that your order will be filled at that price. The market might have moved in the past minute. Then, again, the current quote always contains a certain time lag; the price in the pit might very well be different. Let's assume March S&P futures are quoted as follows: "Last, 162.25; 30 bid; 35 asked." In the financial short-hand used here, the assumption is that you understand that the market price is in the 162 area and the only significant price is the last two digits. Hence, "30 bid" means "162.30 bid" and "35 asked" means "162.35 asked." The bid price will *always* be lower than the asked price since buyers, understandably, will always want the lowest available price and sellers the highest available price. For the trade to be consummated, of course, both buyer and seller must agree on a single price.

In this example, it is obvious that the market is moving higher—at least temporarily. The last trade was 162.25, and now buyers are willing to pay another tick for the same futures contract. The sellers, meanwhile, are no longer willing to sell at 162.25—where a trade was consummated a moment ago—and now are insisting on 162.35 as an asking price. There is no guarantee that the market will trade at this level. Sellers might begin asking less and price might decline. But at the present, the market is "30 bid, 35 asked."

Assuming prices stay stationary (which is an assumption you'll want to make for hypothetical purposes only), let's say you intend on buying index futures and tell your broker to "Buy one March S&P 500 at the market." He'll read the order back to you and give you an opportunity to give your confirmation. The order is then sent to the floor, where it is hand-signalled or run into the pit. At the time the order reaches the floor broker, whose responsibility it is to fill the brokerage firm's orders, the market might be, in the parlance of the floor, "bid 30, asked 35." The order, which the broker holds in his hand, will, once filled, be folded and thrown on the floor where it will be picked up by a runner who will return it to the trading desk for key-punching into the clearing house computer. At the same time, the price at which the order was filled will be confirmed verbally and sent back through the appropriate channels to the client. This verbal confirmation may only take a matter of seconds.

At the time the order filler receives the order by hand or hand-signal, he will quickly determine if the order is a market order or whether it prescribes a limit. Seeing that your order is a market order to buy, the broker will quickly yell out the bid.

"Thirty on one March," he'll yell into the crowd.

He may leave out the word "March" since the bulk of all index trades are in the nearby contract. Moreover, back-month traders traditionally have their own area in the pit where the spreaders are apt to congregate. Upon hearing the bid, chances are the sellers will eagerly begin offering.

"At 35," will come a chorus of offers. "Sell 'em at 35!" Sensing the opportunity to pick off the "paper," as a public order is known on the floor, the sellers will eagerly offer at the higher price in hopes of gaining the "edge" on the trade, or the difference between the bid and the asked. For the professional floor scalper, who bids and asks continuously throughout the day in hopes of gaining small profits, this difference of one tick constitutes a living.

With split-second timing, chances are the broker handling your order will yell out "Sold!"—and the trade will be consummated with one of the other sellers getting his price of 162.35. Each broker then scribbles down the price and the opposing broker's badge initials and clearing firm and the trade is accomplished.

The order then follows a reverse flow, back to the firm's floor people, back to the account executive, who may be sitting in a brokerage house anywhere in the world, and, finally, back to you—all within minutes, even seconds.

When you use a market order, you will typically buy at the asked price and sell at the bid price. Depending upon the liquidity of the market, the "edge" you give up on a market order will range from one tick to three or four ticks, but rarely more. The "edge" is the price you pay for wanting to be in the market at that instant. You can insist on a "limit" order, in which you specify what you are willing to pay, but in this case there is no guarantee your order will be filled since no trader may want to trade at your price. This is the tradeoff you encounter when you insist on a limit order versus a market order. With a market order, you know you'll be in the market, albeit at a slightly disadvantageous price; with a limit order, you are trying to be more selective, but you run the risk of missing the market entirely.

Market orders can be troublesome under certain circumstances, however. In a "thin" market, which is characterized by relatively few buyers and sellers, market orders are apt to result in what is known as "slippage"—or money lost due to poor executions. There is a very understandable reason why this occurs. With fewer buyers and sellers, the "edge" is apt to widen as buyers insist on lower prices to purchase contracts and sellers insist on higher prices to sell, causing the bid and asked to separate. This widening of what is known as the "spread" between the bid and the asked price is likely to result in a poor fill.

When using market orders, it is important to try to gauge the likelihood of slippage occurring. To gain a feeling for the activity on the floor, I frequently attempt to contact floor sources to see whether it's busy or not. If the market is slow, the likelihood is that the bid and asked have widened and the fill is apt to be bad. Another time to look for bad fills is in a so-called "fast" market, when prices are breaking or rising at a rapid rate. Fast markets account for some truly awful fills, which are often far away from the market price.

Despite the drawbacks, market orders can be useful, and, for many traders, they are the only way to go. A market order allows you to know immediately your position in the market. If you use a limit order, you often don't know whether the order has been filled or not and the waiting period can be difficult. In my own experience using market orders in the S&P market, I've been able to sell S&P futures just two ticks off the high using market orders. Could I have improved my fills by using limit orders? Perhaps. But the agony of not knowing my position would not have been worth it. Besides, you can't do much better than two ticks off a top or bottom. I'd be the first to admit that such fills contain an element of luck; under different circumstances, I've received some pretty bad fills using market orders as well. As a general rule, use market orders when you want to be in or out of the market, no matter what—and save the limit orders for times when you have the luxury of letting the market come to you.

Consider the following case—when you might use a limit order. As the name suggests, whenever you use a limit order, you impose a limit on the broker filling the order. Whenever you specify a limit, it is understood you will take that price "or better." For instance, you instruct your broker to purchase one September S&P 500 futures at 167.65. If the order can be filled at 167.60, 167.55, 167.50, or whatever—as long as the price is "better" than the specified limit of 167.65—it will be filled. But if the broker can't get that price, the order will remain unfilled. And it will probably remain unfilled even if the market trades at that price. The reason? Again, you have to go back to the concept of the bid and the asked. When the market is trading at 165.65, the buyers are likely bidding 65 but the sellers are probably asking 70. You may not find a seller willing to "give up the edge" and agree to trade at your price. If you can't (or, at least, if the floor broker handling your order can't), then the order will remain unfilled and will be sent back to your broker marked *unable*. For sellers, on the other hand, the "better" price will be a higher price. Thus, a limit order to sell one September S&P futures at 167.65 might come back filled at 167.70, 167.75, 167.80 or higher—but never lower.

There's another consideration involved here. And that's simple human nature. Put yourself in the broker's place. The pit is crowded, the broker has a "deck" filled with orders, and a flow of market orders comes his way. The market orders *must* be executed immediately. He may or may not get around to "working" your limit order. But to expect him to bid or ask repeatedly for your order is unrealistic. He'll do his best, but he won't waste his time if the market temporarily trades near the limit but then retreats. Rather, the order will go unfilled.

You should indicate "day only" anytime you place a limit order. Otherwise, the order might find its way into the floor broker's "book" or "deck," as the unfilled orders are known, and come back filled a week or two later—long after you forgot about the trade. You can, of course, always cancel an order once you place it. But you run the risk that the order's already been filled. One good way to enter a limit order is to specify that you want it on a "fill-or-kill" basis. Thus, you might instruct your broker to "Sell three June Kansas City Value Line Index contracts at 170.00 fill-or-kill." If the order can be filled at that price or better immediately after it hits the floor, it will be filled; otherwise, the order is automatically killed and you won't have to worry about it coming back filled at some later date. The fill-or-kill provision allows you to probe the market for the best possible price. It is not an order that brokers love. But whose money is at stake?

How often should you use this order? If you are entering into the market, you may have the luxury of time to select your price. You might try the fill-or-kill strategy two or three times. But if they remain unfilled, it is probably best to go with a market order. There's nothing more disappointing than watching a good trade get away from you because you wanted an extra $25 or $50. If you insist on using limit orders for any period of time, it is bound to happen to you, so just accept it and wait for another trade. The real danger, however, rests with using a limit order to get out of a winning position and watching the market reverse, prior to its being filled, and take you into losing territory. If you have ever been caught in this situation, you know that it is best to minimize the damage by taking the loss at the market and forgetting the trade. Again, it is a matter of perspective. Some traders are really enthusiastic to get that extra tick and are willing to fight for every dollar. But is it worth it? Probably not. If you are trying to earn thousands, why insist on the extra $25 or $50?

Another type of order with which you'll want to familiarize yourself is the *stop-loss order*. The stop-loss order is nothing more than an order designed to "stop" losses by activating a market order at a specified price. Buyers, therefore, will use stop-loss orders to sell their positions; and sellers will use stop-loss orders to buy back their short positions. The buy stop (short position) is always placed over the market and the sell stop (long position) is always placed under the market. Unfortunately, stop-loss orders sometimes don't serve the purpose they are designed for. Oftentimes, a stop-loss order will merely contribute to a flurry of buying and selling and cause a momentary panic in the market as everyone wants to buy or sell at once. If you have ever been caught in a market in which the stops are "run," you'll know what this means.

Stops become market orders as soon as they are hit. The more stops at the same price, the more panic will exist when the stops are hit. Remember, the floor broker must execute the market order at the best possible price. If a flurry of, let us say, selling results from the stops being hit, prices are bound to fall as the floor brokers begin offering lower and lower prices in order to draw out buyers. It is not uncommon for prices to decline by a point or more in a matter of minutes when stop selling begins. The result of all of this is a fill which is far away from the initial stop-loss point.

Should you use stops? Probably. Unless you can watch the market carefully, you really don't have much choice. But you must be cautious in your approach when using stops. The floor sees stop orders as "red flags" that are meant to be "run." After all, for the floor, the stops constitute easy money. They take down the market to a level where stop-loss orders trigger selling, and then a flurry of sell orders, like a string of dominoes, creates more selling and the move is underway. One Chicago floor trader told me that you never want to sell on one of these stop-inspired breaks because to do so only "adds fuel to the fire." But how many traders, who are often panic-stricken on such a decline, can ride out the running of the stops? More often than not, the move is short-lived, and the professional buying (or covering of previous short positions) creates support and the market rebounds right up again—minus the dollars of the well-intentioned buyers who placed stop orders under the market. Because this pattern is often quite unpredictable, I frequently try to ride out any initial sharp decline if I am holding long positions. After all, to join in the fray at that particular junction insures a bad fill. I then wait for the inevitable rally—created by the very profit-taking that precipitated the decline—and then use the rally as an opportunity to take losses on the long positions and put on the short positions.

We will comment further on this strategy later on. But there is another general rule involved here as well: that is, *never hold a stop-loss position on the open.* This is another reason for day-only orders. But if you are coming into the market long or short, wait until after the market opens to place the stops. The reason for this rule is the relative ease with which the stops are run on the open. These mini-panics, created by an open which is, more often than not, purely technical and "out of line," are, as we shall see, "engineered from within," in the words of a legendary trader, and designed to create this very confusion. Don't be a victim. Pull the stops on the open.

WHEN MISTAKES OCCUR

A final word about orders: mistakes occur. As a stock index trader you'll be paying for your mistakes soon enough; everyone does. But make sure you don't end up paying for the mistakes of others. As a rule, traders are honorable people and this is especially true where the floor is concerned. Thousands of dollars ride on a nod of the head, a flick of the wrist, a single word yelled out in the bedlam of the pit. One's integrity is vital to the successful operation of the floor; and a less-than-honorable person would soon find himself isolated. No one would trade with someone who was known for backing out of a trade. In fact, it rarely happens. Despite this, mistakes occur and trades are occasionally mishandled. When it happens to you, make sure you simply refuse to take the trade. But make sure you are right. If you specify a given limit on an order, for example, and it isn't filled as you've requested, simply refuse the trade. Obviously, someone will have to take the trade—but since it wasn't your mistake, it shouldn't be you.

There are a number of people who stand between you and the guy on the other side of the trade on the floor. One of them will be responsible and one of them should be willing to take such a mishandled trade. First, there is the floor broker. He may have misread the order and executed it at the market when it clearly called for a price limit; for that matter, he might have bought when you clearly said sell. Typically, the floor broker will own up to his mistakes, regardless of cost, and take the trade himself. Second, there is the brokerage house. The brokerage house wants your continued business and it behooves the firm to treat you honorably. The house should be willing to absorb a loss that it is responsible for. Lastly, there is your account executive. He, too, has reason to give you a fair shake. If it is his mistake, inform him of that fact and let him pay for it. (I've known brokers who occasionally paid the loss of a client following some poor advice, but this, obviously, is a very rare occurrence; if it weren't, the ranks of the brokerage community would be diminished considerably). Sometimes the strangest things occur; I once had an order filled *below the low of the day* (I was selling, of course; these things never seem to work in your favor), but I realized that the fault rested with the trade-checker whose job it was to report all trades and not the fault of the floor broker—the market had indeed traded at that price, if only to pick off my stop! Frequently, a floor broker who messes up a trade will pay any loss resulting from his error out of his own pocket. The point is, don't believe that you ever have to take a trade that is obviously a mistake; there are remedies available, and one is simply letting the person responsible sustain the loss.

SELECTING THE INDEX THAT'S RIGHT FOR YOU

Now that you have a working familiarity with what a stock index futures contract is, how it trades, the value of a tick, and how to read the newspaper reports, you may want to decide on an index to trade. The selection process will primarily depend on your own attitude toward risk, and what you plan to use the markets for—hedging, speculating, spreading, or whatever. Essentially, there are just three stock index futures contracts—the Value Line Index, the S&P Index, and the New York Stock Exchange Composite Index—with mini-contracts available in both the S&P (S&P 100) and the Value Line contract. From a *volatility* standpoint, the Value Line contract, which is an equally-weighted average of blue-chip and smaller, regional issues, tends to be the most volatile.* This is *not* to say, however, that Value Line is the best market for the trader seeking volatility. Other considerations, such as liquidity and the kind of trading activity you are anticipating, should be taken into account as well. The New York Stock Exchange Composite Index tends to be the least volatile, since it is comprised of geometrically-weighted stocks traded on the Big Board. Moreover, the New York Stock Exchange Composite is a smaller contract whose value tends to be about one-half the size of the larger Value Line and S&P 500 contract. When considering volatility as a selection criterion, you must remember that high volatility means not only rapid gains, but equally rapid losses when you are wrong on the market. With the advent of the new S&P 100 and the scheduled mini-contracts in the Value Line Index, the trader who seeks somewhat smaller risks (and correspondingly smaller gains), might select one of these contracts. The

---

* This is only in general, however. There are times when the S&P Index will outpace the Value Line Index. Because the Value Line Index is composed of many lesser-capitalized, so-called "second-tier" stocks, it will reflect the volatility of this market; the S&P 500, on the other hand, being composed of many blue-chips, will reflect this market's activity. Recent market history has shown that the blue-chips often lead the way, especially after so many over-the-counter issues have been bid up to such high multiples in the early stages of the bull market.

S&P 100 is valued at approximately 200 times the quoted price, or 40 percent of the value of the S&P 500 contract—about $35,000, as opposed to $87,500 for the S&P 500 at recently quoted levels.

As a rule, essentially similar competing products on *different futures exchanges* don't flourish. Generally, one exchange wins the lion's share of the business and the other exchanges concentrate on their primary futures contracts—grains, metals, financials, or whatever. In the case of index futures, however, this has not been the case. Despite the commanding share that the S&P 500 has won, the rival index contracts at the New York Futures Exchange and the Kansas City Board of Trade today still enjoy an undiminished popularity. But there is no denying that the S&P 500 will probably continue to dominate the stock index futures market.

Studies have been undertaken to determine which index best follows the market. But the results concluded that the three averages on which index futures now trade are pretty much equal in their value as hedges against major market moves. You may, however, prefer one index over another due to the size of the index relative to your stock portfolio. In terms of size, the Value Line contract is the largest—valued at over $100,000 at recent levels—and the New York Stock Exchange Composite Index is about half as large. The S&P 500 is currently valued at about $85,000 and the S&P 100 at about $34,000.

If you are planning to trade substantial numbers of contracts and plan to be an active day trader, you are probably best off using the S&P 500 contract. The reason is that the S&P trading pit is the best financed and the pit most willing to take the other side against large orders without price disruptions.

Yet another consideration in selecting an index future to trade will be your intended trading strategy. If you want to trade both stock index futures and stock index options, you will have to limit your selection to the S&P 500 and the NYSE Composite Index, both of which maintain liquid markets for their options. You could, of course, trade the "home-made" American Stock Exchange Major Market Index option as well as an index futures, but one wouldn't serve as a one-for-one hedge against the other, and you'd have needless complications, such as having to maintain different margin accounts for each.*

---

* This may be changing if the Chicago Board of Trade goes ahead with its proposed futures contract based on the Amex Major Market Index. At this point, however, this is just in the talking stage.

After carefully weighing the risks inherent in stock index futures trading, you may decide to *buy options only*. Whether you purchase an option on a futures or one of the "home-made" options traded at the Amex or CBOE would make little difference. The point is, *option buyers limit their total liability to the initial cost of the option premium*. This is in contrast to the stock index futures trader, who risks an unlimited amount in margining his positions. Many investors find this limited risk aspect inviting. As a result, they limit themselves to index puts and calls.

Some investors follow the "home-town" approach when it comes to selecting an index contract—New Yorkers favoring the New York Futures Exchange or New York Stock Exchange index futures and options and Chicagoans favoring those traded on the Chicago Mercantile Exchange and the Chicago Board Options Exchange. But with today's ease of communication, this approach doesn't make a great deal of sense. All the exchanges offering index futures and options are monitored for their financial safeguards and all are capable and honest. Still, I suspect Chicago earns the edge. Chicago is the home of both futures and listed options trading. The Chicago Mercantile Exchange, while perhaps not as large as its cross-town rival, the Chicago Board of Trade, is clearly the most innovative and fastest-growing futures exchange in the country.

As for listed options trading in stocks (and now stock indexes), the CBOE is the premier exchange in the country. When the CBOE first introduced the concept of listed options trading more than 10 years ago, many on Wall Street said the idea would never work. Today, listed stock options are traded in New York, Chicago, Philadelphia, and San Francisco and the concept of listed stock options is widely accepted and utilized in the Wall Street community.* The CBOE is the home of the S&P 500 and S&P 100 index options. Index options are also traded at the Amex and New York Futures Exchange. New narrow-index options are scheduled to begin trading at the Philadelphia and San Francisco stock exchanges in the future.

Lastly, your own finances may be the deciding factor in which index or index option you trade. To finance the margin on a single S&P 500 index futures, you'll need at least $6,500 in cash, and some firms also require high net worth. At the other extreme, you can currently purchase an out-

---

* Readers wishing to learn more about listed stock options trading should consult my previous book, *Sure-Thing Options Trading* (Doubleday & Co., Inc., Garden City, N.Y., 1983).

of-the-money put option on the Amex's Major Market Index for less than $200. But remember, risk is always commensurate with reward. Despite the notion that index trading is strictly a game for the well-heeled, you can see that some of the newer index products are tailored for the investor of more modest means. You may find yourself trading in more than one market—perhaps using an inter-market spread between one index and another, or using one of a half-dozen other market strategies. But whatever contract and strategy you decide upon, make sure you understand the advantages and disadvantages before you get started.

Chapter Three

HEDGING—
How To Use The Index Markets
For Stock Market Protection

In the stock market, as in life itself, there are all kinds of risks. Even under the most promising circumstances, stocks have been known to mount broad, sustained downward movements, and investors have often been at a loss as to protecting themselves against such occurrences. One answer, of course, has been to sell, or at least lighten up, one's portfolio. But tax considerations combined with high transaction fees have often given investors reason to pause. Then, too, the crosscurrents of up and down price movements in the stock market have often been quite temporary. What if you sell your stock holdings just as the market is poised for a substantial advance? It's happened more than once. Even runaway bull markets have temporary down days as the bulls regain their stamina and courage and await the right moment to again stampede into the ring.

Prior to the introduction of stock index futures trading, there wasn't much you could do to offset the paper losses of temporary declines in the market. If you had a certain amount of market savvy and understood the intricacies of the stock options market, you could have hedged a stock position using puts and calls. But this only worked well if you held just a handful of stocks. What could you do if you held a substantial portfolio or managed a large mutual fund? The answer is not much. When the market declined, as it often did, the value of your portfolio declined along with it.

A market decline, of course, is only one kind of risk to which stock market investors are prone. What if a year or so ago you had inherited some money from your Uncle Bernard and you were eagerly awaiting your share of the loot to purchase stock just as the bull market hit? Chances are, you missed out on a great buying opportunity—an opportunity you needn't have missed had you been actively involved in stock index futures as a hedge. Portfolio managers are well aware of the problems associated with moving large blocks of stocks in the market. Often, on a short-term basis, stock index futures can serve as a proxy for these expensive transactions while quite efficiently managing risk.

There are a lot of innovative, new ways to approach stock trading now that we have stock index futures to use as a hedge tool, and we are going to explore some of these trading techniques in this chapter. But before we do, we need to look at some of the kinds of risk stock market investors are apt to encounter and then determine whether the index market provides a viable means of hedging, or protecting against, these inherent risks of operating in the equities market.

MARKET RISK VS. STOCK-SPECIFIC RISK

Any time you hold equities, you are subject to two key types of risk—market risk and stock-specific risk. As the two names suggest, market risk (also known as "systematic risk") pertains to risks associated with the stock market as a whole—broad declines in the major market averages, reflecting bearish sentiment in the stock market; stock-specific risk (also known as "unsystematic risk") pertains to risks associated with a particular company—earnings, management changes, product development, industry risks, and so on. As you can imagine, stock-specific risk can be offset, in large part, by diversifying one's portfolio; diversification permits the risks attendant to a single security to be smoothed out as a whole by the other securities of the portfolio. In fact, this is the very reason why mutual funds have enjoyed such popularity. In addition to the professional management which a fund can provide, the diversification aspect enables investors to virtually eliminate stock-specific risk.

But what about market risk? Isn't even a diversified stock portfolio subject to this type of risk? Clearly, the answer is yes. While unsystematic risk, or stock-specific risk, can be eliminated almost entirely by a diversified portfolio, market risk remains. Thus, during periods of substantial decline in the market averages, owners of securities will experience a decline in the value of their holdings. Moreover, this risk will persist regardless of what those stock holdings are; large and small investors alike tend to experience a loss in the value of their holdings during bear markets. Of course, depending on the holdings, some will lose more than others.

One measurement of this relationship between a stock's volatility and the overall volatility of the market is known as the *beta-coefficient,* or simply *beta.* Thus, high-beta stocks will outperform the market averages in rising markets, but underperform the market in falling markets. That is, they will rise faster and decline faster as well. Low-beta stocks will, conversely, underperform the average on the upside and downside, rising and falling slower than the averages. Typically, stocks that move in concert with the averages will have a beta-coefficient of 1, and stocks that outperform the averages will have higher betas, with the slow-moving stocks having betas lower than 1. Stock brokers are well armed with statistical information to provide you with the beta rating on any given stock.

The importance of the introduction of stock index futures is that they permit you to *separate* market risk from stock-specific risk for the first time. By permitting you to unbundle different types of risk, stock index futures allow you to hedge in an intelligent manner.

WHAT'S A HEDGE?

A hedge is a reverse and corresponding transaction in any investment vehicle to offset risk associated with buying, selling, or holding any asset. Most U.S. investors hold dollars, which depreciate during inflationary times. As a result, they turn to gold, real estate, or other tangible assets which are considered to be hedges against inflation. People are said to hedge their bets. In the futures market, owners and processors of tangible commodities, such as grains or livestock, hedge their *cash positions* by buying or selling futures contracts. The point is, to be an effective hedge, the position must be *opposite* that held in cash; thus farmers who grow grain products *sell* futures, while users who need to purchase grain (in effect, are "short" grain), *buy* futures.

An adverse price movement on one side of the hedge, therefore, is offset by a corresponding gain on another side of the hedge. Turning to the stock market, the cash equivalent is clearly stock ownership; and the futures used to hedge the cash ownership of securities are stock index futures. Those who are short stocks can, of course, hedge their positions in the stock index futures market as well.

THE SHORT HEDGE

Since the vast majority of the readers of this book will be individual investors who may be seeking some protection for their stock portfolio, or speculators who may want to occasionally hedge a portion of their portfolio, we'll deal with the most common type of hedge first, the short hedge. The short hedge is employed by the owner of stock as a protection mechanism to protect against loss. Contrary to the critics of stock index futures, who see them merely as a form of gambling or worse, stock index futures serve to make the ownership of equities *safer.* By lessening the risks of stock ownership, therefore, stock index futures indeed serve a vital purpose: rather than drawing investment funds away from the equities market, stock index futures, by allowing investors to manage risk, serve to enhance the raising of funds required to finance new investment ventures. This is a significant advantage both for the owners of securities and the economy as a whole.

The fact is, potential investors in the emerging companies of the future—thanks to the special systematic-risk managing qualities of stock index futures—can now invest large amounts with lesser risk. They are no longer faced with a feast-or-famine situation. Should an investor find himself in a market that stumbles or begins to move down, he can still hold his stocks, secure in the knowledge that his hedging activities will retain his portfolio's value, and perhaps even earn him a profit. The need to unload great quantities of securities during momentary panics should not be as great and the overall performance of the stock market, given sufficient hedging in the index markets, should begin to reflect this new attitude.

Significantly, stock index futures come in varying sizes. With the introduction of the S&P 100 contract, you can now hedge a portfolio consisting of stocks valued as low as just $30,000. But it is important to know precisely how to hedge your portfolio as well as the attendant risks.

Let's consider a hypothetical portfolio consisting of the following stocks and values:

Table 4
STOCK PORTFOLIO

Stock	Quantity		Purchase Price	Value
Computer Sciences	3,000	@	$18	$ 54,000
Kroger	400	@	40	$ 16,000
Zayre	700	@	50	$ 35,000
Cyclops	200	@	30	$ 6,000
Norton Simon	700	@	33	$ 23,100
Exxon	4,000	@	35	$140,000
			Total Value	**$274,100**

Assuming the owner of the portfolio anticipates a temporary selloff in the market, he can hedge his stock portfolio by *selling* stock index futures. Let's assume the S&P 500 stock index contract is currently trading at approximately 175.00. Since the value of the stock index contract at that level is $500 times the index price, the total value of the contract is $87,500. Because the would-be hedger's stock portfolio is about three times the value of a single S&P 500 contract, the hedger must sell three contracts (value: $262,500) in order to undertake a hedge that is approximately equal in value. Over a three month period during which time the portfolio is fully hedged, the change in value of the stock portfolio and the stock index contract may appear as follows:

83

Table 5
STOCK PORTFOLIO

Stock	Quantity		Current Price	Value
Computer Sciences	3,000	@	$13	$ 39,000
Kroger	400	@	35	$ 14,000
Zayre	700	@	66	$ 46,200
Cyclops	200	@	37	$ 7,400
Norton Simon	700	@	18	$112,600
Exxon	4,000	@	30	$120,000
			Total Value	**$239,200**

During the three month period, the stock portfolio has lost $34,900 in value, or about 13 percent of its initial value. During the same period, however, the major market averages have been declining, including the leading S&P 500 average. We'll assume that September S&P 500 futures have declined from the 175.00 level to just 153.00. The 22 point decline in the September S&P futures translates into a profit of $11,000 per contract, or $33,000 for three contracts. As a result of hedging, therefore, the loss in the stock portfolio of $34,900 is offset by a *gain* in index futures of about $33,000. The net loss is just $1,900 (plus transaction costs) on a 13 percent decline in the value of the stock. Moreover, by hedging one's portfolio in this manner, the holder of stock does not incur substantial transaction costs from selling stock. The initial value of the stock portfolio is still intact and he is free to resume gaining profits simply by "lifting" the hedge (buying back the short position) and holding the stock during a subsequent rally.

The calculations on this hypothetical short hedge would appear as follows:

Table 6

Cash Stock Portfolio	**Stock Index Futures**
Initial stock position: Investor holds stock valued at $274,100	Initial futures position: Investor sells 3 September S&P 500 futures at 175.00. Value: $262,500
Three months later: Investor holds stock valued at $239,200	Three months later: Investor buys 3 September S&P 500 futures at 153.00. Value: $229,500
Paper Loss: $34,900	Realized Gain: $33,000

Net Gain/Loss: − $1,900

All hedging is a defensive strategy designed to protect existing cash positions rather than to generate a profit. Hedgers take a position in the futures market which is opposite their existing cash positions and also as similar in value as possible.

It is important to note that had the value of the stock *risen* in the example above, the stock index futures most likely would have risen as well and the short positions would have lost money. Under the mark-to-the-market provisions of the futures market, the investor would have had to post additional margin to maintain the short positions, despite the fact that the loss in futures was offset by an increase in the value of the stocks. In order to accomplish this strategy, therefore, it is important that the investor have sufficient cash reserves to post additional margin. Had the market risen, the gain on the cash stocks would have been offset by the losses on the futures and the net value of the portfolio would have been maintained. The only loss, therefore, would be an "opportunity loss" resulting from having stock profits "locked-out" by the hedge.

ADJUSTING THE HEDGE
FOR HIGH- AND LOW-BETA STOCKS

The amount of market, or systematic, risk in a stock portfolio will depend on the volatility of the stocks held. When the volatility of the portfolio is more or less identical with the volatility of the market in general—when the beta is 1.00—the number of contracts required to effectively hedge the portfolio will be determined by the cash equivalents of the two. Thus, a stock portfolio valued at $30,000 will be hedged by a stock index contract with a comparable value. But how do you hedge a portfolio of stocks with a higher or lower volatility than the market averages? In this situation, a gain in the market averages will generate an even larger gain in the stock portfolio if the beta is larger than 1.00; conversely, a decline in the stock market averages will result in a still greater decline in the individual high-beta stock portfolio. In order to effectively hedge this portfolio, therefore, you must compensate for the higher beta of the individual portfolio.

For example, let's assume you have a stock portfolio valued at $160,000 and the beta of the stocks in the portfolio is 1.5. This would mean an increase in the value of the market of, say, 10 percent, would translate into a gain of 15 percent in this particular portfolio; since you are hedging to guard against downside risk in this example, the same 10 percent decline in stock averages would typically translate into a 15 percent decline in the portfolio's value. Knowing you have a stock portfolio with a beta of 1.5, let's assume S&P 500 futures are trading at 160.00, or about $80,000 per contract. To arrive at the *number of contracts* you would need in order to hedge a portfolio with a beta of 1.5, you would have to divide the portfolio value by the value of one contract and multiply by the beta of 1.5, as follows:

$$\frac{\$160,000 \text{ portfolio value}}{\$80,000 \text{ futures contract value}} \times 1.5 = \begin{array}{l} 3 \text{ futures contracts} \\ \text{for a value of} \\ \$240,000 \end{array}$$

Looking at a low-beta portfolio of just .50, or the equivalent of a 10 percent rise or decline in the market averages translating into a 5 percent rise or decline in the portfolio, the required hedge would be just one contract, using the same portfolio and contract value, as follows:

$$\frac{\$160,000 \text{ portfolio value}}{\$80,000 \text{ contract value}} \times .50 \text{ beta} = \begin{array}{l} 1 \text{ contract for} \\ \text{a value of } \$80,000 \end{array}$$

Institutional investors, whose portfolios may value in the millions of dollars, will have specialized problems when it comes to deciding on the portfolio's beta. One approach is to derive a weighted beta for the portfolio based on the respective betas of the stock groups. For instance, the airlines, comprising 5 percent of the portfolio, might have a beta of 1.00, but the oils, representing another 5 percent share of the portfolio, might have a beta of 1.44. By taking the *percentage* of the portfolio representing different beta ratings and weighting the results, you can then arrive at a *weighted beta average*. This weighted average can then be used in the formula above.

BASIS RISK

A hedge serves to eliminate what is known as *price risk*, or the risk of declining prices on a stock portfolio. But what it cannot eliminate is the risk of a basis change while you hold the hedge—known, understandably, as *basis risk*. The *basis*, quite simply, is the *difference between the cash index and the nearby futures price.* Because the cash index price is determined by the value of the securities comprising the index and the futures by trader sentiment as reflected by the bid and asked price, the basis can—and will—change from day to day. Unfortunately, this basis risk cannot be hedged against. But since a hedge effectively eliminates price risk, most traders aren't that concerned with the basis risk, since it is most certainly the less volatile of the two.

PREMIUM MARKETS AND
DISCOUNT MARKETS

Because a futures contract's price reflects the market sentiment of all the buyers and sellers in a market, one side or another can often gain the upper hand and take a market "out of line" with the cash index. In fact, this bias toward the future value of the cash index often causes what is known as a "premium" or a "discount" market to develop. As the names suggest, a premium market exists when the futures trade above the cash index, and, conversely, a discount market conveys the opposite—futures under cash. While this basis risk, as we've mentioned above, cannot be hedged against (Who's to say if index traders will have a bullish or bearish bias two months from now?), the astute hedger can earn himself some meaningful profits by simply paying attention to the current premium or discount.

Today, the nearby futures might be 1.40 points over cash. To the hedger looking to sell index futures, this might be an attractive situation since, in due time, the futures will *become* the cash index price. The high premium merely reflects current estimates of still higher prices ahead. But to the hedger, who, by definition, is both long and short the market—long securities and short index futures—this premium provides an opportunity to lock-in virtually "risk-free" profits on the futures transaction. Assuming the market declines between now and when the hedger lifts the short position, the premium of futures over cash is certain to evaporate. Thus, in addition to picking up profits on the short hedge, the hedger earns himself a basis profit as well—all in the name of conservative money management principles, of course. In general, sellers should look for high premium markets to put on their hedges.

Conversely, discount markets are attractive to hedgers looking to purchase futures. Let's say a large pension fund is looking to purchase securities, but hasn't finished its preliminary research on which specific issues to pick up. A discount index futures market might prove attractive to such a fund. In fact, a large pension fund recently made itself a profit of millions of dollars by purchasing about 500 S&P contracts in lieu of stock prior to the big rise in the stock market. The fund was essentially short securities (since, in the event of a decline in prices, it could have picked up shares at lower prices) and it hedged by buying index futures in a discount market—again confirming how the rich get richer, a not uncommon phenomenon on Wall Street.

THE LONG HEDGE

In the above example, the pension fund used what is known as a *long hedge*. The long hedge is utilized to protect against an upward move in prices. Perhaps the most common type of long hedge would result from a desire to purchase stock at a later date due to the inability to raise cash at the present moment. For example, an investor might be awaiting the settlement of an estate in order to purchase securities, or an investor might be bullish on the stock market but uncertain regarding specific stock selections. The long hedge, in this instance, would serve as a proxy for long stock. Moreover, the investor who is an aggressive short-seller of stock might want to utilize a long hedge to prevent catastrophic loss in the event of a bull market. Although the long hedge is more apt to be used by the portfolio manager or institutional investor, the average small investor may have an opportunity to use this hedge as well.

Let's consider an example that may very well have occurred during August, 1982. A small investor, let us say, was looking for an opportunity to begin purchasing stocks because he felt a substantial rally was imminent. Having earned substantial paper profits in the real estate market over the past several years, he was attempting to sell some property in anticipation of using the proceeds to purchase stocks. But due to the recession, the real estate market was slow, and the investor was having trouble raising the capital to purchase the stocks. While continuing to attempt to sell his property, the investor realized that the market might take off to the upside and he didn't want to miss the move. Assuming he anticipated putting over $100,000 into the stock market when the real estate was sold, he might have decided to use a long hedge to protect himself in stock index futures. For the margin of just $13,000, the investor could have *purchased* two September S&P futures. Any rise in the market averages would mean his subsequent purchase of stock would have to be made at a higher level—an increased cost. But the gain on the stock index futures would offset any increased cost resulting from a market rise. Let's assume the investor was able to purchase two September S&P futures at 110.00 and later sold the two contracts a month later at a price of 130.00. The calculations would appear as follows:

Table 7

Cash Market	Futures Market

Initial Position:
    Investor decides to purchase $100,000 in stock but cannot due to illiquidity of real estate holdings
	Initial Position:
	    Investor places a long hedge against anticipated purchase of stock by buying 2 September S&P futures at a price of 110.00.
	    Value: $110,000

One Month Later:
    Investor sells real estate and realizes $100,000 in cash which he will use to purchase stock. However, the cost of the stock has increased by $20,000 in past month.
	One Month Later:
	    September S&P futures rise to 130.00 and the investor sells his 2 contracts.
	    Value: $130,000
	
	Gain: $20,000

Opportunity loss: $20,000	

Net Gain/Loss: $0

In the above example, the long hedge worked quite nicely. Had the market declined during the period when he held the long positions, the loss on the futures would have been offset, at least in part, by the lower security prices. But as it developed, the stock market was in the early stages of a bull market and never looked back at the August, 1982 lows. Rarely can a hedge provide you with a one-to-one, dollar-for-dollar protection. But even an inadequate hedge is better than no hedge at all when you have a volatile stock market. Remember, in all types of equity ownership, or would-be equity ownership, there are benefits and risks. The hedge is designed to protect against the inevitable adverse price risks which every equity investor will encounter from time to time.

THE SPECIAL HEDGING NEEDS
OF INSTITUTIONAL INVESTORS

In developing the stock index futures concept, special consideration was given to the needs of institutional investors. The economic justification for stock index futures trading, after all, rests with the market professionals who use the index contracts to transfer risks to willing speculators. Portfolio managers, corporate finance officers, underwriters, stock options specialists, block traders, and market makers all can use stock index futures to manage the risk inherent in dealing with stock market transactions. In order to visualize the special needs of these professional hedgers, let's consider how stock index futures can enhance their market performance.

The Portfolio Manager. The portfolio manager is charged with the responsibility for buying and selling large blocks of stocks often valued in the millions of dollars. His most obvious risk rests with the prospect of a market decline at a time when he is long stock. Unlike the small investor, the large institutional investor often cannot simply sell his shares without unwelcome consequences. For one thing, an order to sell a large block of stock will likely result in a lower overall selling price. The market simply may not be able to absorb a fund's block of stock without a price decline. For another, the transaction costs of selling off stock holdings can be an important factor in a fund's decision to liquidate stocks. And, like the small investor, a fund manager has to think about the tax consequences.

Portfolio managers can be both long and short hedgers, depending upon their position in the market. Anticipating a market rise, a fund manager might decide to purchase index futures in order to cash in on a bull market move before he has actually decided on the specific stocks he will later buy. The hedge, in this instance, will serve as a temporary proxy for the stock purchase. And the profits will help purchase the stock at the original market price before the bull move occurred. More often, a portfolio manager will be long stock and anticipate a selloff in the market. Rather than liquidate his stock portfolio—which he may deem a sound one for the long haul—the portfolio manager will sell stock index futures as a hedge against the decline should it occur.

Many large institutional stock portfolios tend to be representative of the market as a whole, since they are widely diversified. As a result, in such

91

portfolios stock index futures tend to provide excellent hedges; due to portfolio diversification, all specific-stock risk has been eliminated. By carefully tailoring a hedging program designed to combine short-term risk management with long-term portfolio objectives, the institutional manager seeks to control market risk as well. To illustrate a typical portfolio, we'll assume the portfolio manager holds six stock groups in a small, $9 million portfolio with a weighted beta average of one (The weighted beta average is derived by taking the individual beta rating of each major group and then multiplying by the percentage of each group in the portfolio). We'll also assume that the nearby Standard & Poor's contract is trading at 170.00, or about $85,000 in contract value (170.00 X $500 = $85,000). To arrive at the number of contracts required to fully hedge the position, the manager will use the following formula:

$$\frac{\$ \text{ Value of Portfolio}}{\$ \text{ Value of Contract}} \quad X \quad \begin{array}{c} \text{Weighted Beta} \\ \text{of Portfolio} \end{array} \quad = \quad \# \text{ Contracts}$$

OR

$$\frac{\$9 \text{ Million}}{\$85,000} \quad X \quad \text{One (beta)} \quad = \quad 106 \text{ contracts}$$

To make the calculations simple, we are assuming a weighted beta average of 1.00. The weighted beta averaged is derived by multiplying the beta for each industry group by the dollar value of the group and dividing the sum by the portfolio value.

Continuing the example, we'll assume that the portfolio manager sells 106 S&P contracts in placing the short hedge and that the overall portfolio value declines by 10 percent as his anticipation of a selloff is realized. On a $9 million portfolio, the 10 percent decline will translate into a $900,000 paper loss on the stock, an amount that will be offset by a corresponding *gain* on the short hedge.

For the portfolio manager, the short hedge is preferable to selling stock for several reasons: One, the futures market can easily absorb a sale of 106 contracts; two, transaction fees, involved in selling the securities, are avoided; and three, tax considerations and overall long-term bullish sentiment might have dictated holding the stock.

The short hedge can also be used to lock-in future stock liquidations. By selling index futures against long stock, the hedge serves to establish a sale price *before* the shares are actually sold. In the event the stock's price moves higher after the hedge is placed, the gain on the subsequent sale of the stock will offset the losses on the short hedge. Should prices decline, of course, the loss on the stock will be offset by the gain on the short hedge.

Portfolio managers can frequently see the need for a stock liquidation at some point in the future. This might be due to a greater demand for cash to pay benefits in a pension fund or a shift to a different investment. The manager may believe that the market is stronger now than it will be at the time the cash is actually needed. Of course, he has the option of simply liquidating the stock. But the short hedge enables him to lock-in profits (by selling index futures) and still continue to hold the stock for whatever period of time he has available to him. The number of contracts used to place the hedge will be based on the value of the stocks to be sold and their respective beta coefficients.

Looking ahead to a future acquisition of stock due to an inflow of cash, the portfolio manager will rely on the long hedge to purchase the market now prior to the actual acquisition of the stocks. This hedge serves to fix the cost of acquisition. He'll then sell the index futures after he purchases the stock. If his market judgment of immediate higher prices is wrong, however, the futures position will lose money. If he is still bullish on the stocks, he will then be in a position to purchase the shares at the lower prevailing market price.

Equity underwriters and market makers. The underwriter or market maker earns a profit not by investing in stocks, as does the institutional investor, but by participating in a portion of the proceeds of a new issue brought to the market. For these individuals, the vagaries of the stock market are a constant source of worry, since an adverse move in the market can wipe out whatever profit is available in a given underwriting. While underwriters work in different ways, a chief source of their income is often derived by purchasing newly issued stock from a firm and reselling it at the retail level. Thus, the underwriter's earnings are the difference between what he pays the firm and what the stock will bring in the market. Obviously, this is a risky business. A break in the market will mean the underwriter will have to offer the shares at a lower level, perhaps at a loss. By hedging in index futures, the underwriter or market maker can lock-in an acceptable price and thus guarantee himself a profit.

The underwriter's liability is considerable during the time between when he decides to do the underwriting and the period when the underwriting is completed. Since not all the stock can be sold on any given day, the liability will change as a greater and greater portion of the entire stock offering is sold. During this period, the underwriter's liability increases if general stock prices decline. As a greater number of shares are sold, however, the liability will begin to decrease until it will cease to exist when all the shares are sold. To accomplish a meaningful hedge, therefore, the underwirter must lift a portion of his hedge as the stock is sold.

For purposes of illustration, let's assume an underwriter agrees to sell 100,000 shares of a stock at $20 a share in hopes of raising $2 million in capital. The underwriter's risk is that the market might decline over the period of time during which he is offering the shares and he will have to sell the stock at a slightly lower price. We'll assume he is indeed able to sell the shares over a four-day period, but at progressively lower prices. As a result, the net proceeds fall short of his goal of $2 million, as is indicated below.

Table 8

Day	Number of Shares Sold	Price	Net Proceeds
1	20,000	@ $20	$400,000
2	10,000	@ 19-1/4	192,500
3	40,000	@ 19	760,000
4	30,000	@ 18-5/8	558,750
		Total	$1,911,250

By hedging this transaction, however, most of the unrealized income from the stock sale can be earned back in the index futures hedge. We'll assume that on the day the stock is issued the nearby S&P index futures are trading at 130.00, or $65,000 a contract. As the market averages decline—and the sale of more and more shares is realized—the index hedge is partially lifted. By the fourth day the hedge is completely lifted. For purposes of simplicity, we'll assume the weighted beta average is one. The key transactions are indicated in the table below.

Table 9

Day	Stock Liability	S&P Price	# of Contracts	Profit on Short Hedge (realized)
Starting	$2,000,000	130.00	31	—
1 (20% sold)	1,600,000	128.80	25	$3,600
2 (30% sold)	1,400,000	125.00	23	$8,600
3 (70% sold)	600,000	124.00	10	$47,600
4 (100% sold)	0	123.50	0	$80,100

The original stock offering fell short of its goal by $88,750. But due to the short hedge profit of $80,100, more than 90 percent of this loss was recaptured in the index market. Although this hedged stock offering fell $8,650 short of its original profit goal, this is quite an improvement over what the unhedged position would have been. The number of contracts used to hedge the position is calculated by taking the market value of the index contract and dividing it into the stock liability on any given day. Hence, the initial liability of $2 million requires 31 contracts, since each contract is valued at 130.00, or about $65,000. Note that as the stock liability decreases the number of contracts required to hedge the remaining position likewise decreases. The profit on the short hedge lists the realized profit only. Actually, the profits are greater at the outset because the hedge would have included paper profits as well. As all the profits are realized on Day 4, however, the paper profits would cease to exist.

Because the underwriter is hedging only a single stock, the hedge does not eliminate the specific-stock risk, only the market risk. Some risk will remain, but it will be only a portion of the original risk. Of course, by including the stock's beta in the calculations this can be accounted for.

Floor specialists and block traders. Market makers, such as the specialists and block traders, often hold large inventories of stock that are subject to market risk. Although hedging in index futures cannot eliminate unsystematic risk, it can provide an important margin of safety to market makers, who may find themselves taking significant positions overnight. In order to accommodate large block traders and hedgers, who may need some additional time to decide on their hedging needs, the index futures markets are open 15 minutes after the close of trading on the major stock exchanges.

These specialists and block traders will use the same formula indicated above to calculate the number of contracts required to fully hedge their positions. Considering the huge growth of assets under management in recent years—close to $700 billion in pension funds alone—the need for sophisticated hedging strategies will continue to grow. For the individual speculator as well as the hedger, this vast influx of capital into the index futures market should spell opportunity in an unprecedented way.

Chapter Four

INDEX OPTIONS—
Limited Risk, Unlimited Potential

The newest wrinkle on the booming index concept, index options, as we said in Chapter Two, consist of two key types—the options on an established index future and the options on an index on which there are no futures, the "home-made" options. Regardless of which type of option you eventually decide to trade—if you decide options trading is for you—the principles are similar. Like stock options, there are just two index options, *puts* and *calls*. The *put* option gives the holder the right, but not the obligation, to *sell* the index at a mutually agreed price, known as the *strike price*; the *call* option gives the holder the right, but not the obligation, to *buy* the index at the strike price. The price one pays to purchase an option is known as the *premium*. Like futures prices, option premiums are decided by open-outcry in the trading pits where the various options change hands. The only significant difference between the index options on futures and the index options not based on futures is the method of delivery. In the case of options based on futures, the holder of an option who exercises receives a futures contract. Call buyers receive *long*, or buying, positions as if they had bought at the strike price; put buyers receive *short*, or selling, positions as if they had sold futures short at the strike price. Rather than exercise an option, a put or call holder can always sell his option for what it will bring in the market. Because stock index futures are settled for cash and not delivery of a representative index consisting of stock, even an option holder who exercises will receive a cash settlement. It is simply a matter of deciding whether to take delivery of the futures contract or sell the option outright. As for the "home-made" options offered on the American Stock Exchange and the Chicago Board Options Exchange, settlement is in cash since no underlying futures contract exists. The profitable option, therefore, when held to delivery, will be marked-to-the-market based on the actual settlement price of the index. The difference between the strike price and the settlement price will then be paid in cash.

LIMITED RISK

The key difference between index options and index futures is that an investment in an option is limited to the cost of the premium. You can lose the entire premium you pay to purchase an option. But you can never lose more than this amount. In the case of futures, however, both buyer and seller can lose much more than the initial margin deposit. Thus, the futures trader faces unlimited risk, but the buyer of put or call options (not the seller) can only lose the amount of his initial investment.

When you purchase a put or a call option, you pay a non-recoverable premium. This is unlike the futures buyer, who receives his margin back in full when he closes out his trade at a profit. The put or call buyer, in order to profit, must earn back his premium cost in the market. The futures buyer, on the other hand, profits immediately on any rise in the price of the futures contract, whereas the option buyer may find that even a profitable move in the index may result in a loss because he failed to recover his premium expenses. Thus, the primary risk is that the underlying index will not move in the direction anticipated by the investor during the life of the option. The option buyer must also contend with what is known as *time risk*. This is the portion of the premium known as *time value*, or that portion of the premium deemed valuable by the remaining time to expiration. This will be zero at the time the option matures. Thus, to profit, the option must overcome this declining time value in the underlying index.

THE FEATURES OF AN INDEX OPTION

Borrowed from the successful concept of the listed options market, which commenced trading more than 10 years ago in Chicago, the brand new index options promise to have the same appeal because they have *standardized contract terms*. Every option contract is quoted in terms of underlying futures, or, as in the case of the Amex or CBOE options, in terms of 100 shares of stock. Every contract is standardized in the sense that it is identical with every other having the same terms and is, therefore, a liquid trading vehicle. Put and call options are standardized according to *delivery month* and *strike price*. Thus, every June S&P 100 call is identical with every other having the same strike price.

From the buyer's standpoint, the purchase of a put or a call is simplicity itself. Let's say you decide you are bullish on the stock market and decide to purchase one January Major Market Index 130 call for a premium of 6, or $600 for the index option contract, which is quoted in 1/100ths of its prevailing price. Such an option gives you the right but not the obligation to buy, or "call" the option at the strike price of 130. If the Major Market Index rises to, let us say, 146 prior to the expiration of the contract in January, you can either exercise the option—that is, buy the index at 130 and sell it at 146, for a profit of 16 points, or $1,600—or you can simply sell the option in the market, in which case you'll receive a comparable amount because the option now has a *cash* or *intrinsic value* of the difference between the strike price (130) and the prevailing market price (146). Of course, had the market price declined below the strike price, the option would retain only a portion of its value—known as *time value*—since its intrinsic value would now be zero.* After all, you can't make money by paying more for something and later selling it for less. As you can see, *buyers of call options expect the market to rise.*

---

* For the buyer of a call option whose premium consists of time value alone, the risk is that the index will not rise above the strike price by expiration. This risk, known as *time value risk*, is a very real one since an option will inevitably lose all its time value by expiration and will ultimately be valued at its cash, or intrinsic, value alone.

Figure 1
CALL BUYERS EXPECT THE MARKET TO RISE

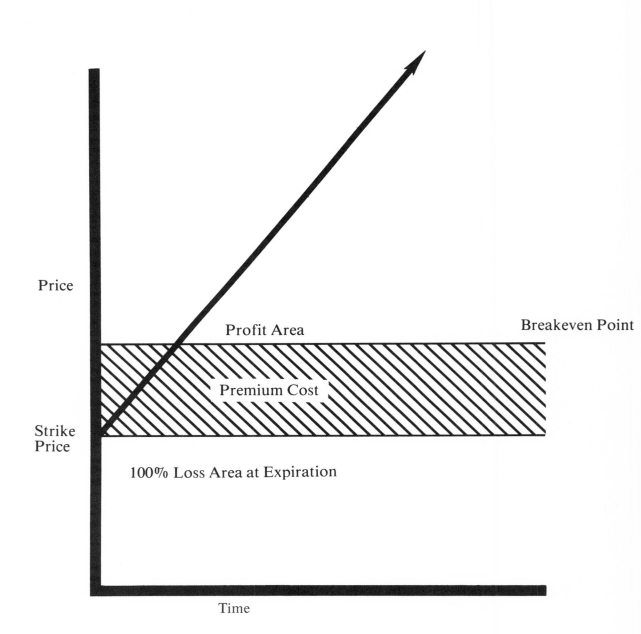

The *put option buyer*, however, is a bear on the stock market, or at least the particular index on which he purchases a put option, and he *expects prices to decline*. Remember, the put buyer has the right to sell, or "put" the statistical index's hypothetical shares to the option writer at the strike price. Thus, if you purchased a June S&P 100 195 put for, let us say, a premium of 7, or $700 plus commissions, you would have the right to *sell* the index at 195 at any time prior to the maturity of the option. Let's say the market declines to 185 after you purchase the 195-strike put. Well, you now have a 10-point profit. You can either exercise the put option or sell the option in the market for what it will bring. This will be *at least* 10 points, or its intrinsic value represented by the difference between the strike price and the market price, plus whatever time value it retains. Because you paid a premium of 7, however, your profit will probably only be 3, or $300, since you have to recoup your premium cost in the market. If you can't get at least 7 in the market, you will lose part of the premium cost. But you might want to recoup a portion of your cost if you decide the market is bullish. The S&P 100 195 put will *lose value as prices rise* (remember, the put provides the right to *sell*), and you may decide to sell the option for whatever it will bring if prices threaten to move higher.

Figure 2
PUT BUYERS EXPECT THE MARKET TO DECLINE

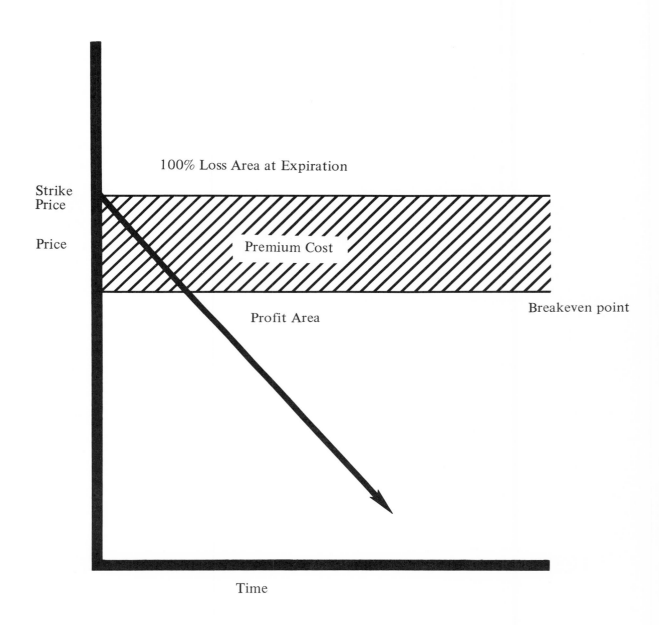

The premium level of an option is determined by a number of factors. First and foremost, the value of the underlying index will be a factor since the option covers the right to purchase or sell the underlying asset. Second, the relation of the strike price to the market price of the index will be vital. In-the-money options, those with cash value, will, quite naturally, sell for higher premiums than options consisting of time value alone. Cash, or intrinsic, value of a call option can be separated quite easily from the call's time value by subtracting the strike price from the market price. (For puts, of course, the relationship between strike and market price is reversed). Hence a New York Stock Exchange Composite Index September 80 call has three points of cash value when the underlying futures price is at 83. Whatever value the call retains in excess of the three point cash value is time value. Third, all other things being equal, the amount of time left to run in an option will determine higher or lower value. For this reason, an S&P 500 March 160 call will sell at a discount to a S&P 500 June 160 call, the latter having a greater amount of time to run. The longer time period prior to expiration of the option will mean the holder of the option will have more time for the option to prove profitable—hence its higher cost. In general, the time component of an option will be greater when the option trades near its strike price, or is at-the-money. An option is a *wasting asset.* This means that as time passes its value decreases until, at expiration, all time value will cease to exist. Lastly, highly volatile index prices will mean higher option prices. The greater the volatility, the higher the premium. Since a put or call buyer needs volatility to recoup his premium cost, the higher volatility option will command the highest premium.

Option values will change significantly as market volatility changes the relationship between the strike price and the underlying index. For the call option, which gives the holder the right to purchase the index at the strike, market prices *above* the strike will have cash value and hence be considered *in-the-money.* Market values below the strike of the call option will have only time value—the value based on the remaining time to expiration—and will be considered *out-of-the-money.* Options having strike prices identical to the market price are said to be trading *at-the-money.* For put options, the terms are reversed since the put gives you the right to sell the underlying index. An *out-of-the-money* put option will have the market price *above* the strike price; and an in-the-money put option will have the market price *below* the strike price. *At-the-money* puts, of course, like at-the-money calls, will have the strike price and the market price at the same level.

The relationship of the strike price to the market price will be the key consideration in determining an option's value. Out-of-the-money options, whether puts or calls, will be less expensive to purchase than in-the-moneys. Unfortunately, the likelihood of such options proving profitable over the life of the option is far less than it would be for the at-the-moneys and the in-the-moneys. At the other extreme, deep in-the-money options will be the most expensive; but these in-the-moneys aren't such a good deal either, since the option buyer is primarily purchasing cash value and not the time value which enables the buyer to gain genuine leverage. As a rule, and this has been corroborated by statistical studies, the best option to purchase is trading slightly in- or out-of-the-money, or the at-the-moneys. In such options, the buyer is purchasing time value, which is the main idea of option buying.

OPTION PREMIUM QUOTATION

When you purchase a put or call option, you pay an option premium to the option writer. This premium, in the case of an option on a futures contract, is quoted in terms of the underlying contract—or index points instead of dollars. The dollar value of an index point is $500 times the quoted price. Thus, an S&P 500 December call quoted at 2.90 actually costs $500 as much, or $1,450 (2.90 X $500 = $1,450). The same form of quotation is used in the NYSE Composite Index options. Options on futures, like the futures themselves, are quoted in increments of .05, or $25 ticks, although the cash indexes are quoted in .01 increments. This method of quotation serves to avoid cumbersome conversions when you deal in both futures and options.

The index options traded on the options exchanges, however—as opposed to those traded on futures exchanges—are quoted in terms of dollars and points, just like listed stock options and stocks. This form of quotation applies to all Chicago Board Options Exchange and American Stock Exchange options. Thus, a quote of 9¾ for an October Major Market Index call translates into a dollar amount which is 100 times as much, or $975.

LARGE AND SMALL OPTIONS

In terms of size, you have the Standard & Poor's 500 index options traded at both the CBOE and CME, on the one hand; on the other, the AMEX and CBOE offer the smaller options, such as the Amex's Major Market Index and the CBOE's S&P 100, which was formerly known as the CBOE 100. As more index options become available, the investor's choice will become more complicated. Which option is right for you? That will depend on how you want to use the index option, if at all. If you plan to use options in conjunction with futures trading on the underlying indexes—there are a number of sophisticated strategies you can employ—you will want to use the NYSE Composite Index or S&P 100 or 500 options, which are traded side-by-side with their underlying futures contract. If the volatility and risk of the futures market has you worried, however, perhaps you are better off using the new Amex options which not only are smaller than the S&P 100 and 500, but don't require the same kind of financial commitment.

Since risk is commensurate with reward in any investment, you will most likely lose less in the Amex options, but you will also gain less when you are a winner. One other feature of the popular Major Market Index (it frequently appears on the Most Active list among the Amex options) is that it closely resembles the Dow Jones Industrial Averages, which are perhaps the most widely quoted average in the world. Dow Jones & Co., however, the firm who owns the rights to the average, has declined to give permission for the use of its index in conjunction with a futures or option contract. The Amex wanted to fill the gap in introducing the Major Market Index and has found a ready audience. Calls on the nearby Amex contract, depending on whether they are in- or out-of-the-money, are available for $100 to $500 a contract. This is quite reasonable when you consider that you can pay more than $10,000 for an in-the-money nearby call option on the Standard & Poor's 500 traded on the Chicago Mercantile Exchange. But it's important to know what you are buying, too. The same call that costs more than $10,000 has $10,000 in cash value. In other words, if, for instance, you paid $10,000 tomorrow—the vast bulk of the option being intrinsic value—if you wanted to turn around and sell the option, chances are you'd get your $10,000 back, give or take a couple of hundred dollars. Why tie up that much money when you are really only interested in the leverage possibilities involved? You shouldn't. It makes no sense. On the other extreme, a very cheap option is apt to be trading far out-of-the-money with little, if any, chance of ever proving profitable.

OPTION WRITING

Just as there is a buyer and seller for every stock index futures contract, there is a buyer and seller for every option contract. But where index options are concerned, the limited risk aspect disappears when you turn to the writing, or selling, side of the equation. The option buyer, as we know, is limited in his liability to the premium cost. This is the most he can lose, period. But the writer, or seller, who takes the other side of the option transaction can lose an unlimited amount of money. Why? The option seller must pay the profits to the option buyer. In the case of a call, we know that a rise above the strike price will result in profits for the buyer. Moreover, since the price can rise to infinity, at least theoretically, the liability is likewise unlimited since the writer must be the one to provide the profits to the buyer.

Let's take an example. Let's say you purchase a December S&P 500 call with a strike price of 175. You might pay $800 for the privilege, or about 1.60 points. The option *seller* receives this premium immediately. But in return, he must promise to pay the buyer the profits if the market goes above the 175 strike price. In order to demonstrate his ability to fulfill his side of the contract, the seller must post margin—just as the futures trader does. Moreover, the margin requirement changes daily since the option, like the futures, is marked-to-the-market. In other words, in pursuit of the modest $800 premium, the seller *might* have to post a large amount of money in order to hold his position. In fact the writer can lose many, many times his maximum $800 profit on the trade—if the market soars and the price of the call option along with it. But the writer has a way out. Should he choose to do so, the writer can fulfill his obligation by buying back—or "covering"—his short position. He may have to do this at a loss—paying, say, $900 for an option that only provided him with $800 in income—but this is the price he pays in order to be free of his obligation to the call buyer.

There are two types of option writing—so-called *naked,* or *uncovered,*

106

writing and *covered* writing. Naked writing means that the seller of the option does not own the underlying index future. In the case of the indexes that don't have futures, all option writing is naked—unless, of course, you managed to purchase all the stocks comprising the index.* The Amex Major Market Index would be an example, although the Amex's recent agreement with the Chicago Board of Trade to form a link for the purpose of trading futures on the Major Market Index would perhaps create a hedging opportunity for writers of the Amex index. As for options that *do* have underlying futures contracts—such as the NYSE Composite Index options traded on the New York Futures Exchange—the writer of a put is considered covered if he has a short position and the writer of a call is considered covered if he has a long position.

The risk associated with a covered position is much less than the risk associated with an uncovered position. For example, let's say you write a June NYSE Composite Index call option with a strike price of 100. As the writer, you want the underlying index to remain stable or decline in price lest it be called away from you above the strike. Thus, your risk is that the index should rise. Above 100, the index call will have intrinsic value and will certainly be exercised. Moreover, the risk is unlimited since the price of the index can, theoretically, rise to infinity. For the covered writer, however, who owns the underlying NYSE Composite Index futures, the exercise of the call will merely mean a loss in profit opportunity. Upon exercise, the writer simply gives up his profits in the futures contract to the option holder. Had you written the option at 100 and purchased the long futures at 90, your profit on the transaction would consist of the profit in the futures—in this instance, from 90 to 100, or ten points—and the option premium, which you receive as the writer. All the profit above the strike price of 100, however, would go to the holder of the call.

When a call option is exercised, the holder of the option receives a long futures contract at the strike price. Since the market is now higher than the strike price, the option has a cash value (or paper profit) equal to the difference between the strike price and the market price. The writer of the call receives a *short position* at the strike price when the option is exercised. If the writer already holds a long position, the short, or selling, position will simply serve to liquidate his position and he will be "flat" the market, or without a position. For puts, the situation is reversed. The put buyer, upon

---

* From a writer's standpoint, this is an important difference since the "home-grown" options, unlike options on futures or stock options, cannot be effectively hedged. Be aware, therefore, that the writer's potential for loss on these options is unlimited.

exercise, receives a short position at the strike in his account and the put writer receives a long position, again, at the strike price.

Considering the risks, why write options? Primarily because option writing can be a pretty consistent source of income. Only a fraction of the options purchased ever result in profits for the buyers. As a result, the odds favor the writers over the buyers. For the buyer, remember, the premium cost must be overcome in the market. For the writer, the premium is a sure-thing. Because he receives the premium, he has a cushion of profits with which to withstand market adversity. The buyer, in contrast, has no cushion of profits. The buyer must see a movement in a favorable direction before he can even start to earn profits.

In general, when the market runs, either down or up, the buyers of puts and calls, respectively, will make money. But when the market is stationary or moving only slowly at best, the writers make money by selling declining time value. As the option nears expiration, its time value must go to zero. Assuming you write an at-the-money option, therefore, and prices remain the same, the entire premium must disappear and you, the writer, will receive the whole thing. For the buyer of the option, hoping for price appreciation, the stationary market means the time value will go to zero and the option will become worthless; he will lose his entire premium, a 100 percent loss.

For those options that *do not* have an underlying futures contract, all writing must be naked. This presents a substantially greater risk unless a comparable hedge against adversity can be found.

Figure 3
CALL WRITERS EXPECT THE MARKET TO STABILIZE
OR DECLINE

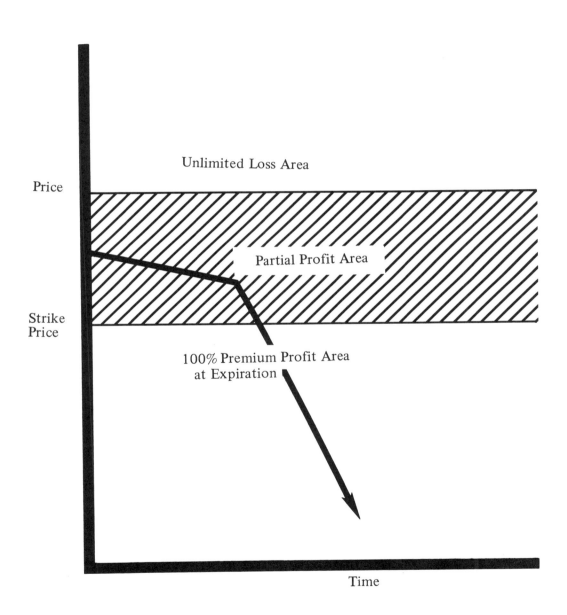

NAKED WRITING—AN EXAMPLE

Let's assume you are bearish on stock market prices and you decide to write a S&P 100 September 165 call on the CBOE. Assuming it is now July 1, the option will have about 2½ months to prove profitable for the buyer, prior to expiration. If the S&P 100 index is currently trading at 163, the 165 call will be out-of-the-money since it wouldn't make sense for the buyer to purchase the index at 165 if the market price is below that level. In return for writing the option, you will be paid the full premium price. This might be 5, or $500 for the contract. If the call option expires out-of-the-money, or worthless, at expiration the full $500 will be yours to keep. The broker, of course, will require a margin deposit when you write the option and you won't be able to withdraw the premium until the position is closed out or expiration occurs. Should stock market prices increase, however, during the time you hold the short call, the premium may increase in value to, say, 6, or $600. You will now have a loss on the position and will be requested to post additional margin. Please note that the option doesn't have to be in-the-money for the option to retain a substantial premium; the time value might increase as the call option approaches the strike price. But at expiration, if the call option doesn't have a cash value (the market price is higher than the strike price), the option will expire worthless and the writer will keep the entire premium.

We'll assume the call writer receives a premium of 5 for selling a S&P 100 September 165 call when the index is at 163. If the index remains at 163 at expiration of the September 165 call, the calculations would appear as follows:

Table 10

Date	Option	Index Value
July 1	Investor writes 1 S&P 100 September 165 call for a premium of 5. Receives: $500. Deposits margin to insure integrity of option contract.	S&P 100 index trades at 163
Third Friday of Sept.	S&P 100 September 165 call expires worthless. Investor receives full $500 premium. Margin deposit returned in full.	S&P 100 index trades at 163
	Profit: $500	

110

Figure 4
PUT WRITERS EXPECT THE MARKET TO STABILIZE
OR RISE

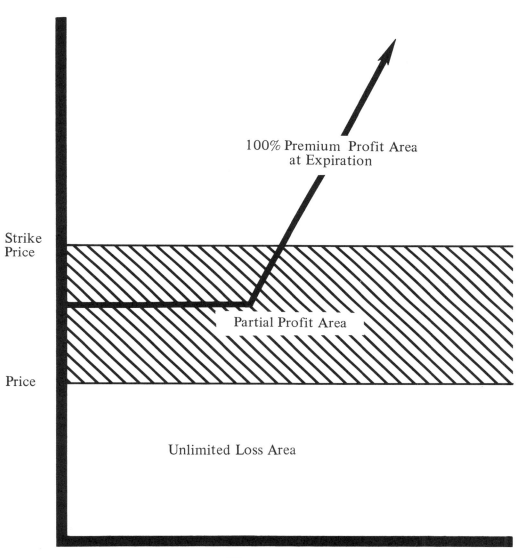

COVERED WRITING—AN EXAMPLE

When you write a covered call, you own the underlying security that might be called away from you, and therefore, you are hedged against loss. For instance, when NYSE Composite Index September futures were trading at 94.50, the NYSE Composite Index September 98 call was available for a premium of 1.00, or $500 (like the index futures, the NYSE Composite Index options are quoted in prices that are 1/500th the value of the option). By *writing* the NYSE Composite Index September 98 call for a premium of 1.00, or $500, and simultaneously buying one NYSE Composite Index September futures at 94.50, the investor virtually assures himself a profit at any price above 93.50. Why? Well, the premium of $500 insures the investor one point of profit cushion on the downside. Should the futures decline by one point, he will lose that amount, or $500, on the futures position; the premium he *receives* for writing the out-of-the-money call, however, provides him with one point of protection; hence, the 93.50 breakeven point on the downside. On the upside, the investor can profit on the futures all the way to the strike price of 98; above that level, the profit on the futures will go to the buyer of the call, since the option will surely be exercised. Thus, the point of maximum profit will be at the 98 strike, where the investor will earn the difference between 94.50 (his purchase price on the futures) and 98.00 (the strike price), or 3.50 points, $1,750. Added to this will be the full $500 premium on the September 98 call, which will be completely worthless to the hapless call buyer at that level. The total profit will be the sum of the two, or $2,250 minus transaction costs *at the strike price or higher*. Above the price of 98, the covered writer cannot earn more on his investment. The futures contract will be called away from him at the 98 strike and he will retain the difference between this purchase price and the strike price *plus* the income he received for writing the call.

Let's assume that at expiration in September, the NYSE Composite Index is at 102.50 for the September futures. The investor's short call option will most certainly be exercised (this is done automatically with all in-the-money options at expiration) and the covered writer will have earned the maximum profit on the transaction. Moreover, the buyer of the option will be satisfied because the call he purchased for a premium of 1.00, or $500, is now worth its intrinsic, or cash, value of 4.50 points, or $2,250 (102.50 − 98.00 = 4.50). The calculations would appear as follows:

Table 11

Date	Option	Futures	Index Value (nearby futures)
August 1	Investor writes 1 NYSE Composite Index Sept. 98 call for a premium of 1.00. Receives: $500	Investor buys 1 NYSE Composite Index Sept. futures at 94.50 as hedge against his short call. He deposits margin of $3,500	94.50
End of September	Investor has 1 NYSE Composite Index Sept. 98 call exercised and is requested to provide 1 long NYSE Composite Index September futures at strike of 98. He retains writing premium of $500	Investor is credited with the sale of 1 NYSE Composite Index September futures at a price of 98. Since he originally purchased this same contract at a price of 94.50, he receives the difference as a profit of 3.50 points, or $1,750	
	Gain: $500	Gain: $1,750	
	Net Gain:	$2,250	

In this instance, both the covered option writer and the option buyer made money. Had the writer been uncovered, however, he would have most certainly lost money. He initially received a premium of just 1.00, and the same option was later valued at 4.50. Had the option writer not been covered by a profitable long futures, he would have sustained a loss of 3.50 points—or the difference between what he received for the option and what it was worth at expiration.

While the above example involves long futures and writing calls, the same principles would apply were you to sell short futures and write a put. The short futures position serves as the protection should the market decline and the put prove profitable to its buyer. For example, let's say you sold short September NYSE Composite Index futures at 93 and wrote an out-of-the-money September 90 put for 1.00. Your maximum profit of

113

4.00 points would exist at the strike of 90. At that price, the short futures position would have a profit of 3 points and the September 90 put would expire worthless, giving you another point. Below 90, however, the put buyer would begin to profit and your loss on the put you wrote would just be offset by the short futures position. Hence, you wouldn't gain more profits below 90. In the event of a price rise, the put provides one point of protection; hence, the one point loss at 94 on the futures position would exactly offset the writing income derived from the put premium. Above 94, however, the position would have a net loss since the one point premium isn't sufficient to offset losses on the futures position. As you can see, the short-futures/write-a-put strategy is most effective in a market that declines, and offers only a relatively modest protection against a price rise.

Figure 5
LONG FUTURES/WRITES CALL

Investor buys NYSE Composite Index Sept. futures at 94.50
and writes out-of-the-money Sept. 98 call for premium of 1

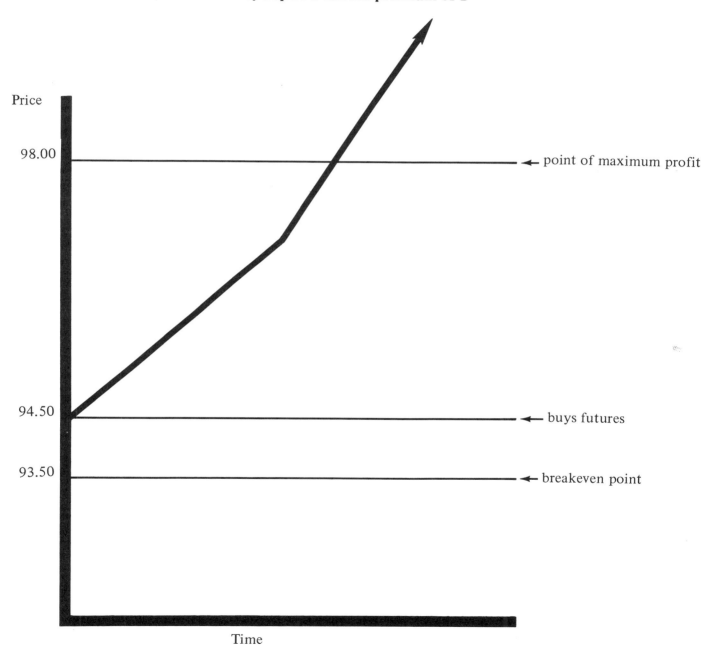

But, you might ask, doesn't someone have to lose to supply the winners with their profits? Most certainly. In the example on page 113, the sellers of the futures at 94.50 were losers, since the market subsequently rose to 102.50. In addition, the covered writer might have enhanced his profits by not writing the call option at all. Instead, he might have simply purchased NYSE Composite Index September futures at 94.50 and held on. But this assumes the advantage of perfect foresight. By using a covered writing strategy, the investor insured himself of $500 of protection on the downside (the premium from the call) and a maximum profit of $2,250 at the strike price or higher. He has created a band of prices within which the trade becomes a sure-thing, and he has some pretty good odds on his side. It is important to recognize that had he *not* hedged his position by taking the long futures contract, he could have lost considerably more on the trade than he ever had the prospects of winning—which was just $500, the maximum profit on the call. A very poor risk/reward ratio, as will be discussed later.

SELECTING THE BEST OPTIONS TO BUY AND WRITE

When you consider the combinations of option durations mixed with varying strike prices, the number of available options to buy or write become truly overwhelming. At any one moment in time, there might be options of three different maturities trading at 10 or 12 different strike prices—and that's just for the calls. There may be a comparable amount of puts available. Which one do you choose?

The first step in your selection process depends on whether you want to be a buyer or a seller, and, of course, whether you're going to concentrate on puts or calls. Remember, although most of our examples will involve calls, the same principles apply to puts. Certainly, your analysis of future market behavior will have some impact on which option you select. If you are certain of a rapid and significant price rise in an index, for instance, the out-of-the-money call will offer considerably more leverage than the in-the-money call. The same is true of shorter—versus longer—duration options. Because of the lower premium costs, the shorter-term option offers higher leverage—but the market must cooperate if you are going to emerge a winner.

Let's look at a hypothetical example using the NYSE Composite Index calls. We'll assume that at a time when September futures are trading at 92.70 with about six weeks to expiration, and December futures are trading at 93.35 with about 18 weeks to expiration, the following calls are available at the following strike prices:

Table 12
NYSE COMPOSITE INDEX—Calls

Price = $500 times premium

Strike Price	September	December
88	5.25	7.20
90	3.90	5.85
92	2.70	4.65
94	1.75	3.70
96	1.10	2.80
98	.60	2.20
100	.35	1.75
102	.20	1.20
104	.10	.85

From the buyer's standpoint, the most inexpensive option is the September 104, trading at just .10, or $50 for the call. A bargain? Hardly. Chances are slim that the NYSE Composite Index will trade above 104 within the next six weeks. But even this call, which will likely remain out-of-the-money, may still increase in value if the NYSE Composite Index sustains a substantial rise. If, for instance, bullish news pushes the Index up to, let us say, 98—then perhaps the September 104 might appear to be more valuable and the buyer could make money. But, in general, the far out-of-the-moneys don't make sense.

At the other extreme, you have the deep in-the-money options. The December 88 call, with 5.35 points of intrinsic value, is trading for 7.20, or the intrinsic value plus 1.85 points in time value. This call will cost you $3,600 plus commissions. The trouble with the in-the-moneys, however, rests with the leverage potential. Even if the option does prove profitable, the initial investment cost, on a percentage basis, does not make it inviting. With a deep in-the-money call (or put, for that matter), you are paying for something which is not providing a return—namely, the option's cash value. You are running a very real risk that, in a declining market, you might lose the entire premium. Too risky. The idea of purchasing an option in the first instance is to achieve high leverage coupled with limited risk. Why not risk no more than is necessary? And why not concentrate on purchasing simple time value? With an in-the-money or out-of-the-money option, you are purchasing just time value alone. Let's look at the September 90 call. The premium is 3.90, or $1,950. But 2.70 points of that cost is cash value. This makes more sense than the September 88 call, but in the event of a decline in prices, you would lose the entire $1,950. With the December 90 call, of course, a decline in prices would result in more than $2,500 lost. How about the 92-strike calls?

The September 92 call is available for 2.70, or about $1,360, and the December 92 call is available for 4.65, or about $2,325. Both options offer you the same opportunity—the right to purchase the index at a price of 92—but the cash values are slightly different. The September call has about .70 points in cash value and the December call has about 1.45 points in cash value. More importantly, the December call offers the call buyer three times as much time for the option to prove profitable. This is significant, since the chance of the option moving higher is obviously greater over the next 18 weeks than it is over the next six weeks. But how do you make a hard-and-fast decision? One method is to rely on how bullish you think the market is. If you think the stock market will make a sustained rally over the next six weeks, the September 92 call probably makes sense. But if you are this certain of a substantial rise, why not save some premium money and pick up the September 100 call for just .35, or $175 instead of paying $1,350 for the lower-strike call? In fact, chances are neither option will prove profitable, least of all the higher-strike September 100 call. Perhaps you should concentrate on a longer-duration option, maybe even the March call. One way to make an intelligent decision concerning which call to purchase is to make the different duration calls comparable by measuring them on a *per-week cost basis*. For instance, the September 92 with a premium of 2.70 costs about .45 points, or $225, on a per-week basis for the remaining six weeks prior to expiration; the December 92, trading at 4.65, with 18 weeks to expiration, costs about .25, or just $125, on a per-week basis. Comparing the two, the longer-duration December 92 call makes more sense. The initial cost is higher, but the December 92 call provides you with triple the amount of time of the shorter-duration September 92.

Another way to view the decision to purchase a call is in terms of the breakeven point. If you are paying 2.70 points for the September 92 when September futures are at 92.70, the breakeven point for the call is 94.70 (or the sum of the strike plus the premium). The December 92, however, with the larger premium and the somewhat higher futures price, will have a breakeven of 96.65 (92 strike plus 4.65 premium). This is a judgment call, but the likelihood is probably greater that December will trade at 96.65 before its expiration than the September 92 will trade at 94.70 before its expiration. On a per-week basis, the September futures must gain an average of .33 points each week to reach breakeven, whereas the December futures must gain an average of only .18 points each week to reach breakeven. We all know that neither the index nor futures will likely move in a steady line from one price to another. In any case, chances favor the longer-term option to be a winner.

And this raises another question: why be a call buyer at all? As a rule, most options expire worthless. True, during runaway bull markets, the call buyer will make himself a lot of money. But as a rule, you are far better off writing options than buying them. Assuming little or no movement in price in the above example, the put *writer* would receive a premium of 2.00 for writing a September 92 put. Remember, for the put to prove profitable, the index price must be *below* the strike price at expiration. Thus, if the index price stays *above* 92 for the next six weeks, the put writer picks up two points, or $1,000. For the September 92 call buyer to earn such a profit, the index must rise to 96.70 by expiration, or two points above breakeven. All in six weeks! The put writer who sells a September 92 put only needs the market to stabilize or stay above 92 to earn a comparable amount. This is why the professional percentage players prefer writing options to buying them. While the risks might be larger under certain circumstances (and these can be hedged against), the likelihood of having a winning position is also greater.

If you look at the premiums for the September and December NYSE Composite Index calls, you'll find the shorter-duration options, from the writer's standpoint, tend to make the most sense. The writer, unlike the buyer, wants to earn premium income for writing those calls (or puts) with the *highest per-week income value.* Understandably, these are the shorter-term options. Options tend to lose their time value only grudgingly. Thus, a given option might retain its time value at a pretty high level until expiration approaches. Then, the time value will tend to disappear quite rapidly since, by definition, at expiration an option will have no time value. In fact, a certain option spread, known as a *horizontal spread,* is based on this propensity for soon-to-expire options to lose value faster than deferred options. In a horizontal spread, a trader will write a nearby option and purchase a longer-duration option. The profit will result from the change in the differential between the two, or the shorter-term option losing value faster than the longer-term option gains value.

In terms of higher or lower strike prices, the writer faces the same dilemma (but in reverse) as the buyer. The out-of-the-moneys will tend to have low premiums, making the potential—which, you must remember, is strictly limited to the premium cost—not worth the reward. Sure, you could write a far out-of-the-money September 104 call, for a premium of $50 in the above example, but what if lightning strikes and the stock market soars? For a potential profit of just $50, the writer might lose thousands. It is not worth the risk. Conversely, deep in-the-moneys require higher margin requirements. Moreover, for the in-the-moneys to prove profitable, the market *must* move in the direction anticipated. For call writers, the market must move down, or at least stabilize, in order to earn a profit. And even then the writer has the problems resulting from margin calls if temporary market adversity sets in. Thus, from a writing standpoint, the options that are slightly in- or out-of-the-money provide the best risk/reward ratio. Options trading at-the-money or slightly in- or out-of-the-money provides reasonable premium income to writers coupled with declining time value. Lastly, another reason for concentrating on those options trading near-the-money is that of liquidity. Most of the action takes place in these options; thus, you have a far greater opportunity to achieve a good fill.

HOW PUTS AND CALLS
CAN MAKE YOUR FUTURES TRADING
MORE PROFITABLE

In addition to covered writing strategies, puts and calls can be used in combination with futures for a variety of strategies from the buying side. Options are incredibly versatile when used in conjunction with futures trading. Consider a situation in which you are long index futures. Your risk of holding futures is a price decline. Why not pick up a little insurance on the position by purchasing a put? Then, if prices decline, the loss on the long position will be offset, at least in part, by a corresponding gain on the put option (depending, of course, upon the strike price of the option and the put's premium cost). For example, let's say you purchase a September NYSE Composite Index futures at a price of 94 and simultaneously buy a September NYSE Composite Index 94 put for a premium of 2.00, or $1,000 ($500 X 2 = $1,000). Now, no matter how high or low the price of September NYSE Composite Index futures trade, your risk is strictly limited. The most you can lose is the put's premium cost of $1,000. This is in sharp contrast to the unlimited liability you face if you hold a long futures position and the market declines *without* protection of the put.

For short sellers of futures, a call option can provide meaningful protection. Although calls typically cost more than puts because investors tend to be optimistic on prices, a call option purchased in conjunction with being short index futures serves to limit the risk to the call's premium. Considering the bull market we've recently seen, this should be welcome as inexpensive insurance.

For example, let's say you are bearish on stock prices over the next four months and that the NYSE Composite Index December futures, with about four months left to expiration, are selling at 94. You might want to sell December futures in anticipation of the decline, but at the same time you may want to hedge by purchasing a call option. Assume the at-the-money December 94 call is available for 4 points, or about $2,000. Let's say you take the position and are now short futures and own one call. Should prices fall to, say, 87 prior to the expiration of the December contract, you can take profits on the futures and allow the call to expire worthless. The transactions would appear as follows:

Table 13
SHORT FUTURES/BUY CALL

Futures	**Options**
Investor sells 1 NYSE Composite Index December futures at 94. Posts $3,500 in margin.	Investor buys 1 NYSE Composite Index December 94 call for a premium of 4, or $2,000.
Four months later the investor buys (covers) 1 NYSE Composite Index December futures at 87 for a profit of 7 points.	Call option expires worthless four months later.
Gain: $3,500	Loss: $2,000

Net Gain/Loss: + $1,500

The purchase of a call in conjunction with an opposite futures position can also be used to lock-in a profit when, for whatever reason, you wish to retain the futures position. For instance, let's say you sold December S&P 500 futures at 180 and the price has declined to 160, representing a $10,000 profit. Because you anticipate lower prices long-term, but are uncertain about the near-term, you might decide to purchase an at-the-money December S&P 500 call with a strike price of 160. We'll assume the premium is 4.60 points, or $2,250. Now you are protected should prices rise. In that event, the loss on the futures will be offset by the gain on the call. Should futures continue to decline, the call's premium will be lost, however. Let's assume that prices rise to 163 by expiration. At that point, the original 20-point profit on the futures will have been reduced to a 17-point profit. But the call, which cost 4.50 points to purchase, will retain a cash value of 3 points. Thus, the 20 point profit will still exist. The cost: $2,250. The transactions would appear as follows:

Table 14
SHORT FUTURES/BUY CALL

Futures	Options
Investor sells 1 December S&P 500 futures at 180 and the market declines to 160, representing a $10,000 paper profit.	When December futures trade at 160 the investor purchases a S&P 500 December 160 call for a premium of 4.50 points, or $2,250.
At expiration, December S&P 500 futures trade at 163 and investor covers his short position for a profit of $8,500.	At expiration, December S&P 500 futures trade at 163 and investor exercises his December 160 call for a return of 3 points, or $1,500.
Gain: $8,500	Loss: $750

Net Gain/Loss: +$7,750

With perfect hindsight, one can see that the investor would have been better off by taking his original $10,000 paper profit instead of purchasing the call. The reason the call didn't protect the entire position was due to the call's $2,250 premium. Only $1,500 of this amount was recovered by the subsequent rise in the market and the net gain was only $7,740. Had the market risen sharply, however, to 167, the call would have recovered $3,500 minus the original cost of $2,250, or $1,250. This would have been used to offset, in part, the $3,500 loss on the futures position. Had the S&P index continued to decline to 155.50 or lower, the gain on the futures would be larger than the call's premium and the option would expire worthless, but useful nonetheless since it provided peace of mind and locked-in a substantial profit.

If you are really one-sided about the market, but prefer to limit your risk, one alternative is to purchase calls in conjunction with being long index futures. It is the rare futures trader who hasn't at some time wished to draw on his paper profits to finance additional contracts. This strategy, known as *pyramiding*, can be extremely risky, however, and the call buying strategy in addition to long futures can limit your downside risk. Say you purchase one NYSE Composite Index September futures at 94 and also

123

purchase a NYSE Composite Index 94 call at the same time. Now, if prices rise, you own not one but two long futures at 94—your original futures purchase plus the one you'll receive when you exercise your call. On the downside, this strategy has the advantage of limiting your risk. The most you can lose on the call is the premium cost. And even then, you can sell the call at a loss along with the long futures. Looking at the reverse situation, you can also enhance your leverage by buying puts along with short futures contracts. Using puts and calls in this manner serves to enhance the outright position while limiting the risk in the event of price adversity.

As you might imagine, there are endless varieties of option/futures strategies. You can take multiple put or call positions in conjunction with futures: for instance, you can buy two puts for every long futures, or vice versa. Or you can buy three calls for every long futures if you are really bullish on the stock market and want to enhance your leverage. And you can concentrate your efforts on finding deep out-of-the-money options selling for very low premiums that will magnify your investment ten-fold *if* your market timing is correct—to name just a few of the more popular strategies.

WHEN THE WRITER'S RISK RISES

When you are writing one of the "home-grown" options for which no underlying futures contract is traded, you have an additional risk. Because such index options react to a broad spectrum of underlying securities, the likelihood of any stock portfolio which you do hold corresponding to the index in a one-to-one relationship is extremely unlikely. As a result, it is quite unlikely a writer of one of these options can be fully hedged.

An example of the kind of risk involved might be provided by a writer of one of the new oil and gas specialty indexes. You might hold one or two oil stocks and, therefore, write an option on the Amex oil and gas index. Having written, say, a call in anticipation of picking up some writing income from near-term weakness, you might think you are indeed "covered" if oil stocks rise. After all, a rise in oil and gas prices would push the index higher along with your stocks. Since you are, in effect, "short" a call, the rise in the index would create a loss in your index writing position; however, being long oil stocks, you would no doubt profit from a rise in share prices. The problem here, however, rests with the correlation of your portfolio with the index. If you hold just one or two companies whose shares are *falling* while oil and gas issues in general are mounting a rise, you are going to lose on both fronts. Be cautious, therefore, when you write options that are not easily hedged. This is especially true of the "home-grown" options that don't have underlying futures contracts.

OPTIONS AS A HEDGE

Put and call index options can be used as a stock market hedge much in the manner of index futures. The most common strategy will be to purchase puts against a portfolio of long stocks. In the event of a market decline, the loss on the portfolio will be offset, at least in part, by a corresponding gain on the put. Unlike the short hedge using futures, however, the put buyer must pay a premium cost. But this cost should be seen as a form of insurance to help guard against portfolio losses. Taking this insurance metaphor a step further, you would view the selection of the strike price as a form of the amount of deductible insurance you are willing to assume. For instance, let's say you purchase an out-of-the-money put with a strike *below* the current market. The premium of such a put will be lower than an at-the-money or in-the-money put, but the holder must be willing to assume the additional risk. The difference between the current market and the strike then represents an unhedged potential loss in the event of a market decline.

By using calls, options can be used as long hedges against stock in the same manner as long futures served in the chapter on hedging. In addition, you can write options in order to generate income, which can be used as a cushion against loss. But writing naked options, due to the unlimited risk involved, should only be undertaken in a sophisticated option writing program in which you are prepared to take immediate defensive market action to prevent unwanted loss.

Why use an index option instead of an index futures as a hedge? When you use index futures as a short hedge—and, paradoxically, this is especially true if you don't need the hedge—a continued favorable move in

125

the direction of stock prices will require you to post additional margin on the losing futures position. This, obviously, will require additional cash, and perhaps a great deal of cash. Not every hedge is needed. Indeed, many hedges eventually only serve to *lock-out* additional profits, as we've seen in some of the examples we've covered. So if you have a fair-sized stock portfolio and you go ahead and hedge by selling futures, a rise in the stock market will result in greater stock profits, but the short futures position will only continue to lose money. You can't tell your broker you will pay him the losses when you take profits on the stock. After all, by then the market might have declined and you won't have any profits. The futures market demands that payment be made daily. Hence, you must have lots of cash to continue to hedge the stock position—or, as an alternative, an index option. The index option premium cost, however, is a one-shot deal—one which is limited in risk. Sure, you can subsequently liquidate an option if you don't want to hold it any longer. But most importantly, *no matter how far the market moves against an option position, the buyer's liability is only limited to the cost of the premium*. Now, if you have a fair-sized stock portfolio and you decide to hedge by purchasing *index put options*, your risk is strictly limited. You buy the options and you forget about them, just like insurance. If you ever need the protection, the put is there to help out. Otherwise, the premium cost is simply the cost of doing business in the stock market.

One drawback for institutions is that a portfolio must exactly duplicate the broad averages in order to be perfectly hedged. While arbitrage specialists attempted to construct portfolios to conform with market averages, the randomness of the index futures prices prevented them from picking up small, arbitrage profits due to fluctuations in the basis. The use of index options as opposed to index futures, however, would only serve to limit the risk—not create a more perfect hedge. Again, the notion of the insurance policy applies.

BULL AND BEAR OPTION SPREADS

A slightly more sophisticated—and complicated—method of using index options is known as the *option spread*. The option spread consists of two or more options which are simultaneously purchased and sold. You can use puts or calls in spreads, but generally you stick to one or the other. The principles of spreading are the same whether you use puts or calls, although one variation of spreading, known as a *straddle* or *combination*, utilizes a variation of both puts and calls. To keep matters simple, we'll concentrate on call spreads here.

When you place a spread position, by buying and selling two or more options of different strike prices and/or expiration dates, you do so with the idea that you will profit if the market trades within a certain area or price zone. In many ways, a spread is simply a proxy position for an outright put or call position. But it has advantages, notably a lower overall cost over the outright option position, as will be discussed.

It is important to understand that a spread consists of both a long and short position. That is, one option you buy and another you write, or sell. Since we are focusing on calls, let's assume you purchase a S&P 100 September 165 call and simultaneously write a S&P 100 September 170 call. In this illustration, the lower-strike call will be more expensive, since you are using a call which enables the buyer to purchase the index at a lower price, and it will result in a net spread *debit* when you place the spread. In other words, you will pay more for the lower-strike call than you will receive for the higher-strike call. Let's say the September 165 call is trading at 3 and the September 170 call for 1. If you place this spread, therefore, you will pay 3 for the September 165 and receive 1 for the September 170. Your net cost is 2, or $200 for the spread. This type of spread, one which is purchased for a net debit, is known as a *bull spread*. Understandably, the spread will make money if the index price rises—very much as an outright purchase of a call will. Moreover, the bull spread shares the same feature with the outright position of being strictly limited in risk. The most you can lose on the spread is the initial cost, or net debit. In this instance, that cost is 2, or $200. Unlike the outright purchase of the call, however, the spread's maximum potential is limited. The maximum profit on the spread will exist at the higher strike price of 170. Above that price, the purchaser of the short September 170 (the call you wrote) will gain whatever profits are available. The maximum profit on the spread is also known in advance. It is 3, or the difference between the strikes of the two calls (5), less the net debit (2).

Let's assume the S&P Index is at 162 at the time the spread is placed. At that price, both the September 165 call and the September 170 call will be

127

out-of-the-money. In order for the 165 call to have value at expiration, the index must trade above 165. What will happen if the index is at 173 at expiration? Both options will have value and the bull spread will return its maximum profit of 3. First, the long September 165 call will have a cash value of 8 points (173 − 165 = 8). Second, the September 170 call, which was *sold* for a credit of 1, will now have a value of 3 (173 − 170 = 3). For the spreader, this represents a loss of 2 points on the September 170 call. Remember, the spreader *sold* the September 170 for a credit of 1. Given the rise in the index, the investor must buy it back at a higher price, thus sustaining a net loss of 2 points. That is, he must supply the profits for the buyer who paid one point for an option now selling for three points. The net credit on the spread is now the difference between the plus and minus values of the two calls. The September 165 has a value of 8 points and the September 170 has a value of 3 points. The difference is 5 points. But since the spreader initially paid 2 points for the spread, his net profit is just 3 points.

Once the index price reached the higher strike of 170, the spread could return no more profit. The reason is that the short September 170 call locked-out additional profit above that point. Thus, the point of maximum profit is 170 for the S&P index at expiration of the September options.

The transactions would appear as follows:

Table 15
THE BULL SPREAD

Buys one lower-strike call and simultaneously writes one higher-strike call

September 165 Call	September 170 Call
Buys 1 September 165 S&P 100 call for 3. Cost: $300	Writes 1 September 170 S&P 100 call for 1. Receives: $100
Index Price: 162	Index Price: 162
Upon expiration, index is at 173 and the September 165 S&P 100 call has a value of 8. Receives: $800	Upon expiration, index is at 173 and the September 170 S&P 100 call has a value of 3. Pays out: $300
Gain: $500	Loss: $200
Index Price: 173	Index Price: 173

Net Gain/Loss: +$300

128

Figure 6
THE BULL SPREAD

Investor buys Sept. 165 S&P call for 3 and writes Sept. 170
S&P 100 call for 1

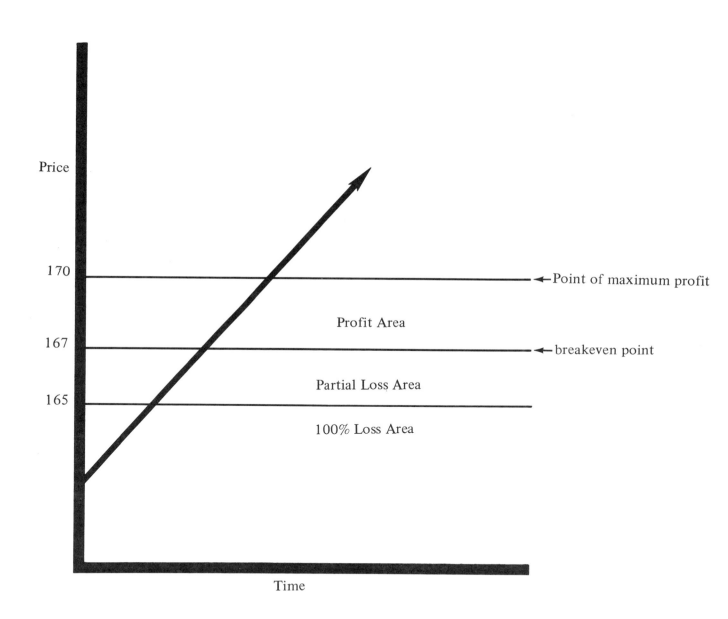

129

If upon examining this transaction, you conclude that the most profitable route would have been to simply purchase the September 165 call for 3 and later sell it for 8, resulting in a net profit of $500, you'd be correct. But what if the index was valued at 170 or lower at expiration, or if both options were out-of-the-money at expiration? In this instance, the spread would have been the superior strategy. The net cost of the spread was $200, as compared with $300 for the outright position. If this doesn't seem like a lot in dollar terms, you have to think in terms of the percentage advantage—the spread is one-third less than the cost of the outright long September 165 call. If you are doing a large number of spreads, this percentage difference can be significant. It can even spell the difference between a profit and a loss in the trade. For instance, if the index is trading at 168 at expiration, the outright buyer of the call merely breaks even (transaction costs aside), while the bull spread investor earns 50 percent on his invested capital.

Moreover, it helps to look at the spread in terms of the probabilities for the underlying index. With the index trading at 162, there is a reasonable chance it might rise 7 or 8 points (to the point of maximum profitability on the spread) in six or seven weeks, the time left to expiration. But 10 points or more? Probably not. As long as the point rise is moderate as opposed to extreme, the bull spread is clearly the better deal. And if, as often happens, the trade doesn't work out at all and results in a loss? Well, the loss is then limited to just $200 rather than $300. For a certain price range, therefore, the bull spread is a heads-you-win, tails-you-don't-lose-as-much situation.

What if you are a bear on the market? The spread to use is known, understandably enough, as the *bear spread*. Turn the bull spread on its head and you'll have the bear spread. With calls, using the same example as above, you *sell the lower-strike call and purchase the higher-strike call*. Again, the lower-strike call will be more expensive; thus, you will *receive* the premium of 3 points for *writing* the lower-strike September 165 S&P 100 call and pay 1 point for *buying* the higher-strike September 170 S&P 100 call. The net result: a *credit* of 2, the maximum profit on the spread. Now, however, you want the price of the index to stay below the lower-strike call in order to receive the full profit.For example, if the index is still at 162 at expiration, both options will expire worthless. As the writer of the lower-strike September 165, you get to keep the full premium of 3 points. At the same time, you lose the entire one-point you paid for the higher-strike September 170 call. The net of 2 points, or $200, is yours to keep. If prices rise, however, you could be in a bit of trouble with this spread—but even here your potential loss is limited to the distance between the strikes minus the initial credit, or 3. Why? Well, above the higher strike of 170, you have protection from your September 170 call. Won't you be losing on the September 165 short call? Sure. But only as far as the higher strike of 170. Above that price, the losses on the short September 165 call will be offset in full by the gain on the September 170.

Let's assume that, upon expiration of the options, the index settles between the two strikes—say, at 168. Now what will you have? Taking each option in turn, look at the September 165. In the bear spread, you *sold* the September 165 call for a net credit of 3 points. In the bear spread, remember, you write the lower-strike call and buy the higher-strike call. At a price of 168, the September 165 call will have a cash value of 3 points. Thus; you've lost what you gained, or the September 165 is a wash. Meanwhile, however, the September 170 will expire worthless since the index at 168 is below the 170 strike price. Your loss, therefore, will be one point, or the cost of the higher-strike call. The transactions would appear as follows:

Table 16
THE BEAR SPREAD

Sells one lower-strike call and simultaneously buys one higher-strike call

September 165 Call	September 170 Call
Sells 1 September 165 S&P 100 call for 3. Receives: $300	Buys 1 September 170 S&P 100 call for 1. Pays: $100
Index Price: 162	Index Price: 162
Upon expiration, index is at 168 and the September 165 S&P 100 call has a value of 3 Pays: $300	Upon expiration, index is at 168 and the September 170 S&P 100 call expires worthless Gain: $0
Index Price: 168	Index Price: 168
Gain/Loss: $0	Gain/Loss: −$100

Net Gain/Loss: −$100

As with the bull spread, here again you might see the wisdom of not spreading at all. After all, at 168, had the bear spreader simply written the September 165 for a premium of 3, he would have broken even. As it stands with the bear spread, he loses a hundred dollars. But with higher prices, the bear spread begins to make sense for its protection value. If you make a mistake and write a naked index call, you can be in real trouble. But with the bear spread, all the potential losses above 170 are offset by corresponding gains on the long September 170 call. Spreads may seem more complicated, and in some ways they are, but they can be a handy tool to have in your arsenal when you go into the market looking for profits.

ADVANCED INDEX OPTION STRATEGIES

In addition to those strategies that involve simply buying or writing options, bull and bear spreads, option hedges, and options used to increase leverage, there are a number of advanced techniques that are variations on the same theme. They involve somewhat more sophisticated market operations, but are ideal for tailoring a specific strategy to a specific market condition. Some of them serve to make a certain strategy more effective, such as rolling an option to achieve greater protection, and others are designed to capitalize on a particular type of market condition, such as straddle buying or writing. Let's look at some of these advanced strategies and see how they might help you enhance your profits in the options market.

Ratio Writes. Index options lend themselves to specific market situations, owing to their liquidity and easy adaptability. If you recall the section on option spreading, you'll remember that an option spread consists of one long option and one short option, such as in the bull spread when you buy the lower-strike call and simultaneously write the higher-strike call. The benefit of this strategy rests with the lower initial cost than the purchase of a call, coupled with all the advantages of call buying—notably high leverage—in the event of a price rise in the underlying index. But why limit yourself to purchasing just one call and writing just one call? Why not change the ratio of purchased-to-written calls in order to capitalize on specific market conditions? For example, instead of buying just one September S&P 500 call and writing one

September S&P 500 with a higher strike, why not write, say, two calls against just one lower-strike purchased call? After all, by doing so you will lower the overall cost of the spread since you will achieve greater writing income. The greater income thus generated will serve to offset the cost of the lower-strike call.

When you vary the number of options you spread in this manner, it is known as a *ratio write*. The most common type of ratio write is known as the *two-to-one ratio write*, although you may have three-to-one ratio writes, four-to-one, and so on. But let's concentrate on the two-to-one ratio write in order to see the benefit of this spreading strategy. *The two-to-one ratio write involves the sale of two higher-strike options and the simultaneous purchase of one lower-strike option of the same type and class*—S&P 500 calls, Amex Market Value Index calls, or whatever. You must remember that in any option strategy, there is a tradeoff between risk and reward. Thus, in a two-to-one ratio write you immediately gain a reduction in the cost of the spread (since the writing income is greater) but you likewise magnify the risk in the event of an upward move in price (only one written call is covered by the lower-strike call). The point is, the two-to-one ratio write is a great strategy when the market is treading water. But it can prove troublesome if the market soars. Let's consider an example.

Suppose you are mildly bullish on stock prices but anticipate a period of stagnant market movement—a period when the market will just be marking ground. And suppose the Major Market Index, traded on the Amex, is at 116 with calls available at strikes, ranging in 5 point intervals, from 110 to 130. You don't want to buy calls because you don't anticipate any sharp upward movement in prices, and, on the other hand, you don't want to write calls (especially the in-the-moneys) because you anticipate stable prices. You might decide on a middle ground—namely, two-to-one ratio writes. With the Major Market Index at 116, you might decide to surround the price with the lower and higher strikes. Thus, you would purchase the in-the-money 115 October call for, say, 5 points and write *two* out-of-the-money 120 October calls for, say, 2½ each. Your cost is commissions. The two out-of-the-money 120 October calls will generate $500 in income and the one in-the-money call will cost you the same amount. If the market cooperates and remains stable or slightly higher, you will have a profit.

The October 115 call will have a value of one point, or $100, if the index

133

stays at 116 at expiration. Above 116, the profit picture improves—up to a point. At 117, the long call will have 2 points in value; at 118, 3 points in value; at 119, 4 points in value, and so on. At the higher strike of 120, this two-to-one ratio write (which, you must remember, didn't cost a dime, commissions aside), will have a value of 5 points, or $500. At 120, the lower-strike October 115 call will have a value of 5 points and the higher-strike October 120 call will have no value, resulting in a *gain* of 5 points of writing income. This, alas, was used to purchase the in-the-money, lower-strike call. The net profit: $500 minus commissions. Above the higher-strike of 120, however, the profit picture begins to dim. Here, you are losing on just one call because only one call's loss is offset by a gain on the long October 115. In the table below, the gain or loss on this two-to-one ratio write is indicated with expiration at several different price levels.

Table 17
EXAMPLE—PROFIT/LOSS TWO-TO-ONE RATIO WRITE

Buys 1 October 115 call for 5/
Writes 2 October 120 calls for 2½ each

Price Level[*]	Value of 1 October 115 call	Value of 2 October 120 calls	Net Gain/Loss[**]
115 and lower	$0	$0	$0
116	$100	$0	+ $100
118	$300	$0	+ $300
120	$500	$0	+ $500
122	$700	$400	+ $300
124	$900	$800	+ $100
126	$1,100	$1,200	− $100
128	$1,300	$1,600	− $300

As you can see, the two-to-one write creates a trading band within which the strategy is profitable. Once outside that band, however, at least to the upside, the two-to-one ratio write becomes unprofitable.

Rolling Options. When the market changes, the most intelligent approach for the investor is to change as well. One such flexible strategy is known as *rolling*. When you roll an option, you switch into another option

---

[*] At expiration
[**] Commissions not included

of a higher- or lower-strike, or perhaps into a more distant option. As the names suggest, you *roll-up* an option when you switch into an option with a higher strike, you *roll-down* an option when you switch into an option with a lower strike, and you *roll-out* an option when you switch into a more distant month. In the example of the two-to-one ratio write, you might have rolled-up the option to protect against higher prices. For instance, as prices approached the higher strike of 120, which was also the point of maximum profitability, the investor might have liquidated the two-to-one ratio write in its entirety, and rolled up to the next two higher strikes—in this case, by purchasing one October 120 call and writing two October 125 calls. This strategy of rolling up would have permitted the investor to make still more money as the market rose above 120. Specifically, it would have involved selling the long October 115 call for a profit of at least 5 plus whatever time value the option retained and buying back the two short October 120s—undoubtedly at a loss since the now at-the-money calls would probably be worth more than 2½ points each, depending on the amount of time left to expiration.

In a declining market, the investor stands to earn the lion's share of the call premium simply because the likelihood of the option ever proving profitable becomes less and less as prices decline. But as long as that investor holds the short call, he is liable to the call buyer. Having declined, the market can always mount a rally and the call could prove profitable to the buyer and a loser to the writer. As a rule, once a substantial portion of the call premium is earned, it often pays to buy back the call and again write another lower-strike call in order to generate a continuous flow of writing income. For instance, you write an out-of-the-money October 120 call for 2½ and the market declines. The call's premium might decline to, say, 1. You now buy back the call for 1 and earn a profit of 1½ points, and you write a lower strike call for, say, 2½ again. The market declines once more and you buy back the second call for, say, one-half point, earning a 2 point profit—and you repeat the pattern. This strategy is known as *rolling down*. When you think about it, this strategy makes a lot of sense. Why continue to hold a call—and risk the unlimited liability associated with being a call writer—when you have already gained more than 50 or 60 percent of the available income? It is better to roll down and insure that you'll earn at least the rapidly declining time value. A small portion of this time value will persist until expiration no matter how far out-of-the-money the option trades.

Lastly, you want to *roll out*, by moving into the next adjacent contract month, when the option approaches expiration. Of course, you don't *have* to roll out your options, but you should be aware that you will be posting margin and as long as you hold a short option there will be risk associated with the position. Under certain circumstances, such as when you are uncertain whether you wish to continue writing, you may wish to simply let your options expire—in which case, you'll capture the entire premium. But if you are an aggressive writer and want your margin money working hard at all times, you will be on the lookout for an opportunity to capture the greater time value in the more distant contract months by rolling out.

Straddles. An index option straddle involves both the purchase *or* sale of a put and a call at the same strike price. First, let's look at the straddle buyer. The straddle buyer, by virtue of owning both a put and a call, can either buy or sell (or even both buy *and* sell) the index at the strike price. Such a buyer might be confused about the future direction of prices, or he simply might consider the premium cost worth the risk. Remember, when you own a straddle, you own both a put and a call and you must overcome the cost of two premiums. Since this isn't always an easy task to accomplish, you must consider the cost of the straddle against the likelihood of a significant move, up or down, from the strike.

The straddle writer's view of the market is the opposite of the buyer's. The writer wants the market to stay where it is when he writes the straddle—at the strike price. While this is unlikely, the writer has the income of two premiums to offset any losses. The point of maximum profitability for the writer is, of course, the strike price. But the writer also creates for himself a trading band within which he is assured a profit. His risk, however, is significant since the market can rise to infinity against the call or fall to zero against the put.

Combinations. Combinations, which, like straddles, can be purchased or written, are identical to straddles with one exception: the strike prices are different. Thus, instead of buying a straddle with a strike price of 115 for both put and call, the combination buyer would buy, say, a 120 call and a 110 put. The cost of the combination should be considerably less than a straddle, since both options can be out-of-the-money when purchased. But this means the buyer must overcome more adversity on both options in order to earn a profit. The combination writer, on the other hand, will earn two premiums when he writes the option and there is the possibility that

136

both options will prove profitable. But the income will be less than the income generated from a straddle—again, because out-of-the-money options have lower premiums than in-the-money options.

Butterfly Spreads. The butterfly spread is nothing more than an overlapping bull and bear spread, or a spread consisting of three strike prices and four positions. The middle strike in a butterfly is the shared strike and will have two long or short positions depending on precisely what market action you are anticipating. The best way to illustrate this spread is through the use of an example. Suppose the following calls are available on the CBOE at the time the September S&P 100 is trading at 164.50:

Table 18

SEPTEMBER CALLS

Standard & Poor's 100

Strike Price	Premium
170	1 ¼
165	3 ¼
160	6 ¼

With six weeks left to expiration, you may wish to capitalize on steady prices by putting on a butterfly spread with *two short options in the middle*. To accomplish the butterfly spread, you buy the lower-strike 160 for a premium of 6¼ and also purchase the higher-strike 170 call for a premium of 1¼. Your cost is the sum of these two options, or 7½. At the same time, you write *twice as many of the middle-strike calls*. Thus, you sell two 165 calls and *receive* the premiums amounting to 6½. Your net cost is just one point. Now, if the S&P 100 index at expiration is, let us say, 165, the butterfly spread will have a value of 5 points, or the cash value of the 160 call. At 165, the two short 165 calls will expire worthless as will the higher-strike 170 call, which remains out-of-the-money. At the higher strike of 170, the two 165 calls will have a cash value of 5 points each, or 10. But since the butterfly spreader *sold* those calls, they constitute a loss. At the same time, however, the long 160 call will have a value of 10, and the loss will be offset. However, since the butterfly was put on for a net

137

debit of 1 plus transaction costs, the spreader will have a loss of that amount at the higher strike, or higher. At 160 or lower, all four calls will expire worthless and the cost is the initial one-point debit. Here, again, as with ratio writes and simple call or put writing, a profit band exists within which the butterfly will return a profit. Before you attempt to use a butterfly spread, try to work out your transaction costs. With the maximum profit of just several points, you have to be careful about these costs.

You can also place the butterfly by turning this situation on its head. Suppose you purchased two 165 calls (the middle strike) and wrote one in-the-money 160 call for 6¼ and one out-of-the-money 170 call for 1¼. Now you would have a net credit of 1. But now you want the market to move away from the middle strike. At 165, the two long calls would expire worthless. However, the short 160 call would be worth 5 and would be exercised against you. Your loss would amount to the difference of the net credit of 1 and the cash value of the in-the-money short call of 5, or 4 points. At the higher strike of 170, the two long 165 calls would have a combined value of 10, but this gain would be offset by the 160 call, which would also be worth 10. Nevertheless, you would gain the initial net credit of one point. At the lower strike of 160, you would collect the initial net credit of one point since all four options would expire worthless.

The butterfly is a highly sophisticated spread that requires excellent market timing and agility, since even a half or a quarter point loss in the execution can impair the spread's profitability—which on a point basis, granted, is small, but on a percentage basis can be quite attractive.

THE FUTURE

With monthly volume of about one million contracts in index options after about six months of trading, the future for these versatile new financial instruments appears bright indeed. In fact, market analysts expect index options to become more popular than index futures since the limited-risk aspect of option buying, coupled with the lower initial cost of entry, is expected to catch the fancy of a wide spectrum of investors. In a recent cover story in *Business Week,* Chicago Board Options Exchange president Charles J. Henry summed up the enthusiasm for his exchange's new S&P 100 contract by saying: "These are the fastest growing securities products ever, and we've hardly scratched the surface." Perhaps in response to the avalanche of new index options scheduled for release in the future, the Securities & Exchange Commission recently put a moratorium on new options—in part, to give the brokerage community a breather in training their people in the intricacies of these new instruments. Such is the mark of a security product experiencing explosive growth.

Part II

RULES FOR SUCCESS

How The Stock Index Futures Game
Is Really Played

Chapter Five

THE PSYCHOLOGY OF THE FLOOR

Games Your Broker Never Taught You

Once you've mastered the mechanics of the stock index futures market and acquainted yourself with some of the nomenclature of this somewhat arcane art, you are faced with a much more formidable task—that of learning how to trade. Certainly, many are called into the whirl of this fast-paced and enormously lucrative undertaking, but comparatively few find themselves among the chosen. The path to profits is strewn with the wreckage of the impetuous, the uninformed, and the merely unsuited speculators—all in pursuit of the "holy grail" of market mastery that forever seems to elude them. Many are looking for easy answers. But they often fail to ask the proper questions.

"Which way do *you* think the market is headed?" is probably the question I'm most frequently asked when I'm on the seminar circuit. But the question belies the inquirer's true motivation: namely, a hot tip, an easy solution, an avoidance of the real question, which is *why does the market behave as it does?* As for the question of market direction, the honest answer is that "God himself doesn't know." In the interest of showmanship, however, most pundits would marshall some facts and stammer out an answer—higher or lower, the chance of being correct is still fifty-fifty.

THE KEY: KNOWING HOW TO TRADE

The first thing you'll probably observe about such an answer, once you turn it over in your mind for a minute, is that it is essentially meaningless. Given the notorious volatility of stock index futures, both buyer *and* seller might ultimately be proven right—or wrong! Timing is just too critical to rely on a tip such as this, no matter how well-reasoned. You might win a trade or two relying on an expert's opinion, but ultimately you'll have to be your own man. Consider the following scenario: you are bullish on the market and I am bearish. Backing up your opinion with cash, you buy stock index futures and I sell them. After five minutes of trading, prices decline and my position is the profitable one. But who's to say the situation won't be reversed an hour later? Anyone who has traded stock index futures *knows* how short-lved certain declines and rallies can be. How can a hot tip help you in such a volatile market? It can't. Besides, even if someone's opinion helped you to gain entry into the market at a propitious moment, you'll still need another to know when to liquidate. "He who buys on Smith's tip," goes the old adage, "must also sell on Smith's tip." And sooner or later, you may not want to rely on Smith anymore. The point is, *knowing how to trade is the key to stock index futures profits*—not tips, opinions, or even reasoned analyses drawn up in advance of a market campaign.

There is a world of difference between having a market opinion and genuine market knowledge. Lots of people have opinions about the stock market; ask any cab driver, maitre'd, or, for that matter, stock broker and you'll have all the opinions you'll need. As a general rule, the number of opinions offered is usually in inverse proportion to the amount of knowledge held by the individual dispensing the advice, however. Opinions are found in abundance on Wall Street, and I suggest you avoid listening to them if possible.

Genuine market knowledge is something else again. An investor who knows his way around the market is apt to be neither so certain about the future to be rigid in his thinking, nor so uncertain as to be indecisive and unable to make up his mind. Flexibility is the key. The results of a Wall Street study done some years ago indicated that the overly cautious, known as risk-averters, had trouble making up their minds. They'd wait until they were certain they had a "sure-thing" before investing. This, of course, invariably proved to be the worst possible time. On the other hand, the "crap-shoot" approach to investing isn't likely to yield good results either. Clearly, the middle path is the road to take—where you are willing to take chances but aren't reckless.

THE BEGINNING OF MARKET KNOWLEDGE

In the back of your mind somewhere, if you are like most of us, you must be thinking—if so many people lose trading stock index futures, then someone must be making all the money, right? After all, the money doesn't just disappear into thin air. On the one hand, you have the self-proclaimed experts, not a few of which will charge you a handsome fee for divulging their secrets. On the other hand, you have the market professionals—those who risk their own funds in the market. Perhaps it will pay to learn a little bit about how the stock index futures game is really played by the professionals before joining the ranks of investors who plunge in blindly, thinking stock index futures trading is easy to beat.

Before we deal with specifics, I want to stress the importance of *attitude* in sizing up a good trader, especially the attitude that allows for flexibility. We've already touched upon the subject of opinions. I'm frequently reminded of an extreme example of the opinionated versus the flexible trader that I encountered among floor traders in Chicago. The best trader I ever met used to tell me that he couldn't make a call on the market before the opening. "Let's see how it opens," he'd say, noncomittally, "and then I'll have some idea what to do." Meanwhile, the floor would be rife with rumors about possible market moves. Once the market opened, after about five minutes of carefully watching prices, he'd begin buying or selling, looking for one short rally or decline to make his profit for the day. Having made his *daily* profit (it could be, and I'm not exaggerating here, $500 or $50,000), he'd close out his positions and go home—often well before the close. Occasionally, he'd take a position and find himself losing money. But it never really bothered him. He knew how to get it back. Looking back now, I realize he knew how to trade in the most profound way, sometimes being the lone buyer in a sea of sellers. If he thought he was right, he'd buy and buy and buy; in time, with raising prices, he'd have a profit and the short sellers would be tripping over themselves to cover and buy back their shorts. Their panic was often a sight to see.

It was about the same time that I encountered an example of how *not* to trade. I was introduced to a young gold futures trader who had some success in the 1980 bull market. Unfortunately, his initial success had gone to his head and he was busy trying to repeat his success in the most reckless fashion imaginable. While gold was still trading at over $800 an ounce, he was buying more contracts, hundreds at a time. He was absolutely certain that gold had to go over $1,000 an ounce. It never did. He lost a fortune. In looking back, I realize that this trader, in his youth and inexperience, had what the Greeks used to call *hubris*, or excessive pride. Thinking he was invincible, he invited his own demise. It was the very opposite of the humility exhibited by the other trader, who was cautious on the open and careful to close out his trades prior to the close each day. Where one was cautious and bold, the other was simply reckless and foolhardy. You know which one won.

What is important about this? That genuine knowledge of the market is quite different from boastful opinion. The market is always right, the investor occasionally. Fortunately, in order to make a success of yourself, you don't have to be correct 100 percent of the time. But you do need to know how to trade.

FINANCIAL SURVIVAL

It is not by accident that the jargon used by exchange members is often couched in military terms. One hears of this or that trader "taking a hit," as if he'd been gunned down by M-16 fire. A "hit," of course, means a trader has taken a serious loss and his ability to continue among the member ranks may be in jeopardy, in which case you'll soon hear about him being "blown away"—with the same results of a soldier who steps on a landmine, and is later "buried." Understandably, except for a sigh of regret, the popular response is "the less said the better." After all, others among the living may soon join him.

Life goes on, and with the opening bell, things return to normal—a sort of daily six hour period of absolute pandemonium, in which the periods of tranquility are few. During the day, the floor might mount a "search-and-destroy mission," in which the stops are routinely "gunned" with the predictable results of nearly everyone getting "wiped out." When this particular market phenomenon occurs, the traders who have bought the market might first find their sell-stops hit as prices reverse. Being adverse to risk and trying to play the game by the book, the longs (buyers) place sell stops right below the market to limit losses in the event of market adversity. Sounds logical, doesn't it? After all, limiting risk is the first rule of trading. But, as often happens, once the panic selling dries up, the buying begins in earnest and the market goes up. Having cleaned out the longs, the short sellers are then in jeopardy as the market continues its rise unabated, often taking out the intra-day highs. Sure enough, soon the short-sellers are panicking, rushing to cover their short positions, and bidding up prices to unrealistic levels in the process. Once the buying stops, however, and more rational heads prevail, chances are the market will return to some middle ground, perhaps unchanged, up slightly, or down a fraction on the day. Sound familiar? It should. It happens on a routine basis in the stock index futures market.

On a normal day, the stock index futures markets are in chaos; this is broken, on occasion, by periods of outright panic, when the chaos turns to frenzy—so emotional is this most volatile of markets. When it does, stops are run, the basis moves up or down without rhyme or reason and traders find themselves in a "fast" market in which fortunes change hands in minutes, even seconds. A discount market might change into a premium market as sentiment changes from bullish to bearish and back again. The overall feeling is one of speed coupled with enormous psychic energy. When the market goes in this fashion, the entire exchange floor seems to utter a deep, throaty groan and the trading pit seems to sway back and forth, pulsating in the psychically-charged atmosphere. It is amid such a background, in which emotion more often than rationality reigns, that one has to operate. Unless you understand the psychology of the floor, with all its seeming confusion and occasional misleading signals, you are going to be at a distinct disadvantage. Like everyone else in the stock index futures market, the floor trader operates with his own interests in mind. By knowing how his interests might conflict with yours, you give yourself a fighting chance not to fall victim to the many pitfalls that await the unsuspecting investor.

IF IT'S NINE O'CLOCK, IT MUST BE SHOWTIME

Every weekday morning at precisely nine o'clock, a buzzer rings on the floor of the Chicago Mercantile Exchange, signalling the start of trading in the Standard & Poor's trading pit. By that hour, the day is well underway for hundreds of other traders who have been trading foreign currencies and gold, and a number jam into the already crowded S&P pit. There is hardly room to stand, let alone move; and the later-comers at nine o'clock have to stand at the edges of the multi-tiered trading pit where hundreds of others have already assembled, awaiting the start of a new day. As the open approaches, hands sweat, hearts pound, and the conviviality of troops going into battle gives way to the seriousness of the task at hand—surviving another day with thousands, and even hundreds of thousands, of dollars in potential profits or losses at stake, sometimes riding on a single trade. As every trader knows, the hazards are real. A flick of the wrist, an arched eyebrow, a wave of the hand, and the shouting of a bid or offer at the wrong moment can make or break a trade. Mistakes here can be costly. Every trader knows the familiar war stories and every trader knows his fellow members will gladly "bury" him if he isn't careful. At the open, pandemonium breaks out. But this is just the beginning. There are six hours and fifteen minutes left in the trading day—time enough to earn the best-paying wages in the world or get one's brains beat in while trying.

While the average floor trader is well acquainted with the potential risks of trading stock index futures, the public often isn't. This is unfortunate because, in general, the unsuspecting public supplies the profits that make the men and women on the floor rich. But this doesn't mean the floor doesn't earn its money. The pressure of living in such a fast-paced, unforgiving environment is unbelievable. To soothe the tension some turn to drink or cocaine. The bars in Chicago's Loop frequented by the floor exchange members have video price screens mounted where television sets normally hang. These bars are well populated during trading hours, even before noon. At night, the scene moves uptown to the Rush Street area, where talk of the market continues. Others work off their tensions in health clubs and gyms, one favorite being the fashionable East Bank Club on the banks of the Chicago River close to the exchanges. For those who indulge in neither drink nor exercise, the latest rage has been to cultivate

148

one's primary instrument, the voice, through professional vocal instructors. Taught by the same people who teach professional singers, the voice lessons are intended to preserve the voice and to enable a trader to better amplify his bids and offers over a six hour period. The makers of antacid pills and throat remedies find a ready market among the floor trader population as well. There are even doctors who specialize in the ailments of floor traders, presumably charging substantial fees to such well-heeled clients.

Much the same story, no doubt, could be told of the pressures of other businesses. Yet few activities combine the risk and pace of stock index futures trading, even within the futures industry. In a recent issue of *Business Week*, a leading Merc spokesman and trader, Leo Melamed, was quoted as saying: "Most commodities have moments of calm—but not the S&P. You literally have to close out your position if you want to get a cup of coffee or smoke a cigarette."

Compared to gold, soybeans, or even pork bellies, long thought to be the "fast" markets among high-rollers, stock index futures seem propelled by extra high-octane jet fuel. One Merc trader, who has taken positions in virtually all of the 17 major agricultural and financial commodities listed on his exchange, was recently quoted as saying of the S&P: "This is the biggest, fastest market I've ever seen." He now trades only the S&P 500. And for good reason. Stock index futures offer the fast track, the quickest way to make a market killing in the shortest period of time. Now let's look at how some of the players trade this market.

A SCALPER'S STRATEGY—
THE NICKEL-AND-DIME APPROACH

Whether your approach is long-term or short-term (and these designations are strictly relative depending upon your audience), a good place to begin an examination of floor trader psychology is the professional scalper. While there are many notions on the "best way" to trade index futures, the general categories are relatively few. A scalper strategy is one of them. And although this strategy doesn't lend itself to off-exchange trading, the public trader must understand the role of the scalper in order to understand the forces that can help or hinder him in the market.

First and foremost, the scalper has a mind-set that is oriented toward the short-term. For the scalper, five to ten minutes at the outside represents a long-term trade; at other times, the job can be accomplished in seconds, so why risk holding a stock index futures contract when it might move against you? And that's the key to the scalper's psychology. He reasons thusly: *I don't care which way the market moves as long as I can make a small profit; I just want the edge.* The edge, you may remember, is the difference between the bid and the asked. In other words, when buying, the scalper wants to trade at the bid, *his* bid; when selling, the scalper wants to trade at the offer, *his* offer. Because he is relatively indifferent to the direction of prices, he will oftentimes both bid and ask at the same time. That is, he will offer to sell at one price and bid at a slightly lower price simultaneously. By doing this, he might buy from one trader at, say, 165.80 and immediately sell to another at 165.85, profiting from the one tick difference. This may not seem like a lot of money, but when you consider that a scalper pays no commissions and may scalp a tick or two more than one hundred times a day, the profits add up. But his task is not an easy one. What happens if the market runs against him soon after he takes a trade? Because his profit is so small, he must limit his losses quickly. Not to do so only invites disaster. Even one bad mistake in liquidating a loss immediately can result in a week's profits gone on one trade. In light of this risk, you can see why a scalper might not want to hold a position more than a few minutes, or even seconds.

The function of the scalper is an important one for the public trader to understand. The scalper, in pursuit of numerous small profits, provides the necessary liquidity that makes a market efficient. Without an abundance of such risk-takers on the floor, the bid and asked prices would most certainly be farther apart and the cost of trading, in terms of good fills, would almost certainly be higher, for buyer and seller alike.

There are some words of caution that should be given at this point. First of all, you should be particularly wary of market orders when trading is "thin"—as reflected by fewer scalpers than normal and corresponding wider bid and asked prices. One strategy used when trading is to inquire of the floor to determine the sources of the current activity. (This is done by simply asking your floor contact, over the phone, who is doing most of the trading. Floor brokers tend to be very aware of who's doing the buying and selling). If it is slow, I might find myself paying an extra tick on a market order; on the other hand, if it is active, it suggests the competition between buyers and sellers will keep the bid and asked prices close together and I won't have to pay more than one or two ticks at most with a market order. For example, if the bid is 165.15 and the asked price is 165.20, you can pretty well count on being able to buy at the asked price and sell at the bid price using a market order. If the competition between buyers and sellers were to dry up, however, and the market were to become thin, the spread between the bid and the asked would almost certainly widen and my fill would likewise reflect this slippage.

Additionally, you should consider the nature of the market at the time you are placing your order. You'll find your fills are much more acceptable during periods of relative calm, a normal market. But as soon as a market breaks, say, a key support and becomes "fast," the proportion of buyers to sellers will shift drastically to the sell side and the ultimate fill price will probably bear little resemblance to the price on the board at the time the order was entered. There is nothing illegal or unethical about these poor fills. The problem rests with the traders themselves who, caught on the wrong side of the market, all want to sell at once. Understandably, at such time the buying pretty well dries up. As a result, the panic rush to sell sends prices lower and lower as each successive offer drives the price down. Sooner or later, of course, bargain hunters will begin buying and prices will rise again.

Another factor to consider is the number of contracts changing hands at a given price. If you are doing large numbers, you may want to ease them on a few at a time. An order to sell 200 contracts might be taken with relative calm, but it might also precipitate a severe price drop if the market isn't liquid enough to absorb that number at that time.

THE GREATEST LIQUIDITY
AT THE OPEN AND THE CLOSE

The greatest liquidity in the market exists at the open and the close, when the likelihood of a large number of traders being in the pit is highest. The reason for this is relatively simple. At the open, market forces have had a full day to accumulate since the prior day's close, and chances are the market will be taken out of line on the open, the result of pent-up buying

151

or selling accumulating overnight. Over a weekend and on the heels of Friday's money supply numbers, the market may well be even more ripe for a sharp rally or decline. To capitalize on the situation, a large number of floor traders are apt to be on hand, waiting to buy or sell the initial "spring" effect that often accompanies an open fueled by news.

At the close of trading, on the other hand, a different phenomenon is apt to be influencing prices. At the close, the *locals*, or floor traders, who speculate for their own accounts, are *evening up* their positions. That is, if they were sellers throughout most of the day's session, they will be short contracts and will become buyers in order to cover. By liquidating their positions, they go home *flat* the market, or without a position. Without the burden of commissions to think about, scalpers and other floor traders are quick to enter and exit positions, not only because their cost of trading is minimal, but because they *know* how risky it can be to hold a position overnight.

Another reason why many floor traders will close out their positions by the end of the trading day has to do with margin. Like the public trader, the floor trader must post margin for all positions taken overnight. But on an intra-day basis, virtually no margin is required of a floor trader—as long as he is good for his losses, of course. This is an important point to remember, since it illustrates why the floor is often willing to absorb large orders in return for gaining the edge. If a hundred-lot order hits the pit, a scalper will gladly take the other side in hopes of picking off a tick or two. After all, a single tick profit on one hundred contracts constitutes a profit of $2,500—and the entire trade can often be accomplished, from start to finish, in two or three seconds. If you told your broker to sell one hundred December S&P contracts, however, he'd be careful to see that you had more than a half-million dollars in your margin account before taking the order. The scalper's freedom to take large positions and easily jump from side to side is often an intimidating factor for many new traders, who tend to be wedded to a single market position and an often much too one-sided point of view concerning prices.

Despite the stiff competition presented by the floor for the public trader, the scalper is often the public's best friend. Not for altruistic reasons, certainly. But by providing the necessary liquidity, the scalper allows other traders to easily enter and exit the market without price disruption.

The time of greatest illiquidity will exist in any market that is particularly slow, such as a holiday market just prior to or after Christmas, or during periods of the day when the pressures of the open are over and the enthusiasm toward the close has not yet begun. Typically, this mid-day slowness occurs sometime between mid-morning, when the traders go out for breakfast, having made their money on the open, and lunch time. Whenever the market is *thin*, or illiquid, you have to be careful; fills are notoriously bad in most futures markets when trading is slow.

A well-known story, which is perhaps apocryphal, concerns an unnamed grain pit during a slow period of trading. With only a half-dozen traders standing around in the pit, a broker with a client's order enters the pit and begins bidding. His bids, however, are soon met with blank stares by his fellow floor traders. Rather than agreeing to take the other side of the trade, his fellow traders decide to become buyers themselves. Each successive bid is higher, and the hapless broker soon realizes that they simply want to take advantage of the situation. They want to bid up the price to an unrealistic level in order to *sell* to his client. Sensing what is going on, the broker walks out of the pit and over to the phone. He calls the client and asks him if he still wants to do the trade at the market—which is now bid five or six cents higher than it was a minute ago. Yes, the client indicates, he wants the order filled at the market. So the broker returns to the pit where an artificial bidding war soon causes the price to rise once again, and as soon as the broker calls out his bid, the other traders jump all over him in their eagerness to *sell* at the higher price. The order having been filled, the price soon retreated to its previous stable level five or six cents lower.

A DAY TRADER'S STRATEGY— PICKING THE TREND

Stock index futures are perhaps the most popular day trading vehicles ever introduced in the futures market. One indication of the popularity of index futures among day traders is the relation of the volume to the open interest. On a typical day, the volume in the S&P 500 contract outpaces the open interest by about 8,000 contracts. This is in sharp contrast to the relationship of open interest to volume in other contracts.

That day trading in stock index futures is popular among investors in general comes as no surprise to floor traders, whose outlook tends to be toward the short-term. Indeed, the index futures have all the hallmarks of an excellent day trading vehicle. The liquidity is excellent (meaning you can enter and exit the market without giving up too much of your profit), the volatility is high (providing excellent opportunity for profit), and you can always be sure the action will be intense. To make money day trading, the last thing you want is a sleepy market that spends most of the day in the doldrums. Moreover, given the abundance of new index products, there is a game available for investors of every means.

The day trader specializes in finding the daily trend. He may rely on a host of short-term indicators to pinpoint his activities on any given day, but above all he wants his profits quickly and steadily. He is a percentage player, who prefers to make a few well-chosen trades and jump to the sidelines with his profit. He is comparable to a guerilla jungle fighter in the investment world, where he hides in the forest until the time is right and then strikes and retreats back into the bush. The day trader knows his terrain and knows when conditions favor his mode of operation. He is aware that superior armies (namely, the well-financed institutional investors) might have greater firepower. But he also knows how to keep his opponent off balance. In short, he is a consummate professional at what he does and he earns the respect of those who must compete with him.

When the public investor decides to trade stock index futures, he decides to do battle with the guerilla floor trader. More often than not, the novice investor is walking through dangerous territory which is entirely new to him. At the same time, he is trying to outfight the professional floor trader who, if nothing else, is better equipped to out-maneuver him at almost every turn.

GUNNING THE STOPS ON THE OPEN

Evidence that the unsuspecting investor might have walked into an ambush in the financial jungle often begins at the start of trading every day, right at the open. For it is at the open that the public is often the most vulnerable and the floor most at ease with the situation in which it knows it has the upper hand. Take a recent Monday morning in the market, following a surprise money supply report the following Friday. First of all,

154

the floor trader rarely holds a position overnight, let alone over a weekend. A weekend is especially perilous due to the release of the weekly money supply figures the previous Friday. Essentially, the money supply affects interest rates and interest rates affect the economy which, in turn, affects public companies, and hence the stock market. The exact relationship of any given government report—money supply, Federal Funds rate, discount in the prime, consumer price index, or whatever—and its impact on the market is totally beside the point. The fact is, how the market *perceives* the report, the psychological impact of the event, is the important factor. And when it comes to stock index futures, even the perception of the event may be insignificant compared to how the market can be manipulated or moved in order to create profits for the knowledgeable insiders. In short, the event is the *excuse* to take the market up or down, or whatever.

Returning to the Monday morning alluded to above, we have a situation where the floor is coming in "flat the market," without a position and rested to resume the daily battle for investment survival. The novice public trader, however, is apt to come in with a position already on—either long or short, it doesn't make a great deal of difference. The trader who comes in long may have made money in the past and has suddenly acquired a great deal of confidence in his ability to select winning trades. Well, remember, the guerillas are safe in their bunker at this point since they are without a position. No matter what occurs on the open, those without a position won't be hurt one way or another. The short seller, who, depending on where he put on his position, might have a winner, is also coming into the market with a vested interest; he wants to see declining prices. One of them, however, is about to step on a landmine.

Prior to the open on this Monday morning, a lot of information has been digested since Friday's close. Chances are, cash bonds traded higher in anticipation of the money supply report—which, for some unknown reason, caught the Wall Street community by surprise—and now financial futures will have a lot of catching up to do. This bullishness will spill over into stock index futures, as investors will scurry to jump aboard the bandwagon lest they miss an important move. Moreover, since the financial futures market opens an hour earlier than the stock index futures market, traders will have an opportunity to see precisely how bullish the market may be. Anticipation is bullish and the rumors begin to spread even before the morning's "call" is announced. Up, up, up—the sentiment is

155

overwhelming. After all, it's a bull market. Why not a continuation of the past few months?

At this point, a mixture of euphoria and despair has settled over the Wall Street community. For the hapless short sellers, the guns are about to roar. The open will certainly be more than a hundred higher (one point) and the loss will be considerable. Those using stops will have them triggered automatically on the open; those without stops will likely throw in the towel shortly after the open when the paper losses become intolerable. For the fortunate buyers of stock index futures, on the other hand, the bullish news is a sheer gift from heaven. They are certain to have substantial profits on the open. But why take profits when you are hot? Why not join the crowd and buy more?

The buzzer rings and the predictable happens on the higher open. First, a flow of buy orders hits the floor as a mob of short-sellers, all trying to cover at once, bids up the price higher and higher. "Ten bid, fifteen bid, twenty bid, twenty-five bid!" the voices roar out, and up goes the price of the S&P contracts. The panicky buyers find calm, knowledgeable short sellers willing to accommodate their wishes as the market mounts a rally. Who, you might ask, would sell under these circumstances? Plenty of people. Scalpers, looking to buy back on the next tick down; day traders, seeing the rally for what it really is, a momentary panic caused by a running of the stops. The scene being played out in Chicago is duplicated in New York. But now it isn't the futures market leading the way, but the cash index suddenly showing weakness as the first of a series of profit-taking downturns assaults the stock market. The cash S&P index, updated each minute, begins to hesitate, and finally begins to head lower. The upward move was overdone. The new trend is down.

Now the tables have turned—and the fortunes of those who only a moment ago thought themselves certain winners or losers with them. The opening breakout that had brokers' phones ringing from California to New York has failed. The sudden reversal, which in the lexicon of Wall Street is known as a *false breakout*, has the market in a new mini-panic. Now the sellers are the ones making money. Despite the initial runup on the open, the market actually finishes the day in negative territory—despite all the bullish news. And two days later, the market is down a full five points off the day's high. The winners? The short sellers with the ability to go against the momentary trend in order to capitalize on the real trend of the day—which was clearly down.

THE CRESCENDO EFFECT

There's a paradoxical principle at work here—one that permeates market psychology and threatens the conventional wisdom. In essence, the principle is a model of simplicity: to wit, *when the market rises on the open, the trend will be down*; and *when the market declines on the open, the trend will be up*. When you think about it, you will see the wisdom of this statement, since the market professionals require the cooperation of the uninformed in order to secure their profits. Moreover, this notion of contrary opinion, which is based on hundreds of years of market knowledge, is routed on a sound logical foundation. "When everybody thinks alike," said Humphrey Neill, the father of contrarian opinion, "everybody is likely to be wrong."

If you want to see the forces at work here in the market, you have to take the situation apart point by point and examine what really happened. First, as a general rule, if you are taking a position overnight, you should always *pull your stops on the open*. Simply instruct your broker each day that a given stop is a "day only order." The stops are "red flags" to the floor and until they get them all, the floor will never be satisfied. How does the floor know where the stops are? They don't. At least, not precisely. But it is no secret that the conventional wisdom calls for placing stops just above the market for short sellers and just below the market for buyers. As a result, the floor has become very proficient at hitting the stops by either bidding the market up—known as *high-balling* the market—or allowing the market to drift down to a point where the longs give up and sell—*low-balling* the market.

Granted, it takes considerable courage to bid up a market in hopes of hitting the stops. What if someone comes in and offers one hundred contracts at that price and you end up buying the top? But that's what wins the game. It works in this fashion. A trader purposely bids the market up. Thus, if the bid is twenty, he might bid twenty-five, or even thirty. If the market is near a key resistance level, one of two things will occur. He will find a seller at twenty-five and be long the market. Or an uneasy local—or, more likely, the "paper," or a public order—will come in and bid it a tick higher, say at thirty. If the sellers stop offering while the bids increase, you have the makings of a brief run on the stops. Now, if the market is bid at, say, thirty, the stops might be hit and a flurry of buy orders will hit the pit

157

at once. Of course, at this point the trader who started the stampede is selling. Generally, in a minute or two, the buying will subside and the run on the stops will be over—just like that. Those whose stops were hit are now all losers. Those who gunned the stops are winners.

This brief crescendo effect explains why markets frequently move in reverse fashion to the day's ultimate trend. By definition, a stop-loss order becomes a market order once hit. Thus, an order to sell index futures at, let us say, 161.00, might be filled at 160.50 if the market is moving down swiftly at the time the stop is triggered. There is no guarantee you will ever get the price you would like. The problem is that most speculators tend to place their stops right where all the other stops are located. Once hit, there is only selling since the buyers in the pit typically have the good sense to watch the prices drop like a rock. In time, however, the bargain hunters in the crowd will emerge and prices will typically rebound. But where does that leave the hapless speculator whose sell-stop got him out at the bottom?

The crescendo effect is particularly evident on days when the market is staging a substantial move. This may even take place over a three or four day period. It happens because many traders, unlike the professionals, think they can withstand an adverse market move by holding onto a bad position.

Let's say the market opens down, hitting the sell stops. In time, the selling will inevitably dry up as the stops are all filled and the market will probably begin a rally. A number of self-styled experts always make it a policy to sell rallies because it makes good sense to them. As the market rallies, therefore, there will be selling. But where does this leave the seller once the market continues to rally? With losses, naturally. And sooner or later the seller will begin to think about covering at a loss. In the meantime, however, his human nature will probably convince him to hold on in hopes of getting out on a decline. But let's say the market continues upward and the seller finds himself in greater trouble. Chances are, the hapless seller will continue to hold his position, thus compounding his initial mistake of not getting out when the getting was good. Not wanting to appear foolish by admitting his error and covering at a loss, he invites additional trouble. Soon the market turns into a roaring bull and it truly appears hopeless. The seller gets a margin call which he probably meets—throwing good money after bad. He calls his broker in disbelief. What's happening? Nothing but a short-covering rally, he is told. Just send in another ten grand. We'll be out of trouble in a couple of days. In due time, other short sellers will run out of money and their buying will push prices still higher; the higher prices, in turn, will cause the big funds, who rely on trend-following methods, to begin to cover, thus adding fuel to the fire and sending the bull market soaring once again.

Is it any surprise that traders who can't take a small loss end up taking a big loss? It happened in the soybean market in the early winter of 1980, it happened in the silver and gold markets in the winter of 1983, and it happened in the stock index market in the summer of 1982, to name just a few examples. Chances are excellent that it will happen again.

The mark of a professional is that he *knows* that he *doesn't know the future;* no one does. As a result, he is willing to take a loss before it signifies trouble.

THE SIGNIFICANCE OF NEW HIGHS AND LOWS

If there is one area where most floor traders would agree, it would be on the significance of new highs and lows. There are intra-day highs and lows, contract highs and lows, weekly highs and lows, and so on. So you have to define precisely what you mean when you speak of a high or low. As areas of important resistance and support (where sellers will halt the upward movement of prices by selling and buyers will halt the downward movement of prices by buying), highs and lows signify key reversal points of breakout areas. They are important because they pinpoint precisely where a trader must be willing to commit himself to the market.

Following the opening each morning, the market will map out an area where it will trade for perhaps twenty minutes to a half an hour. While this is not what most analysts call the *opening range*, it is an important area because it creates a temporary trading band. As the market falls to the lower end of the range, scalpers and other floor traders will be willing buyers; at the high end of the range, they will become sellers. In a sense, this band of prices, which may be 40/100ths to 60/100ths of a point in width, represents the accumulated opinion of every trader in the market up until that point. The *high of the day*, known as the *intra-day high*, becomes the *resistance* and the *low of the day*, known as the *intra-day low*, becomes the support. Whenever an intra-day high or low is penetrated, especially

159

when it is still early in the trading day, the pace of buying and selling will pick up. One reason for this increase in activity rests with the stops. As we've already seen, stops tend to be clustered just above intra- and inter-day highs and below intra- and inter-day lows. A violation of the intra-day highs or lows, therefore, will signify either a genuine move out of the range or a mere penetration of the old highs or lows in order to pick off the stops.

How do you tell a genuine move from a false one? It isn't always easy. But you can put the odds in your favor by paying careful attention to how the market tends to trade. The stock index futures market is particularly perverse and misleading because it will often go into new high or low ground only to retreat and go the other way. You frequently hear the saying, "New highs after eleven." This means that the intra-day high made by eleven o'clock in the morning (Chicago time) will be taken out—*even if the market is headed lower*. It is as if the market has to take one more shot at the top (and, in the process, frighten the hapless shorts out of the market) before taking its intended course downward. The same might be said about the lows—in reverse, of course.

To determine whether a move is genuine or not, pay close attention to how it goes up or down. When you have a short-covering rally—that is, a rally brought on by the panic buying by shorts seeking to get out of their positions at all costs—the market is apt to rally quickly. But then a curious thing happens: *the rally goes dead*. It doesn't necessarily break right away, or fall apart. Instead, things turn lackluster. Usually, this is the quiet before the storm. The shorts, having all covered (bought) in a hurry, are finished buying and few new buyers are available to push the market higher. Until you get caught in one of these rallies (usually buying at the top), you won't appreciate the importance of knowing how to spot this market phenomenon. Once you do get caught, however, you'll never forget it. I remember once buying gold in just such a rally. Within minutes of purchasing gold contracts, I was several hundreds of dollars ahead. Unfortunately, I didn't know at the time that the sudden "deadness" following the quick rally was a sign of trouble. Instead, I interpreted it as a momentary pause and went out for a cup of coffee. About eight or nine minutes later I returned only to find that I'd lost well over a thousand dollars. It was the most expensive cup of coffee I'd ever had.

The more time you can spend analyzing market rallies, the better off you'll be in spotting the false rally or the genuine rally. It is important that you learn how to read the tape. You'll find that the genuine bull rally is another animal altogether. Powerful buying cannot be hidden on the tape. If you simply follow the successive bids, you'll find that in a genuine bull market move, the bids form a readily identifiable pattern. The market will be bid at a price and then a trade will occur at that price; next, an offer might come across the tape at the same price, an attempt by the sellers to knock it down. But the market will hold as a buyer jumps at the chance to buy additional contracts. The sellers might even succeed for a moment or two, and the market may sell off. Within moments, the buyers will bid it higher and the market will rise again. The sellers will again attempt to knock it down, as the struggle between buyers and sellers continues. But chances are the next bid will be higher and the one after that higher still. In short, the bulls will take control.

Assuming you have already purchased contracts, your exhilaration at seeing this pattern cannot be underestimated. When a market cannot go down, it will go up—simple as that. Once the sellers take their opportunity to knock a market down and cannot, they, too, will give up and become buyers. There's no sense in knocking your head against the wall. I remember just such a pattern in the bull market in stock index futures in early 1983. For reasons that are not important here, I had been selling S&P contracts all morning in anticipation of lower prices. The market went my way for awhile, but soon came back up on me and my shorts were all losing money. Rather than fight the market, I knew what I had to do. First, I took the loss which amounted to several thousand dollars. Then, because it was approaching noon, I went out for lunch.

I never like to take a loss without a plan for getting it back. And this day was no exception. Over lunch, which I ate alone because I didn't want to be distracted by the opinions of others, I realized I did the correct thing. Having a loss of several thousand dollars is okay if you are out of the market and the loss is over with; I still remembered my expensive cup of coffee from the gold market a year or two previous. The point is, I needed a short trading break to get back into a frame of mind to go back into the market. The more I thought about the morning's trading pattern, the more certain I was that I did the correct thing. The market wasn't going down at all that day; in fact, I was 100 percent wrong—and I'd paid some losses for my mistake. But making a mistake and not making money are not the same thing. Just because I was wrong on a trade didn't mean the day was going to be a loss. On the contrary, I now realized how strong the market really was.

After lunch, I began buying. Where was the market? Sitting on its highs for the day. "How can you buy up here?", came the inevitable question. Look at how far it has already come. I know how far it had come—because I'd been selling it all morning. At first, I bought just a couple of contracts—to see what would happen. Sure enough, new high ground. Then I began to buy in earnest. Higher bids slid across the tape. The tension was now palpable. Try as they could, the sellers couldn't knock it down. Again, new high ground. It was time to load up. I bought more. And then it took off to the upside. Within a minute or two, the market had moved up over a point and I immediately began to take profits. By aggressively selling, I managed to make a ton of money on my long positions—enough to offset my losses on the day and make a handsome profit besides.

What happened that day was nothing special. After the rally, in fact, the market traded lower. As an experienced S&P trader, however, I knew that the average range was about two points—and that there was still potential to the upside when I jumped on the long side. The key to my success was knowing what to do.

There's no such thing as a free lunch in the stock index futures market. I can't stress this enough. No one is giving away anything down on the floor—not a nickel, not a dime. For you to make money, you have to take it away from someone else—very likely someone who wants to win very badly. But you can do this if you know when to be cautious and when to be bold. Ironically, most investors are the most bold (reckless?) when they should be cautious and the most cautious when they should be bold. In the above example, boldness was called for—and it subsequently paid off. But I shudder to think about what would have happened if I'd hesitated and "watched the market" for awhile or became convinced that I was right and the market wrong.

ALWAYS BUY NEW HIGHS AND SELL NEW LOWS

You'll find few experts suggesting buying high and selling low but, as Damon Runyon once quipped, that's the way to bet. Not just any high or

162

low, of course. But *new* highs and *new* lows. What's the difference? Plenty.

A *new* high can be a new high on the day, a new high on the week, or even a new life-of-contract high. The same is true of new lows. The reason why the market is usually bullish on the penetration of new highs or bearish on the penetration of new lows is that major or minor support and resistance levels are violated at those price levels. Moreover, the penetration of a new high or low signals an activation of the stops at those levels. Naturally, the longer the support or resistance has held, the greater the likelihood that the subsequent move will be a significant one.

There is nothing new about this rule. It was a major tenet of the considerable body of work of W. D. Gann, who was a legendary grain trader. Yet as simple as the rule is, it is quite difficult to follow. For instance, assume the market has traded within a narrow range all day and then it mounts a rally. You want to buy, according to the rule. But your broker is likely to ask you if you are crazy. "Buy up here?" he might say. "If you thought it was going higher, why didn't you buy down at the bottom an hour ago?" The point is, you didn't know an hour ago that the market was headed higher. (Besides, if your broker is so brilliant, why is he working for commissions instead of risking his own funds?) The tape has now told you the direction the market wants to take, and you better get going if you want to catch it.

This rule flies in the face of all the conventional wisdom about buying dips and selling rallies. But, by definition, for a market to rise it *must* take out the old highs. And the same is true for selling new lows.

Timing is everything in the stock index futures markets. Once you learn to buy and sell on an instinctual level, you will no longer be held captive by your emotions telling you to be careful and watch the market for a moment longer. It's the hesitation that will get you in trouble—not the rule.

There's a pragmatic consideration that has to be taken into account here, and that involves the time of execution between when the signal is generated and when you get the order off. Typically, if a new low or high is taken out, one of two things will happen. Either the market will run immediately, in which case you better already have your order in the pit or you will miss the move; or, on the other hand, the market will give you another chance to get aboard. In the case of the latter, wait for the pullback or rally and then *go after the move*. I emphasize this because it is

163

so important. I remember being long S&P futures one day when the market suddenly broke. Down, down, down it went. But while my impulse was to immediately sell, I realized I would only end up selling the bottom and the market would bounce up again, if for no other reason than the sudden break would mean a lot of traders would soon be taking profits on their short positions. So I made two quick decisions. One, witnessing the break, I would now look for a spot to go short. Two, I would wait for the short-covering rally to take the losses on my longs and start selling. Sure enough, the rally came just like clockwork. Up came prices and I put on the shorts. Then the *real* decline began. It was an enormously profitable day. Again, after being on the *wrong* side of the market.

MAKE YOUR MONEY EARLY IN THE DAY

If there's a best time to buy or sell, it's just after the open, early in the trading day. You may have noticed that the open frequently occurs *near the extreme end of the range of the day*. This is not an accident or happenstance. Statistical computer studies have been performed on a number of different futures contracts, and the evidence is overwhelming that the open *is* frequently near the high or the low of the day. Stock index futures are no exception. Think of the market, for a moment, as a giant spring that is pulled apart each morning. You will gather an idea of what I mean. The opening represents the pulling apart of the market—and not a few traders whose hopes are riding on a favorable opening as well! The spring effect simply returns the market to its normal shape. To prove my point, I'm enclosing ten trading days' price information for the September 1983 S&P 500 contract. In this sample of ten representative trading days, you can clearly see that the open is near one or another end of the range.

Table 19

OPEN TO END OF RANGE—SEPT. '83 S&P 500

Day	Open	Extreme End of Range	High/Low	Total Range	Distance from End of Range
1	162.90	162.70	Low	90	20
2	164.25	164.20	Low	150	5
3	164.60	164.95	High	175	35
4	164.45	164.25	Low	200	20
5	166.05	166.25	High	275	20
6	163.70	163.25	Low	175	45
7	166.00	166.35	High	220	35
8	164.50	164.50	High	185	0
9	163.25	163.90	High	270	65
10	161.85	162.10	High	180	25

Average Daily
Range   =   192

Average Distance
of Open From End of Range   =   27

One basic inference to be drawn from the table above is that if you place your stop 70/100ths points away from the opening and it is *hit*, you have a pretty good idea that you did the right thing by exiting the market. More importantly, you can also draw the conclusion that the open represents one of the best times to enter the market. The move away from the open, at least after the misleading price moves resulting from the action of the stops is over, tends to be the "purest" move of the day. By this, I mean the most consistent with the greatest follow through. By concentrating on finding this initial move, you increase the odds in your favor in a dramatic fashion. This is what the professional floor traders look for, and it can stand you in good stead as well. After all, what do you need to make an excellent living trading stock index futures? If you could make just one-half point on two

S&P contracts daily, you would make $500 a day. That's $2,500 a week, or $125,000 a year with two weeks off for vacation.

THE RULE OF THREE

It's fine to know that you have to make your money early in the day, but what are you really looking for? You're looking for a breakout from the daily opening range and you're looking for a significant move that will enable you to earn a nice profit—and run! The question is, when do you take a trade?

You might rely on the rule of three, which states: *look for a breakout from a previous support or resistance on the third test of that support or resistance.* * Following the opening, there is a time of uncertainty when both buyers and sellers are placing their positions in hopes of getting in on a move. Typically, the scalpers will be making money by selling rallies and buying dips. The result is a market that goes up a little and down a little, exhibiting a sort of randomness resulting from the floor playing off the orders coming into the pit. But if you watch closely, you'll see the first two tests of the intra-day highs and lows are apt to hold whereas the third is apt to be the real thing.

THE BREAKOUT PLAY

At this point, you have to make a decision. With the third test about to be made, you have to either get an order into the pit or be prepared to call in a market order as soon as the break into new high or low territory occurs. You also have to know how to mount a defensive play in case the strategy fails. Remember, no strategy is foolproof. For the breakout strategy to work, you have to first wait for the initial range to be established. For the sake of illustration, let's say we are talking about one-half point, from 160.00 to 160.50. Once you understand the parameters, you can call the support at 160.00 and the resistance at 160.50 the breakout areas. As long as the market trades *within* this range, the market is no

---

* Legendary trader W. D. Gann stressed that everything moves in threes, including breakouts based on time intervals of three—three days, three weeks, three months, etc.

better than a crapshoot. By the way, this is why preconceived notions about what the market must do are useless. The fact is, no one knows. The scalpers will be busy buying and selling and trying to get the edge, but this isn't a game you want to engage in. Rather, as a day trader, you want a good and pure move, preferably the first out of the opening range. In general, and I stress *general*, a market will trend in one direction most of the day. This doesn't mean there won't be counter-trend moves. There will be. But you want to get in on the beginning of the first move.

Let's say it is nine forty-five Chicago time and you've been watching the S&P market for forty-five minutes. The market has made two trips up to the resistance and the same number down to the support. It is now mounting its third rally, and the breakout is imminent. The third rally fails and it drifts lower. Then it hits the support and attempts to rally again—and fails. This is the sign that you should start selling.

Meanwhile, down in the pit, the weakness in the market hasn't gone unnoticed. The market breaks below the support and the big money is starting to sell as a chorus of voices shouting "new lows" can be heard as the floor begins to smell blood.

As for the previous buyers who are now long, they are getting ready to sell in a hurry, hitting the bids to get out at any cost. Soon the bargain hunters are trying to support the market. But they, too, find the absence of buying unable to hold prices. They, too, become sellers and pretty soon you have a mini-bloodbath as the sellers panic all at once and offer down the price.

Assuming you are short, you should be prepared for any contingency. One, if the market continues downward, there will come a time when the shorts want to begin taking profits and the market will rally as a result. As a rule, you want to immediately anticipate this rally and cover your shorts. This profit should be your major profit on the day. Moreover, this profit should never be given back through reckless trading later in the day. To safeguard this profit, always make your largest commitment on this trade (but not so large that you aren't prepared to double-up and go the other way if necessary—more on that later). It is only a natural human emotion to want to size up a situation before committing yourself. But this is a mistake. Take your shot early in the day. Chances are, the price around the open represents the highest price of the day—and hence the safest for the sellers—and the market will never return to that level again that day.

167

Having sold on the breakout (by the way, this would be selling new lows), you are now in an excellent position. If you wait, you will only have to sell lower and any rally will result in a paper loss. And what if you are wrong? If you are wrong, and the break proves a false one, you have to take immediate action lest you find yourself in what is known as a *bear trap*. A bear trap exists when the market goes down, trapping the shorts, and then mounts a significant rally. Don't allow yourself to become a victim. Rather, if the market now rallies and goes into new high ground, *first cover the shorts at a loss and second buy twice as many contracts as you previously sold.* Why twice as many? Because you now need only half the distance to generate a comparable profit to offset your loss. The only way you can lose with this strategy is if you are whipsawed again and again.

Figure 7 shows how the breakout play works.

WHY YOU NEED ADEQUATE MARGIN

If there's one thing that separates the winners from the losers in the stock index futures market, it is money. Futures trading is a money game. The well-financed traders profit at the expense of the less-well-financed (known, appropriately, as "weak hands") again and again. Here's why. The trader operating on thin margin *must* earn a profit almost from the outset. He has no margin for error. If he is wrong, the trader of only modest means must close out his transaction at a loss. Typically, however, the thinly-financed trader compounds his problems by holding on in the face of adversity. Because he reasons that he *can't* take a small loss, he often, paradoxically, ends up taking a large one.

While everyone must post margin in the futures markets, the trading public must post more than the floor trader who is a member of an exchange. Because the floor trader is apt to be flat the market at the close of trading each day, his intra-day trading isn't really subject to the rigorous margin requirements that the public must meet. As a result, the floor trader, regardless of his own personal resources, can *act* like a trader who has ample resources. This is an important advantage.

In the breakout play described above, the exchange member has an advantage because he can, as we've seen, take larger positions without

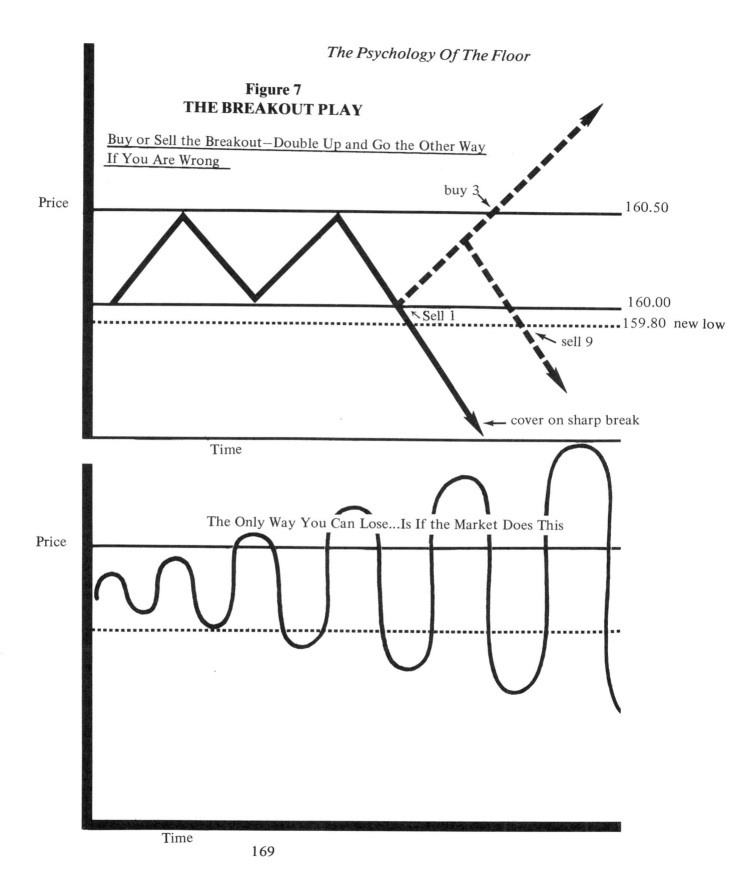

Figure 7
THE BREAKOUT PLAY

Buy or Sell the Breakout—Double Up and Go the Other Way
If You Are Wrong

buy 3

Price

160.50

Sell 1

160.00

159.80 new low

sell 9

cover on sharp break

Time

The Only Way You Can Lose...Is If the Market Does This

Price

Time

169

posting additional margin. For public or floor trader alike, however, this strategy is difficult to execute because it runs the risk of getting whipsawed.

How many times should you be prepared to switch sides and reverse your position? It depends on how the market is behaving. If you have been in a position all day and there are only five minutes left to the close, it doesn't make a lot of sense to reverse. But then again, you have to wonder why you would stay with a position which wasn't working out for an entire trading session. As a rule, look to reverse no more than twice. Thus, if you have a position and it doesn't work, reverse; if that position, in turn, proves a loser, look to reverse once more. And if you aren't ahead on the day by then, chalk it up to bad luck. Using this technique, you should be able to make consistent profits—that is, profits almost every day. Indeed, if you do it right, you can make quite a bit of money. But let me stress that you have to have complete confidence in your approach and never let the market get away from you.

If inadequate margin if often a problem, so also is a trader's tendency to underestimate the volatility of a market. To be a consistent winner, you must be willing to take what the market gives you—reasonable profits, most of the time; extraordinary profits occasionally. So many winning trades turn into losers simply because a trader was unwilling to accept a profit.

You must remember that your financial "stake" is your greatest ally in the market. When the opportunity comes to jump on a trade, you are going to need your margin money as your financial backing. So do everything you can to protect your resources. Nothing. is more frustrating than to know what to do in the market, and have your broker inform you that you are undermargined. Leave sufficient funds in your account, in T-bills or whatever, so that you won't get caught short when the time comes.

If you find yourself getting whipsawed using the breakout play strategy, don't panic. Unfortunately, this will happen. Chances are, the market is just in a small trading range and trendless for the time being. Thus, if you are short and the market goes first in your favor and then against you, it may be nothing more than a random movement. If it breaks into new low ground, you may want to short more contracts. And then think about covering. Anytime the market gives you a truly hard time, you want to get out with the best profit you can. To do otherwise is to invite getting ground up. But one caveat: *do not become a buyer late in a trading session, hoping to pick a bottom.* Covering is fine, but bottom-picking can be dangerous. Occasionally, being a bottom-picker works. Certainly, many try it. But more often than not, the trader riding the trend makes the profit. And the trend starts early. When the gold and silver markets broke in the early winter of 1983, there were many bottom pickers—right at the top of the market. How were they to know gold would subsequently break by over $100 an ounce? After all, a move of that magnitude wasn't expected. But it ruined a number of traders who didn't have a chance once the bottom fell out.

KNOW YOUR MARKET

Another perhaps apocryphal story concerning the grain market occurred a number of years ago when a wheat trader walked off the floor with a mournful look on his face. A friend saw him and went over to inquire.

"Bob, what's the problem?"

"I've just been busted out in the wheat pit," Bob replies. "I'm finished."

"No, you're not," his friend says. "Come over here and trade soybeans with me."

Bob looks at him, and says, "But I don't know anything about soybeans."

Obviously, if Bob knew the wheat market well, he probably wouldn't be experiencing such difficulties. One can only imagine whether he could have done worse in soybeans. But the story does illustrate the notion that one's market is a specialty, and the professional trader wouldn't anymore think about switching from one market to another than he would think about becoming a cattle herder or an oil man. In general, professional floor traders are highly-trained specialists, loyal to one pit and futures contract. This loyalty, of course, stems not from feelings of kinship (although that may be a part of it; I know of one fellow who trades cattle because, although being city born and bred, he enjoys being around cattlemen and driving around in a pickup wearing a Stetson on his head) so much as a strong desire for self-preservation. Anytime a new trader joins the ranks of a new pit, he must learn the intricacies of a whole new market.

A new trader, like the public trader, is at a disadvantage almost from the

171

start. A new floor trader is unlikely to "get the paper," or have floor brokers handling public orders trade with him—simply because they don't know him and they'd prefer to deal with the familiar faces of people they know. The reason for this is two-fold: friends are friends, and where money is concerned, why not help out those you know? The assumption is that the floor trader will profit from the trade, of course. In due time, a friend can be counted upon to return the favor—help with an out-trade, or whatever. This mutual back-scratching is well entrenched in the futures market where a trader who is "out" on a trade—meaning it is unreconciled the next day and has not cleared—will often find the opposing trader willing to help him out by splitting the difference in cash, agreeing to resolve the trade at a price in the broker's favor, or otherwise accommodating the other's needs. The disagreement, resulting in the trade being miscarded, may have arisen due to one or the other trader missing the price, contract month, quantity of contracts, the other trader's badge initials—or even both traders being on the same side of the trade; both buying, for instance.

So-called "out-trades" can be quite costly, since someone has to make up the difference. A few years ago, an out-trade cost a bond trader over $100,000. And this leads to the second reason why brokers prefer to deal with people they know. An inexperienced or new trader might simply miscard the trade, and it will become a big hassle to resolve it the next day. The number of out-trades in the stock index futures pit is among the largest on any futures exchange. The reason being the number of relatively new traders, coupled with the relentless pace of the markets. The greater the volatility of the market, the more likely a trade won't clear because one or both traders missed the other's initials, or price, or whatever. Considering the hectic conditions they work under, it's absolutely amazing that more floor traders *don't* have out-trades.

Out-trades aside, the men and women on the floor of a futures exchange are highly attuned to the risk involved in this perilous undertaking. They know how a moment's hesitation can frequently cost thousands of dollars, how inexperience can manifest itself in a dozen different mistakes—and, above all, how much concentration and sheer mental effort is required to trade stock index futures, or, for that matter, soybeans, pork bellies, or gold. For this reason, they tend to focus on a highly individualized sort of trading in a concentrated way. A trader, for example, who is a specialist in, let us say, spreading forward and back months of U.S. Treasury bond futures, won't concern himself with anything else. His job is to know the spreads, the vital differentials between months, upon which his living rests.

A scalper, likewise, wouldn't think of taking a position trade because it would be counter to his game plan. And, taken a step further, a stock index futures trader wouldn't spend his time trading lumber or unleaded gasoline futures. The dissimilarities propelling such markets are just too diverse.

But apart from the subtleties that serve as demarcations between one market and another, there is a very real reason why one should specialize in one market over another, even within the same general group, such as the growing number of index products. *Markets are different*. They rise differently, and they sell-off differently, and unless you're familiar with the market you intend to trade, you will be operating at a distinct disadvantage to those who do know it well, namely the floor traders.

Not long ago, I spoke with a broker friend who'd become quite proficient at day-trading S&P futures. Despite his success as a day trader, he must have felt there were other worlds to conquer, because he had suddenly switched to taking heavy positions in the inter-market spreads between the Kansas City Value Line contract and the S&P contract traded in Chicago. "But do you know anything about the Value Line contract?" I asked him. No, was his reply, but he had a feeling that one was overvalued in terms of the other. He cited the conventional wisdom about the spread, as if no one else knew this information. While there are indeed obvious differences—the size of the respective contracts, volatility, market price, and so on—I wasn't at all sure that my friend knew enough about this unique relationship between these two indexes *and the underlying futures contracts based on the indexes* to overnight begin taking rather substantial spread positions. Needless to say, he, indeed, had the spread in reverse (contrary opinion would have worked!) and he ended up with a substantial loss simply because he didn't know his market.

Others err because they borrow time-tested stock market techniques and try to apply them to the futures market. For instance, in the equities markets it is a commonly accepted principle that market diversification serves to insure safety of capital. Thus an investor would not think twice about holding a half-dozen to a dozen stocks or more in hopes that one or two losers will be offset by the other stocks he holds in his portfolio. In the futures market, however, where everything is speeded up due to the high leverage involved, the diversification argument doesn't make as much sense.* So you can imagine my surprise when an investor approached me

---

* No doubt, the commodity fund managers will disagree with me on this score, but have you checked *their* record lately?

following a seminar to tell me he traded a portfolio consisting of more than 13 different futures contracts at a time. His story was not unfamiliar. He'd made an appreciable amount of money, but then lost it and was searching for a trading system. By the way, he was a doctor who maintained office hours and performed the many other duties of a busy physician, resulting in little time left over in his busy schedule to follow the market. I reflected on all the hours I'd spent trying to trade just stock index futures and wondered why he hadn't already gone broke.

Now you might very well ask, "what is there to know about a market?" Plenty. How the market breaks, the daily average range, the magnitude of the typical rally, the market's liquidity, the typical basis (relationship of cash to the futures), how the market tends to handle news events—all this information can help you win profits. Moreover, much of it is statistical and a matter of public record. Most of the truly important news is in the tape itself. Once you develop a feel for the market, you begin to sense how it trades and how it reacts to news and events.

WHEN TO PLUNGE

A corollary of knowing your market is knowing when to plunge. By plunge, I mean take a position consisting of more contracts than you normally trade. The reason? To make a significant amount of money during a particularly propitious moment—enough to more than make up for the inevitable slow periods and times when you become the victim of a whipsawing market.

As a rule, you want to think of the short side of the market when you think about plunging, but even this statement needs important qualifications. As a rule, markets tend to rise at a slower rate than they decline, although anyone who witnessed the late-1982 bull market in stocks would tend to disagree with this. Nevertheless, it is the market breaks that provide the real profits to stock index traders. If you think of a market rise in terms of a man pushing a boulder up an incline, you'll see the difficulty prices sometimes have in rising. As he pushes the prices slowly upward, he is occasionally stopped in his tracks and even forced backwards—at least until he marshalls his strength and again reasserts his control. But at the top of the incline, after much effort and concentration, he may find

174

himself on the edge of an abyss. Once the boulder goes over the edge and into the abyss, it disappears under the force of gravity with dispatch. At times, the market moves in a somewhat similar pattern; haltingly upward, but dropping like a rock.

Sometimes for a year or more, Wall Street will see nothing but good times. Share prices by and large move steadily upward and the market reacts with optimism. But there will come a time when investors will want to take profits and, for that matter, will simply cease to be as bullish as they once were and the impetus for higher prices will cease along with their enthusiasm. When that occurs, watch out! The existence of many, many small investors in the equities markets and the stock index futures markets presents a situation in which the market could break sharply. Thinly-financed, such investors are the first to bail out when adversity hits. Moreover, their inability to withstand temporary breaks in the market means a panic situation could easily result with the predictable happening: stops hit, panic selling, and a plummeting market. It is at times like these that some real serious money can be made, and I suggest you keep a ready cash position to avail yourself of such an opportunity.

"If you want to make it down here," a floor trader once told me, "you have to load up on the short side." It's good advice.

Professional floor traders are always looking to "fade," or trade against, the public, and one way to accomplish this is to be a steady short seller. Investors are natural optimists and tend to be long stock index futures in far greater numbers than they are short futures. Since there has to be both a buyer and a seller in every trade, the ranks of the short sellers must come from the floor trader community—those who aren't psychologically adverse to betting against lower prices.

You must, on occasion, be prepared to plunge on the long side as well, however. It is just too pat to try to say you should *always* emphasize one side or another. Which is the best side to trade? The right side, of course.

If you are not what I call a *selective plunger,* you only invite the forces of the market to slowly grind you up. Consider: on *every* trade, you are paying commissions plus you are, more often than not, giving up the edge to the floor. Occasionally, your stops are among the like-minded and by the time your order is filled, you've given up twice what you intended to. Then you have to factor in your bad trades. Nobody's perfect. It adds up.

The antidote to this slow grind is the *occasional killing.* As long as you make it in large chunks, you can afford to give some of it back in little pieces—a fair exchange by any standards.

The precise moment to plunge will only become clear once you work through the material in subsequent chapters. But unless you are familiar with the groundwork, with the theory behind the rules, the reasoning won't appear clear. Put simply, *some trades offer far better opportunities for profit than others;* the more readily you can identify the winning trades, those with the percentage in your favor, the better your record will be. Finding the high-quality trade, however, isn't always easy. You have to process a lot of information and then place your position *before* the opportunity becomes widely recognized. This takes a certain courage and foresight—two qualities that aren't always readily found among the emotionally-driven individuals who often fill the investor ranks.

Lastly, a word of caution. While it is necessary to be a selective plunger, you don't want to be a plunger of the non-selective variety. There's a great deal of difference between an aggressive trader and one who is merely a fool. Perhaps fortunately for some of us, the latter type abounds in the stock index futures market. I know a fellow who would offer to sell *or* buy dozens of contracts at the same price. He didn't want the edge, he didn't have a point of view, he simply wanted the action—the chance to make a quick score. Unfortunately, he also had the habit of trading while under the influence of alcohol—and, perhaps surprising to some, he used to occasionally win while in such a condition. Even substantial sums. But his luck ran out in the stock index futures market. Throwing caution to the winds, he plunged on the short side of the S&P market one day just as the August 1982 bull market was getting underway. Because he was in way over his head, having sold hundreds of contracts, he was blown out of the water the very first day. Underfinanced, he didn't have the money to make good his losses. He'll never trade futures again.

"I WANT THE MONEY"

I recently read an account of the great jockey Angel Cordero. Only three days after being thrown from a horse and nearly crippled, Angel, with more than 5,000 victories under his belt, was out riding—and winning—again. Known for his aggressive style of riding, Cordero had been set down by the stewards over the years. But he remained irrepressible. In talking about his riding tactics, he told a reporter for *The New York Times:*" 'Lots of times I had to take chances to win. I'd be running in behind horses when I had no place to go—I'd just try to make room for myself.' '' Sammy Renick, the former jockey, is quoted as saying of Cordero: '' 'He's a great athlete, and with a terrific will to win. He'll make moves that are so deft, so borderline to impeding another horse, that it's hard to make a call. He'll take advantage of every little opportunity.' ''

This is the mark of a champion. And if you change a few words, the same sentiments might be said of a winning stock index futures trader. The will to win, the notion of making the most of one's opportunities, the rebound from defeats—all are qualities that make the successful trader. One winning floor trader told me the same thing in fewer words. "I want the money," he told me.

When you think about it, it is amazing how few traders really *know* what they are after. If you have ever spent any time in a brokerage house board room, you would think most investors were in the market to impress others with their market opinions. This one can tell you sales and earnings figures for the past ten years of every major blue-chip stock in the Dow Jones Industrials. That one is touting a new computer stock that his brother-in-law purchased two months ago that has already tripled in value. And another wants to know what *you* think about IBM's chances for record level earnings again this year. What does this have to do with making money?

Exactly! And that's why you don't want to lose sight of your reason for trading stock index futures.

Mental toughness is one component in the key to success in the market. While one type of trader is nursing a hangover, the other is psyching himself out to beat the market, his game plan clear in his head. A commercial airlines pilot once assured me that, should anything go wrong aloft, he was trained to react immediately. The same is true of the good trader.

Yet how many traders know when to take defensive action? How many know when they have to plunge? How many put themselves in a position to truly win? How many really want the money?

I can assume you really want the money. And by the time you finish this book, you should also have positive answers to the other three questions posed above.

177

NEWS EVENTS AND RUMORS

During the 444-day tenure of the U.S. hostages in Iran, news stories abounded with up-to-the-minute developments of the year-and-a-half negotiations. Down on the floor of the Chicago Mercantile Exchange, the news often turned to hyperbole, as the imminent release of the hostages was reported no less than five or six times, the rumors sweeping across the huge trading floor like wild fire. Embellished as they were, the rumors often took on a life of their own; but, in time, as more and more were proven unfounded, each was met with greater and greater suspicion. After months of repeated rumors, one finally realized that the actual news, when it arrived, would be met with little more than a shrug; the news was already in the market.

Nevertheless, unexpected new events can cause skittish markets to react violently. The Sadat assassination, which caused the gold market to gyrate wildly, was one recent example of this. But sometimes the news events have been manufactured to move the market. The story is told of a trader, caught holding long gold contracts in a declining market a year or so ago, who ran into the gold pit shouting, "Reagan's had a heart attack!" It lifted a few eyebrows, but ultimately proved a failure. The President was well.

If there's an inference to be drawn from these events, it is that markets will react differently at different times. Not too long ago, gold, which has long been thought of as a barometer of anxiety, would move ten or fifteen dollars an ounce on the slightest bit of international tension; today it seems that nothing short of a nuclear war could make it skyrocket like the old days—indeed, if such an event could be of any benefit to winner or loser. Compounding the difficulty of analyzing news events is that one man's news is another man's rumor. Then there is the offsetting factor: given the number of *different* interpretations concerning an event, one often cancels out another. But when the news becomes one-sided, the opportunities often become available. A favorite gambit of floor traders is to routinely "fade" any front-page story appearing in *The Wall Street Journal.* Consider such headlines as: **STOCKS SOAR; NEW BULL MARKET CITED** or **WALL STREET BULLISH; SKY'S THE LIMIT.** These, and similar such headlines, are a sure sign the market's headed *lower*—briefly, if not over the long-term, in the opinion of the floor. The reason? News stories always lag behind the actual events. Only the most unsophisticated investor, of which there are many, will buy stocks on news like this. Hence, the floor, always attuned to selling anyway as professional "faders" of the public, becomes heavy sellers when the bullish news becomes too one-sided. It is a case of the old market adage, "Buy the rumor, sell the news."

For some reason, which I've never been able to figure out, the consensus of the news media is often accurate to the day in picking major tops and bottoms in reverse. The day *The Wall Street Journal* ran a story on the gold bugs finally turning bearish, the gold market turned a mighty bull and soared more than $100 an ounce in the ensuing two weeks. More recently, stories about the reduced grain crop due to the unbearable summer heat signalled the top in soybeans and other bean products. And in the stock market, where interest rates provide the clue to future direction, rising rates have often been accompanied by rising security prices as well—an incongruous situation without explanation in the conventional wisdom.

But the media can't be blamed. If anyone's to blame, it is our own need to know the reason for an event, even if the interpretation is less than accurate. Readers want to know that this or that event propelled prices higher. If the absence of an easily identifiable reason for a market move leaves a writer in a quandary, the move will be attributable to "technical" factors. This, supposedly, means the market went up because it went up, or some such nonsense. The point is, the attributed factor is always applied *after* the fact; Whatever fits will hang upon the peg of attributive reasons. For example, this morning's *Journal* bring the following words of wisdom:

> Analysts said traders had been expecting a decline in M1, which is cash held by the public plus private checking accounts, of between $500 million and $1 billion. Prices were also hurt by the Fed's announcement late Friday that at its meeting in July the Federal Open Market Committee, the Fed's chief policy-making body, voted for a 'slight further tightening' of growth in the nation's basic money supply. Analysts added that most people believe that at its latest meeting last week, the FOMC voted to maintain its July policy stance. That means that current interest rates are likely to remain near their current levels until early autumn and that the Fed won't adopt a less restrictive policy stance at least until October.

Occasionally, I meet someone who talks like this and I run like hell. The so-called fundamentals have very little to do with the short-term direction of prices, and even if they did, the abundant number of fundamental factors would prove confusing, to say the least. Then what about the long run? "In the long run," as Keynes so aptly put, "we are all dead."

News events serve a legitimate purpose. They serve as an *excuse* to move the market along the path of least resistance. This can work in your favor *if* you can see the process in operation. For instance, taking the mish-mash of financial jargon in the account above, a more realistic version of the same situation might appear as follows.

> Using last Friday's Money Supply report as an excuse to hammer down prices on the open, the floor stretched the market out of line and created panicky selling by the public on the open. Informed buying then entered the market as prices rose steadily throughout the day, despite weakness in interest rates. The market closed on its high as short sellers were quick to cover lest bullish sentiment overtake the market.

But even this account only hints at the forces at work. Chances are, the stock index futures market had been trading at a discount to the cash index—in anticipation of the bearish Money Supply report. Once the report was released, the conventional wisdom says, in effect, oh yes, that must be very bearish; just look, for instance, at the suddenly rising interest rates. The scenario is set up to be played out. First, the bearish news is the *excuse* to take the market down; second, once the damage has been done to the hapless longs and the less-intelligent sellers, the fish are in the barrel and shooting can begin. The market *must* rise. Not only are the *former* short sellers, who anticipated the dire news event (in this case, a bearish Money Supply report), now covering, but they are also aggressively buying. From whom? From the Johnny-come-lately sellers who are now convinced the market is going lower because the market is interpreted as bearish. Remember, it takes two to tango. Unfortunately, one side is always getting the better of the other.

Now, in defense of the hapless speculators who find themselves caught in this situation, it must be said that everything did indeed "look" as if it would move in their favor. On Friday's close, just prior to the issuance of the report, the stock index futures market settled near the high of the day. In fact, if the unlucky longs had only held on, they would have earned profits, since Friday's highs were taken out and new highs established on Monday afternoon. But this is easy to see with twenty-twenty hindsight. The point is, the news event provided the excuse, then the unwary were relieved of their cash. This also points out the reason why day trading is often the smart course to take, especially over a weekend just prior to the issuance of a potential market-moving report.

If a news report can be used to mask a market's true intentions, it can

180

also be used to announce them. Perhaps the strongest and truest sense of a market can be determined by *watching its reaction to news*. There are news events and there are news events; some have a potential huge impact on the market. So you have to watch for news that *should* move prices. When potential market-moving news occurs, therefore, pay attention to how the market reacts. The rules are as follows:

If an important piece of bullish news is released and fails to push prices higher, sell immediately; and, *if an important piece of bearish news is released and fails to push prices lower, buy immediately.*

The importance of these rules should not be underestimated. Bullish markets thrive on bullish news; once a continuation of more bullish news hits the market and fails to advance prices, the likelihood is that all the would-be bulls have already done their buying. As a result, their buying is exhausted and they need new blood coming into the market to bid up prices. Usually, just following a bullish report there will be great anticipation in the market. Let this be a sign to be cautious. When the market fails to respond, prices just seem to go "dead" for awhile. Typically, this is the quiet before the storm. This brief hesitation means everyone is watching everyone else. Once the first bull bolts for the door, the herd is certain to follow. And prices will plunge.

At a market bottom, the bearish sentiment is overwhelming. You should always remember that, by definition, *a market is always the most bullish at the top and the most bearish at the bottom.* On the bottom, therefore, few believe there is much chance for higher prices. Once a news event occurs, seconding their belief, prices should move even lower. Again, we have the mirror image of the top; the bears are waiting for new selling. When new selling fails to develop, the market is poised for a substantial rise.

WHO'S IN TROUBLE?

One way to visualize this overbought or oversold situation is to ask yourself the question, "Who's in trouble?" The more buying you have in a declining market, the more speculators who will sooner or later have to sell. The same is true of selling in a rising market, of course. One advantage the floor traders have over those who must trade off the floor is that the floor can generally see who is doing the buying. This can be shown best by an incident that occurred to a friend of mine in the Merc's Swiss Franc pit one day. Prices were trending lower when the brokers who handle the orders for the big European banks came into the market and started purchasing hundreds of contracts in hopes of supporting the market. Typically, this would be a sign that you would want to follow suit. But as my friend tried to make sense of this market, he noticed that not only was the rest of the pit selling, but that Swiss Franc prices were making very little headway. His approach is to test a market, sort of like putting one's little toe in the water to see whether it's hot or cold. First, he offered to sell a few contracts to see how the market would take the selling. Then he decided to see if he could get away with low-balling the offer, offering to sell below the last offer, an entirely legitimate tactic. Sure enough, a bargain-hunting buyer took the other side of the trade. But now, with this new low tick, the buyers were becoming uneasy; the brokers of the European banks weren't trying to support the Swiss Franc at these prices. They had already tried to support the price at a higher level and were, in fact, holding hundreds of long contracts—all of them now with paper losses. Suddenly, additional selling pushed the market under a support level and, predictably, the bottom fell out; the banks were now sellers, adding to the tumult.

In the stock index futures markets, which are, after all, tied to the major underlying cash indexes, you wouldn't think this type of momentary panic on the part of a few traders could result in similar devastation. But the same characteristics are evident. You might think that no one is big enough to push around the Big Board—and you'd be correct. But as a number of sophisticated arbitrageurs have found to their regret, the basis (relation of futures to cash) can be anything but steady, and a few panic-stricken big traders can move the market sufficiently to cause hundreds of smaller traders to join them in panic buying or selling.

CONSISTENT PROFITS

If there's one overriding strategy that the stock index futures trader can borrow from the professional, it is the notion of approaching the market as a business venture—and keeping an eye on the bottom line, profitability. Despite what you hear about index futures being just another gamble, even a cursory glance at how floor traders conduct their business would suggest otherwise. To make a living at trading index futures, you must earn a profit.

And you can't very well earn a profit if your seed money, or financial stake, is wiped out on the first trade. For this reason, most floor traders look upon their trading activities as a business, not a speculation, although trading index futures can be highly speculative.

It may seem surprising to some, but a number of successful floor traders *do not lose.* They might lose on a trade, but on a daily, weekly, or monthly basis, they earn profits. To make the market consistently profitable, however, they often have to accept small profits in lieu of the big market killing that so many often fruitlessly seek.

We've covered some of the strategies that professional stock index futures traders use. The ones that we've covered would all have been profitable numerous times in the past couple of years since index futures commenced trading. A lot of that profit, however, might have evaporated had the trader not adhered to some of the commonsense rules of trading. This is why you must be rigorous in your pursuit of consistent profits. Don't let temporary market circumstances prevent you from continuing on the path to consistent profitability. The following seven rules will help keep you on the correct path.

SEVEN RULES

1. *Never let a profit develop into a loss.* The goal of every trade should be to make a profit. Obviously, this is not always possible since some trades will simply go against you from the outset. Accept these losses as a normal part of trading. A certain portion of your trades, however, no matter how bad your luck, will move in a favorable direction. To adhere to the consistent profit rule, you must permit yourself to accept the profit on these trades before they have an opportunity to go into negative territory. No matter how well-engineered a market, there will always be a certain randomness involved. When the randomness is favorable to you, accept the profit; when it isn't favorable, don't let a small loss result in a larger loss—close out the trade. As a rule, a profit that develops into a loss is likely to mean trouble. Don't tempt fate by holding on in the face of adversity. Liquidate the position and look for another opportunity to enter the market.

2. *Don't overtrade.* Select your trades carefully. To earn a handsome profit, you only need two or three good trades a week. Better to wait patiently for a good trade rather than jump into the market without rhyme or reason. Moreover, over-trading adds to commission expenses.

3. *Play your own game.* Know what you want in the market and go after it. This includes knowing your own game plan and moving toward a goal with your own interests at heart. Don't switch trading methods in the midst of a market campaign unless you have a good reason to do so. If, for instance, you look for a higher open in order to sell, wait for the market to move in the direction anticipated before putting on the trade. You may very well have the right idea. Otherwise, your impatience may cause you to enter the market prematurely, and you may sustain a loss as a result. On the other hand, you must be flexible enough to know that the market is always right. If your anticipation proves incorrect, be prepared to go the other way—or even stand aside. The best trades are the ones that go your way right from the start. Be prepared for your opportunity when it comes.

4. *Never fight the market.* When wrong, get out! There is no future in trying to outsmart the market when it clearly wants to move against you. Occasionally, you will get whipsawed by switching sides in a volatile market, but this is inevitable. The point is, once the writing is on the wall, you must accept a loss. A corollary of this rule is: *No losses overnight.* Profits, yes. But losses, never. For some reason, once a position turns into a loss, the chances of it regaining profitability on the following day are slim. By steadfastly adhering to this rule, you'll find that despite a short period of losses, the damage will be minimal. They will have to take away your money in bits and pieces. But once you try to fight the market by going overnight, you are prepared to take a bigger loss on the following close, and the problem is compounded. Learn to love a small loss and this will never be a problem. Even the best traders have more numerical losses than profits. The idea is to make five or six times as much money on each profit as you lose on each loss. You'll be in fine shape.

5. *Never trade the same number of contracts on each trade.* As mentioned earlier on, you have to be a selective plunger in order to win. If you trade the same number of contracts each time, chances are the market will merely grind you up. The money lost in slippage (bad fills, etc.), commissions, and inept trades will more than offset your profits.

6. ***Forget the fundamentals.*** Money moves the market, not fundamentals.* No matter how bullish or bearish the market might seem based on the prevailing supply and demand for securities, the big money is going to have its way. Occasionally, the market's direction may coincide with fundamental analyses—but who's to say what caused the move? Rather than waste effort trying to discern the fundamentals, concentrate on trying to read the "footprints" of the major market forces. Fortunately, these "footprints" are clearly discernible in the market tape—*if* you know what to look for.

7. ***When you're hot, you're hot; when you're not, you're not.*** Sometimes, no matter what you do, you can't win; fortunately, the reverse is true as well. Learn to accept the inevitable trading slump, confident that you will once again emerge a winner. Adjust the size of your market commitment to reflect your position in this cyclical wave. One trader I know switches from full-size contracts to mini-contracts when he senses a slump coming on. You could do worse than follow his lead.

---

* For a truly excellent analysis of why this is true, see R. Earl Hadady's new book, *Contrary Opinion.* Available from Hadady Publications, Inc., 61 S. Lake Avenue, Pasadena, Calif.

Chapter Six

GANN, FIBONACCI AND THE GOLDEN RULE
Clues to Market Timing

One of my most vivid memories is of entering a trading room in the Chicago Board of Trade building a few years ago and seeing a number of futures traders, telephones clasped to their ears, cathode-ray video screens blinking in front of them, yelling out orders to buy and sell. Those who could managed to gulp coffee and frantically tapped-out price quotes on the machines in front of them amid the din in the crisis-filled atmosphere. In looking around the room, I noticed a portrait of a man dressed in a conservative business suit mounted on the wall. By the gray, faded look of the portrait it was obvious the photo had been taken many years ago. I remember wondering what the portrait was doing in this particular room, where very little effort had gone into the decoration. Finally, my curiosity got the best of me. I stopped someone and asked him who the man in the photo was.

"That," he replied, with a certain degree of reverence, "is W. D. Gann."

In looking back at the incident now, it stays in my memory. It was very appropriate. For Gann, more than anyone before or since, was the legendary futures trader, the master of market timing who had conquered the cotton and grain markets in his day and, before that, had turned Wall Street on its head. His market predictions were the stuff that made legends, and it is a tribute to him that he is still a father figure to today's new generation of futures traders.

Gann was noted for his market predictions. In 1908, when Union Pacific was trading at 168-1/8, he announced that it would not trade at 169 until it had a good break. The stock shortly thereafter broke 23 points. Then there was the prediction about U.S. Steel. Gann once predicted that U.S. Steel, then trading about 50, would run up to 58 but wouldn't sell at 59. From there he predicted a 16-3/4-point break. It climbed to 58-3/4 and then broke 17-1/2 points. And another prediction involved the Union Pacific high of 184-7/8. Gann said it would trade at that price, when it was currently at 172, but not even an eighth higher. In fact, it hit 184-7/8 eight or nine times before breaking to 172-1/2. His most famous prediction involved September Wheat in 1909. He predicted that September Wheat must sell at $1.20 a bushel by the end of the delivery month or "it will prove that there is something wrong with my whole method of calculation." But by noon on September 30, 1909 (the last day of trading), September Wheat was only trading at $1.08. His detractors confronted him with this fact. "I do not care what the price is now," Gann is said to have replied, "it must go there." By the end of trading that day, September Wheat was trading at exactly $1.20 per bushel, where it closed. Gann was vindicated.

What did Gann know that, before or since, no one else seems to have been able to understand? It is hard to say. The writings he left behind are overwhelmingly difficult. And there are few Gann analysts around today who are able to explain his theories.

AMID THE CONFUSION— UNCANNY ACCURACY

One reason that so much confusion reigns about Gann's work is that he said so many things. Realizing that, at best, trading was an art and not a science, Gann, like most good analysts, worked on the notion that flexibility was important. If scenario A didn't occur, reasoned Gann, then perhaps scenario B would. If prices didn't reverse 45 days after a major high or low, perhaps they would in 49 days. Three-and-a-half weeks often marked the end of a countertrend in the market, Gann said. But one must pay attention to a host of countervailing forces, some of them extending back over years. He plotted charts, he counted market days, weeks, and months, and he formulated incredible theories based on underlying laws of the universe. In the end, he had won an incredibly loyal group of followers. Unfortunately, few, if any, can explain what Gann was saying. And fewer still why Gann's work is so popular today.

One school of thought maintains that Gann's forecasting methods are popular because they work in a limited fashion. Specifically, they work because the abundance of traders following Gann techniques creates its own form of a self-fulfilling prophecy. If, therefore, everyone following Gann's work sees a certain resistance level at a Gann line, then they will sell against the line and the theory will indeed work. This is one theory. But another is that Gann was really on to something. Perhaps there are unknown forces in the universe that create cycles in economic events that do indeed cause prices to rise and fall at predetermined rates. Put another way, there is very little randomness in the Random Walk. On the contrary, there is a reason for everything, and given enough time and study, the reasons might indeed be known someday.

Regardless of where you stand on the theoretical considerations, there is a very pragmatic reason for giving some credence to Gann. Very often his theories work. Now, this could be happenstance, or it could be by design, but the point is, who cares? If it works, you should be interested.

TIME AND PRICE SQUARED

Many people would maintain that what Gann said about time and price is his most valuable contribution to market timing techniques. The problem is, like most of Gann's work, the essence of the theory is hidden by an abundance of details. Essentially, what Gann said was that *a market will continue along its present path, until a sufficient amount of time passes, before a reversal is possible.* On a bar chart marking both time and price, therefore, X amount of time must pass before prices will reverse at point Y.

To illustrate this concept, Gann developed his own price charts. These are currently available from two commercial sources—Lambert-Gann

189

Publishing in Pomeroy, Washington, and Conceptual Investments, in Old Greenwich, Connecticut.* Many traders, of course, maintain their own Gann charts. The primary difference between a Gann chart and a standard bar chart is that Gann charts are constructed in precise ratios between time and price. Thus, a so-called "one-by-one" Gann chart would have a one-day interval in time comparable to, let us say, a one dollar rise in the price of the futures contract. The importance of this chart construction becomes evident when you attempt to draw in so-called "Gann lines." Gann lines, drawn from intermediate- and longer-term highs and lows, tend to indicate a reversal in price *where the lines cross in time.* Thus, by drawing, say, a forty-five degree line from a previous bottom and a forty-five degree line from a previous top (known as a "1 X 1" in Gann chart jargon), the point at which they cross will indicate the *day* (not the price) at which the top or bottom should reverse. This, of course, is a simplification of the theory; nevertheless, it is often uncanny how accurate this simple, yet sophisticated, timing tool can be.

Besides short-term reversals, Gann charts can often pinpoint major reversal points by drawing lines from life-of-contract highs and lows, often going back more than a year in time. The most useful type of chart for day-to-day trading is the daily chart that records open, high, low, close in the form of a bar, and X's and dots in lieu of horizontal lines standard in most bar charts. But the true Gann analyst will complement his studies with weekly charts (weekly highs, lows, and closes) and even monthly charts. Since stock index futures are so new, the ideal manner to track these longer-term reversals is with charts based on the underlying cash indexes.

MARKET DAYS

In addition to plotting Gann angles (for which you might want to purchase a "Gann Angle Finder" available from the same commercial sources that publish the charts), you'll also find valuable a complete systematic accounting of the number of *market days* between major and minor market highs and lows. Since Gann discounted the value of non-

---

* Conceptual Investments publishes the same charts which were previously available from Technical Trading Services in West Palm Beach, Florida. Conceptual's complete address is: 49 Center Drive, Old Greenwich, Connecticut 06870, (203) 661-3330. Gann enthusiasts who are computer-oriented will be pleased to learn that Lambert-Gann Publishing Co., Box 0, Pomeroy, Washington 99347 offers the first complete software package for creating Gann charts.

market days, such as weekends and holidays, on his charts, all Gann charts place no empty spaces for such weekends and holidays. Instead, Monday's price action is plotted next to the previous Friday's. Ideally, days between market highs are plotted along the top of the chart and days between market lows are plotted along the bottom of the chart in order to separate the two. Since you might have a number of market bottoms or tops, you might, after a period of time, have a dozen or more rows of numbers, all measuring the number of days between different market highs or lows.

Once you draw up this information, what do you do with it? You use it as a reference point between different highs and lows—so many days between lows, so many days between highs, so many days between a low and a high, and so many days between a high and a low. The idea is to get more than one number to *suggest* a market reversal might be imminent. And to do this, you must know the *Gann numbers*. There are many Gann numbers because Gann thought so many were important. He placed particular emphasis on the *numbers squared*—49, 64, 81, 100, 121, 144, etc. Thus, whenever you have, say, 81 market days between a previous high and what might be a new high, look for a top to occur. Rather than trust me on this account, do your own studies and see how often a major reversal will occur on a number squared.

But the numbers squared were just one series of numbers that Gann relied on. You must look as well at the Gann numbers, which are derived by dividing the number 365 (number of days in a year) by 8, and then further dividing and multiplying. The key 14 Gann numbers are as follows:

Table 20
GANN NUMBERS

3.00	182
5.82	228
11.82	273
22.50	319
45	365
91	410
137	456

Markets often reverse or make new highs or lows when these Gann numbers are reached. In order to know when one of these numbers is being approached, keep a running count of the market days from previous highs

191

and lows along, respectively, the top and bottom of your chart.

Let's take an example. The life-of-contract high of the September 1983 S&P 500 contract occurred on June 22, 1983 at a price of 173.85. Counting ahead, the Gann analyst would look for another high (although not necessarily a new life-of-contract high) 11-12 or 22-23 market days in the future. By the way, the count begins with one the day *after* the high is made. Counting ahead 23 market days, a new high of 172.45 was made on July 16, 1983—exactly where it was anticipated!

One of the most startling observations about June 22 being the life-of-contract high of the September 1983 S&P contract is that it occurs at the changing of the seasons. Gann emphasizedthat the changing of the seasons were important times for major price reversals. The key dates to remember are March 21, June 21, September 22, and December 21. Often, within a day or two of these dates, prices will change direction. A glance at a S&P price chart reveals a bottom was made just two market days prior to March 21, and the life-of-contract high on June 22 is just one day after the June 21 equinox. According to Gann, the financial year begins on March 21st. His price and time charts begin with zero degrees with this date and move around the calendar with September 22nd representing 180°, or 180 days into the cycle. Based on Gann theories, significant price changes should occur on the 45th, 90th, 135th, and 180th day following the March 21st period low. Significantly, a cycle low occurs precisely 45 market days following the March 21 period low and a cycle high occurs precisely 90 market days following the same date. If you are charting on a weekly basis, you can expect reversals on the 45th, 90th, 135th and 180th week following a major low as well. One wonders what remarkable force in the universe causes such precision in financial markets to occur.

ANNIVERSITY DATES

Gann said that anniversity dates marked an important milestone in a stock's or futures' history. You could have taken the August 9, 1982 low, therefore, which is often cited as the beginning day of the current bull market, and counted ahead exactly one year—and again purchased stock index futures. Had you done so, your timing would have been correct to the day! On August 9, 1983, just one year later, the September 1983 S&P

futures contract made a significant low at 159.25 that held until the maturity of the contract more than a month later.

In reading over this information, you may want to credit these occurrences as mere coincidence. But the more you study Gann, the more these "coincidences" seem to occur. Was W. D. Gann the market genius his followers credit him to be? Gann believed that the mysteries of the universe were ultimately within our abilities to grasp. He reasoned that the essence of all vibrations and rhythm is a sharing of diversities—manifested in cyclical occurrences—at regular time intervals. Given the abundance of recurrent cyclical events in the universe—tides, heartbeats, sleep patterns, menstrual cycles—who are we to argue that financial events are also not among them?

FIBONACCI NUMBERS

Leonardo Fibonacci, who was more popularly known as Leonardo of Pisa, was an Italian mathematician of the 13th century who formulated a series of numbers based on adding the preceding number in order to generate the next number in the series. Starting with the number one, therefore, the series increases as follows: 1, 1, 2, 3, 5, 8, 13, and so on. A list of the first fourteen Fibonacci numbers is as follows:

Table 21
FIBONACCI NUMBERS

1	34
2	55
3	89
5	144
8	233
13	377
21	610

The Fibonacci numbers are used in the same manner as the Gann numbers, primarily as clues of when to expect market reversals. The two series of numbers are particularly useful when both occur at the same point. For instance, let's say a market day is 6 days distant from a previous market high and 8 days distant from a previous market low. The first number is a Gann number (5.82) and the second a Fibonacci number.

193

Using a longer period, you might find a low occurring 410 market days from a previous high and 610 days from a previous low. This confluence of Gann and Fibonacci numbers should alert you to a possible market reversal. Oftentimes, a series of Gann and Fibonacci numbers, all measured from different tops and bottoms, will occur at the same time. Thus, a given day might be 228 (Gann) market days from one top and 144 (Fibonacci and Gann) market days from another top; drawn from prior bottoms, the same day might be 89 (Fibonacci) market days from a prior low and 137 (Gann) market days from another low. Again, these numbers should be used as an alert.

THE DAY-TRADER'S USE OF FIBONACCI NUMBERS

With the introduction of personal computers and five-minute bar charts, the use of Fibonacci numbers as a day-trading tool has become popular in recent years. First reported by market analysts John Hill and J. D. Hamon, the use of Fibonacci numbers in this manner relies on "taking the count" in increments of five—5, 10, 15, 25, 40, etc.—and using *minutes from the open* as the primary starting point. The idea is to pinpoint the *time of day* when market reversals are most likely to occur. While I've never done much research in this area, I suspect the notion of time on a daily basis is important as well. You'll notice that four of the key times using this method occur during the first hour of trading. This is in keeping with the material presented in the previous chapter on making your money early in the day. The times that follow are based on doing a Fibonacci count using 5's, beginning with the opening of the Chicago-based S&P contract.

Table 22

Minutes After Open	Time (Central)
5	9:05 am
10	9:15
15	9:30
25	9:55
40	10:35
65	11:40
105	1:25 pm

THE GOLDEN RULE

The Golden Rule is very simple. It says that you should look for a retracement in prices of .618 times the initial move. In day trading stock index futures, it is amazing how often a retracement will move .618 times the prior move to the *exact tick*. This rule, while simple to understand, should not be underestimated.

Let's say it is Thursday morning and you are looking to sell short March NYSE Composite Index Futures. The market opens at 97.15 and immediately begins to trade lower until it stabilizes at, let us say, 96.65. Rather than sell short on the low of the day, measure the range and take .618 of the range and add it to the low of the day. If the market is indeed about to go lower, it should not rise above this price.

The mathematics of this strategy would be as follows:

First, take the range from high to low.

$$
\begin{aligned}
\text{high} &= 97.15 \\
\text{low} &= -96.65 \\
\hline
\text{range} &= .50
\end{aligned}
$$

Next, multiply the range by .618.

$$.50 \text{ range} \quad X \quad .618 \ = \ 0.309$$

Rounded off, the anticipated pullback is thus 30/100ths. Then you add the anticipated retracement to the low of the day and you have a target sell price.

$$
\begin{aligned}
\text{low of day} &= 96.65 \\
\text{anticipated pullback} &= +.30 \\
\hline
\text{target sell price} &= 96.95
\end{aligned}
$$

The same, of course, works in reverse for buyers. The advantage of this strategy is that it enables a short seller to risk very little if he is wrong. Occasionally, however, the pullback won't be .618 of the prior move, but

40 or 50 percent. In that case the move will be missed. But it does have the advantage of letting the trader know right away if he is wrong, since more often than not the move won't retrace more than 60 to 65 percent.

Now let's see if we can apply the Golden Rule to an actual trading situation. Figure 8 shows the intra-day tick chart for December 1983 S&P futures for September 22, 1983. During the first hour of trading, prices rose from the low of 170.15 to 170.95, suggesting the trend on the day would indeed be higher. Having seen this move, the astute trader could have taken 61.8 percent of the move and estimated a selloff to the 170.45 level prior to a resumption of the move. In fact, the market traded down to that *exact* number and rose 1.80 points on the day. Clearly, by waiting for the .618 retracement, you could have taken a virtually riskless trade. Incidentally, the LSS 3-day Cycle Method's anticipated low for the day was at 170.50 and the anticipated high was at 172.10. You could have improved on these numbers by simply buying the open.

NEVER UNDERESTIMATE
THE IMPORTANCE OF TIME

"Time," W. D. Gann used to say, "is the most important factor of all." However certain you may be of a trend in the market, you must allow time to elapse before a market reversal will occur. In keeping with Gann's emphasis on the importance of time, I've listed some of the more important time periods to watch for—beginning from major or minor tops and bottoms and counting forward. While Gann stressed the importance of market days, he placed importance on calendar days as well. Anniversary dates, for instance, were important, according to Gann. So be prepared for market reversals when you count calendar days. Of course, in order to be able to predict a change in trend, you have to be looking for one to occur to begin with. Remember, flexibility is the key. If the reversal you are so eagerly awaiting doesn't occur within one time frame, look for it to occur within another. Now, for the important time periods.

1. *Seven weeks or 49 days.* The number 7 is lucky in more ways than one. In the recent bull market in stock index futures, a May 6th top was followed by a life-of-contract June 22nd top just 49 calendar days later! But don't expect every top-to-top formation, or other formation, for that

Figure 8
SEPTEMBER '83 S&P 500 FUTURES
September 22, 1983

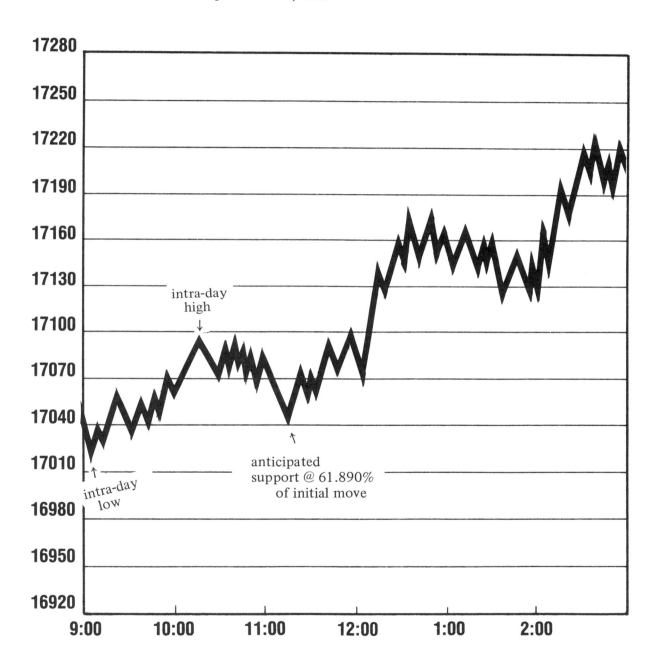

matter, to be exact to the day. The general time frame is what is important. Gann cautions that a reversal often occurs from the 49th to 52nd day following a top or bottom.

2. *Forty-two to 45 days.* Forty-five calendar days is one-eighth of 360 (the number of degrees in a circle) and about an eighth of the number of days in a year. In recent months, the stock index futures markets have made two significant low-to-low intervals marked by 45 market day intervals.

3. *Ninety to 98 days.* This interval marks one-quarter of a year. A major low-to-high interval in the stock index futures market measured precisely 90 market days this past year.

4. *One-hundred thirty to 135 days.* One-third of a year.

5. *Seven weeks down, two-to-three weeks sideways.* Bear moves are often marked by a period of consolidation. If you are following a bear move and looking for a place to begin buying index futures, look for this two-to-three week pattern to occur first.

6. *Two-to-three weeks down followed by failure swing up.* This is a highly significant pattern—in fact, it's the precise pattern that occurred when the September 1983 Standard & Poor's made its life-of-contract high. Following the top on June 22, 1983, the market moved down for just three weeks, bottoming on the third Friday. From there, the market mounted a sharp seven-day rally that *failed* to penetrate the prior high. This failure to take out the old high presented an excellent selling opportunity, as prices declined 12 points from there in two weeks.

7. *Monthly changes.* Within each month, there are important dates which should be watched for major or minor reversals. The important dates are as follows:

   a. *6th or 7th.* In 1983, three reversals occurred on either the 6th or 7th—April 6th, May 6th and July 7th.

   b. *9th to 10th.* Important lows occurred on June 9th and August 9th.

   c. *14th to 15th.* A low occurred on July 15h.

   d. *19th to 20th.* No recent reversals on these dates.

   e. *23rd to 24th.* March 24, 1983 was a minor top reversal.

   f. *29th to 31st.* No recent reversals on these dates.

8. *Thirty calendar days, or multiple of 30.* The March 6th high was followed by the April 6th high just 30 days later. The June 9th low was likewise followed by the August 9th low, just 60 days later. A high occurring on May 23 was followed by a high on June 22nd—and yet another high on August 22nd.

9. *Anniversity dates.* One, two or even three years from a major high or low, you should look at the possibility of another (albeit perhaps not a life-of-contract high or low) high or low occurring. The August 9, 1982 low, which signalled the beginning of the bull market in index futures, was followed by a major low occurring exactly one year later, on August 9, 1983.

10. *Monthly intervals.* The number of monthly intervals are many. First, you should pay attention to the 3rd or 4th month, the 6th or 7th month, or the 10th or 11th month from a major high or low. Longer important monthly intervals exist at 12 months, or one year (anniversity date), 18, 24, 30, 36, 42, and 48 months.

SEASONAL TIME PERIODS

Starting with the first day of spring, March 21, Gann calculates a number of important seasonal dates when price reversals might occur. A list of the important dates is given below. Each date is derived from the calculation indicated. What's surprising is how often a seasonal date coincides with a market top or bottom.

Table 23

Date	Relationship to year and number of weeks from March 21
May 5	1/8th year or 6½ weeks
June 21	¼ year or 13 weeks
July 23	1/3rd year or 17 weeks
August 5	3/8ths year or 19½ weeks
September 22	½ year or 26 weeks
November 8	5/8ths year or 32½ weeks
November 22	2/3rds year or 35 weeks
December 21	3/4ths year or 39 weeks
February 4	7/8ths year or 45½ weeks
March 20	1 year or 52 weeks

NEVER TOO LOW TO SELL,
NEVER TOO HIGH TO BUY

Once you arm yourself with the timing techniques that have helped traders over the years, you'll want to know some of the more general rules used by masters such as W. D. Gann. One such rule, which is a corollary of the rule advocating buying new highs and selling new lows which was advanced in the previous chapter, pertains to the relationship of current price to the price at some time in the future. Price is a relative measurement placed on an asset having a relative value. What seems high in price at one moment in history seems quite reasonable at another moment in time. There was a time, I'm told, when you could buy a brand new Ford for under $1,000; today, you are lucky to roll a new Ford out of the showroom for under $10,000. The point is, just because sellers were willing to sell an asset such as a stock index future at a comparatively low price this morning, there's no reason to believe they will be selling it at any price—given the right circumstances—this afternoon. What may seem low (or high) is just a relative term. And the sooner you can disabuse yourself of the notion of high versus low, the better off you will be in the market.

Many otherwise normal people become quite irrational when it comes to the question of value. Refusing to buy when prices were low (after all, it *looked* like it was going lower at the time), they likewise are paralyzed when prices subsequently trade higher ("I can't buy it now; look how far off the low it's come"). The words "too high"—and "too low"—are relative terms.

I remember a day when the market opened steady and soon began to sell off just after the open. The buyers never had much of a chance. But then the market stabilized and, sure enough, mounted a good rally and ended the day virtually unchanged—after, of course, soaring into new high ground, and causing the shorts to cover in panic. But the knowledgeable traders had a good day. By buying the bottom? Hardly. As one trader put it, "Only a fool would have bought it down there"—although someone obviously had. No, the smart money was buying on the way up, even new high ground, where it was obvious it was still going higher. You must remember this: to make money you only have to buy low and sell high. It doesn't matter if you purchase where some would think it is "too high," as long as you are able to sell still higher up. The same applies to selling into declining markets.

When I'm having a good day, one of my favorite strategies is to add to my position, in a limited fashion, when I know I have the trend in my favor. This provides the "icing on the cake," so to speak, for a good day and serves as a great source of satisfaction—enough to make up for those occasional days when you get battered around. On the kind of day of which I am speaking, the market might open higher. You might have purchased contracts in anticipation of the trend continuing. But you are soon caught in a bull trap and liquidate at a loss. So far, not so good. Yet, as often happens on a day such as this, you can make a lot of money if you are willing to go with the new trend and sell. Having put on short positions, I often like to sell more when the bargain-hunters start buying—but not a great deal more. In case of a reversal, this would endanger my profits. Very often, these late-inning sales turn up winners. Paradoxically, by casting caution to the winds at times like these, you are really embracing good fortune. After all, the trend is clearly in your favor at this point. Why not capitalize on the tendency of the selling to get overdone toward the end of the day- -when everyone expects the inevitable rebound?

This, of course, goes against the conventional wisdom. Isn't the idea to sell rallies and buy dips? Isn't the market "low" when it appears to be approaching a bottom? But what's a bottom? The real bottom occurs when prices reach zero. Until then, there's always the possibility of lower prices.

ALWAYS USE STOP-LOSS ORDERS

This is the oldest rule in the book, but often the least followed. Under no circumstances should you ever trade stock index futures without knowing where you will get out in the case of market adversity. Losses must be kept small if you are to survive. As a day trader, you should make it a rule: *no paper losses overnight*. There is no excuse for violating this rule. Simply place your stop-loss order when you initiate a position and you won't get in trouble. If you have the luxury of watching the market during trading hours, you can trade without stops, however. But you must maintain the mental discipline required to take losses when necessary.

Where should you place your stop? That depends on what market you trade and the volatility of the market at the time you are trading. Since volatility changes, your stop placement will likewise change. You don't want your stops to be too close or too far away from the market; those that are placed too close will inevitably get hit, whereas stops placed too far away will result in larger-than-necessary losses. In general, you have to give the S&P contracts about a point to swing during the day.

Gann stressed that stop-loss orders must be placed above and below prior *swings* in the market, and not just prior highs and lows. But this pertains to longer-term traders, not day traders. When a swing price is violated, chances are the trend has changed. But stops cluttered above prior highs or below prior lows are apt to be caught by random price moves or active forays by the floor gunning the stops.

The problem with stops is that they often are hit at the extreme end of a move or when the market is running. To overcome this drawback, you might want to await pullbacks before exiting the market. But this requires watching the market full time and also having the mental discipline to exit on the pullback—a difficult task since the market always "looks" more encouraging once it reasserts itself in your direction. For example, let's say you are short index futures and await declining prices. Unfortunately, the market moves higher and you are now holding a losing position. Rather than exit on the initial upward surge, however, wait for profit-taking to push the market down a bit—but not necessarily back to where you originally sold short. By awaiting the pullback, you can often save yourself a couple of hundred dollars per trade. The Golden Rule frequently provides the optimum exit point.

If you have traded index futures for any period of time, you are probably familiar with the circumstance in which you have a loss but aren't emotionally prepared to admit defeat. Chances are, you feel foolish for getting on the wrong side of the market, and this may cause you to hang on; or, worse yet, your reaction to market adversity might be to double up your efforts by taking more positions. In either case, you are inviting trouble. And what started out as an intelligent trade now becomes a wild wishing contest. Given the deteriorating circumstances, reason turns to hope, and pretty soon you may feel you *can't* get out because the loss would be unacceptable. This familiar scenario has marked the beginning of the end for more than one stock index futures trader in the past couple of years. Don't let yourself become a victim of this ill-advised strategy. Always limit your losses. And live to fight another day.

NEVER GIVE BACK A PROFIT

Gann believed that the most dangerous thing was to let a profitable trade start going against you. Once achieved, a hard-won profit *must* be realized. This is the hardest lesson for a novice trader to learn. Often, one holds on in anticipation of still greater profits. But given the volatility of the market, chances are a profit unrealized will quickly become a loss. Even after years of experience in other futures markets, I made this mistake when I first started trading the Standard & Poor's 500 contract. I made exceptional day-trading profits as soon as I initiated trades, often thinking there was plenty of time to nail down the profit; but the market often switched directions and the profits disappeared. Don't let this happen to you. Even if a profit is *threatening* to turn unprofitable, close out the position. By doing so, you'll be better prepared to take the profits next time—and you'll avoid the inevitable losses by getting out at breakeven or better.

The right time to get out is *as soon as you realize you've made a mistake.* For instance, let's say you purchase index futures in anticipation of a substantial rise in prices. You know, at the outset, that you are not perfect and that your entry point may well be less than ideal. However, you also know that if prices fail to hold a significant support level, chances are they will trade lower. So you have created in your mind a sort of safety band within which prices can trade *before* you will become concerned. But once prices move your way, you must not hold the position for another trip down into the safety band. Put another way, move your actual or mental stop higher. If prices don't go your way within a relatively short period of time, you want to get out as soon as you realize the mistake. Do not wait until your strategy is based on hope. Usually, by that time the trade is doomed to failure, and you have no recourse except to accept the loss anyway.

Contrary to popular opinion, losses can be a trader's best friend. First, they remind him of the substantial risk involved in trading index futures. Second, since a large number of them are inevitable in a zero-sum game situation such as index trading, they should be accepted, just as, say, strikeouts are to a home-run hitter. If you learn to trade correctly, you'll learn to "love" your losses. Well, perhaps not exactly "love," but at least you won't fight them unnecessarily. By this, I mean you will thank yourself for accepting small losses in lieu of the alternative, which is to hold on in the face of adversity, and often ruin. I once knew of a trader who didn't believe in losses. When he found himself behind in the market, he dug in his heels and held on. It worked for awhile—a very limited while. He later went broke.

"LOOK FOR TROUBLE WITHIN AND CORRECT IT"

Gann believed that a good trader always took responsibility for his actions; he assumed the blame for losses and never blamed anyone else. A good trader, Gann maintained, never guessed, but always took positions based on reason. Excuses only cause a trader to repeat mistakes—costly mistakes. The antidote for the careless sort of trading that abounds in most boardrooms is a willingness to admit mistakes and follow rules.

A recent series of phone conversations with a broker friend brought the truth of this statement vividly before my eyes. In our many discussions about the market over the years, we had formally agreed on a number of rules that make for profitable trading. Although simple and straightforward, the rules are very important: simply put, if you don't follow them, you are inviting trouble. It was for this reason that I was surprised when he told me about his market situation.

Significantly, the following conversation took place during market hours.

"I've got this loss in seven short December S&P's right now," he explained. "But I'm going overnight with them. You'll see, tomorrow's the top."

"Hold it a second," I said. "You know the rule. 'No losses overnight.' " We had agreed many months before that a losing trade during the day never seemed to work out the next day.

He was in no mood to be dissuaded. "I know the rule," he said. "But tomorrow's the top." He had said it in the kind of fanciful voice that traders use when reason has turned to hope.

"Oh, really?" I said, barely keeping the sarcasm out of my voice. "You have some kind of information that can tell you the future?"

"You'll see," he said, and hung up.

The next day prices opened higher and went higher. His losing short positions only went deeper into the red. If anything, the top he'd predicted looked more like a bottom. A few days later we talked again, and this time he was bemoaning another trade that was now going sour on him. He'd long since forgotten the money he'd lost on the previous trade. On the heels of that debacle, however, he had again made the same kind of mistake. Although we both relied on the same trading system and both had identical buy and sell points, he had jumped the gun and hadn't bought at the buying number. Significantly, the numbers were right on the money that day and the trade should have been going well. But it wasn't—because of an inability to follow one's better convictions. Instead of relying on what was a proven method of trading, the impulse to second-guess the market had again won out with predictable results.

That same day I spoke with a friend who takes large positions in the S&P market. He'd been long fifty contracts when the market broke on him. What did he do? He covered and sold one-hundred contracts. Because the market sold-off over three points that day, he ended up making a ton of money. He was playing the game strictly by the rules—the rules that, as an accomplished trader, he knows will work. The impulse to avoid the moment of truth when one must own up to a mistake was never really a part of his decision. He realized his initial mistake in buying the market and immediately took corrective action. There was never any question of blame—nor was there time!

RULES TO IMPROVE YOUR MARKET TIMING

Nothing you do in stock index futures can improve your results more than good timing. So here are a few guidelines to help you know when the climate is best for buying or selling.

Rule #1. Pay attention to anniversity dates and seasonal time intervals. If you know when to look for a key price reversal, you are that much more likely to be prepared when it comes. We've already mentioned the low that occurred a year to the day after the August 9, 1981 stock market bottom. An alert trader could have made a quick six points ($3,000 per contract) by simply going long S&P futures at the September 22nd seasonal top that occurred the following month, and liquidating a week later. I can't stress enough how important these seasonal changes can be. Not only do they often (though not *always*) pinpoint reversals, but, more importantly, they provide the knowledgeable trader with the confidence to take substantial positions. Remember, only by "loading up" when you are right are you going to truly make it in the competitive stock index futures market, where there is a dollar lost for every dollar gained.

Rule #2. Count market days from previous highs and lows. Be sure you keep track of the number of market days from significant highs and lows. You never know when this information will provide just the kind of confirming signal that you need. The number of tops and bottoms that fall precisely 23 market days apart seems far too consistent for this to be merely happenstance. The strongest possible signal exists when you have a number of important signals occurring on the same day. For instance, an anticipated top might be 23 market days from a recent top, but also 144 days from another top and 55 days from another, and so on. Frequently, not only will you get a reversal on such days, but the reversal might be preceded by a "blow-off" top in which prices are bid up into new high ground in the morning, only to collapse in the afternoon. On such days, you can make a significant amount of money if you are prepared for such volatile price action.

Rule # 3. Keep your records up-to-date. Use the same notebook and chart to maintain all your trading information. If you must go out of town, make sure you have someone put aside daily copies of *The Wall Street Journal* or whatever source of information you rely on for daily prices. Nothing is more disconcerting than to have a gap in your information when you want to go back and track the market. Did a significant high occur on the missing date, or not? What was last week's low? If you don't know this kind of price information, you don't have all the information to make the correct trading decisions. One thing is certain, however. The people you'll be competing with *will* have this information—and they'll use it to their advantage against you. If the back data isn't readily available, there are many commercial sources that can provide this type of information.

Rule #4. If you are looking to position a trade, try to put on your positions on a Gann or Fibonacci number day. In general, if you are looking for a longer-term move (it could be six or seven days or even that many months), you put the odds on your side when you wait for a Gann or Fibonacci day to occur. There are many such days. But to make sure you don't miss one, write down the key numbers and place them on your Gann chart. You will then have a ready reference available to spot a potential reversal point in the market. If you are correct, of course, the odds of being stopped-out from such a position are decreased that much more.

Rule #5. Get to know the phone clerks who relay your orders and let them know about your style of trading. Although the phone clerk who handles your order (primarily at the discount firms; this is your broker's responsibility if you're dealing with a full-service house) is frequently among the lowest paid in the firm, his or her responsibility is considerable. A mistake in the order can mean thousands of dollars to you. Since timing is nothing unless the order is appropriately executed, you must convey your orders in a professional manner to the phone clerk. You might indicate that all your orders are market orders, for instance. Or tell the clerk that you always want to place a stop with the order. By doing so, a more personal relationship will develop and the clerk will get to know your style of trading. This will help you in the long run. And if you have a winning year, a bottle of Scotch for a helpful order-taker at the Christmas holiday time might be appropriate. You'd be surprised how a good man on the phones can help you work your order; he can provide you with information about the sentiment on the floor, the nature of the rallies or declines, and a host of other information—all of it valuable. This isn't the order-taker's job, by the way, but it is that little extra that a good floor operation can provide—especially if these unseen individuals on the phone think you're worthy of the information. Even in a sometimes faceless business, the personal touch can go a long way. If you trade through a full-service broker, of course, knowing his floor sources is part of *his* job. Make sure he earns his commissions by seeing to it that you get the fastest possible fills. After all, that's what you are paying for.

By the way, most discounters will provide you with a sample copy of how to relay information concerning an order to a phone clerk. Remember, he or she has to write down the order. If you convey the order correctly in the first instance, it will save precious seconds in getting the order filled. Here's the right sequence of information you want to provide.

1. Your name and account number.

2. Whether you wish to buy or sell, number of contracts, the name of the futures, contract month, and type of order (at the market, limit, fill-or-kill, or whatever).

3. The same information for the stop-loss order, if any.

After you give the order, the clerk will read it back to you as follows: "This is for account # 58031. You want to sell 8 March S&P 500 contracts at 191.95 or better. Is that correct?" You give your affirmation. And then he'll read back the stop as well. Once you give your verbal okay, he'll handle the order from there.

What happens if, after placing an order and seeing the price trade at your price limit, you don't receive a confirmation on the "fill" at once?

Chances are, the order has been filled but the runner, whose job it is to carry the confirmation back to the floor phone, hasn't picked it up yet. When the floor broker fills the order, he throws the order onto the floor where, among a pile of such orders, it may remain for a minute or two. When the flow of orders heats up, a virtual blizzard of "paper"—public orders—will result and amid the pandemonium it may not be physically possible to pinpoint your precise order. Things can become especially chaotic right on the close when the trading pace picks up, so don't expect instant confirmations during the last five to ten minutes of trading. Then again, if you have placed a limit order, the price generally has to trade *through* your limit before you can pretty much be guaranteed a fill. For instance, if you are buying Standard & Poor's 500 futures at, let us say, 191.05 or better, unless the price goes to 191.00, you may not be filled. Why? Because the 191.05 price may have only resulted in one trade. After that, the bid may have gone to 191.10 or higher, in which case your bid of 191.05 would be unacceptable. Conversely, if you are selling on a limit order, you want the price to go one tick higher to assure yourself of a fill.

SHORTCUTS FOR THE GANN ANALYST— MAKING THE NUMBERS WORK FOR YOU RIGHT AWAY

If you had your choice, you'd probably never want to get mixed up in this Gann business at all. As mentioned earlier, Gann is hopelessly complicated. I've never found anyone who could make any sense out of his pronouncements, despite the volume of work that has appeared under his name. As a pragmatic gesture, therefore, I've tried to take just one little portion of Gann and concentrate on making it intelligible. In doing so, I've developed a number of shortcuts which can easily be learned and used by the novice stock index trader. Here are a few shortcuts to help you size up the market using Gann principles.

Shortcut #1. How to take the count in predicting upcoming tops and bottoms. Start with a major or minor bottom or top and project out using Gann and Fibonacci numbers. The count begins with one on the day after the top or bottom, using market days only. On your calendar, when you reach a date signified by a Gann or Fibonacci number, make a notation. When the date in question arrives, check to see whether some sort of reversal occurs. A typical list might appear as follows:

Table 24

Beginning Date	Market Days	Target Date	Occurrence
Aug. 9, '83	23	Sept. 12, '83	top—Sept. S&P @ 169.40
Aug. 9, '83	9	Aug. 22, '83	top—Sept. S&P @ 166.35
Aug. 9, '83	34	Sept. 27, '83	1 day after top—Dec. S&P @ 172.60 on Sept. 26, '83
Aug. 9, '83	12	Aug. 25, '83	bottom—Sept. S&P @ 160.30

Shortcut #2. How to use Gann angles to pinpoint price reversals. Construct a chart (or, preferably buy one) using a 1 x 1 scale of one tick up corresponding to one day over in time. Next, draw 45 degree angles from several tops and bottoms. Where the angles cross in time suggests where prices should reverse. There are, of course, many other angles that Gann relied on, but the 1 x 1 he considered the most significant.

Shortcut #3. How to use weekly highs and lows to detect a change in trend. Simply jot down last week's high and low. When one is violated, consider the trend persisting in that direction. On a violation of last week's low, for example, be a seller in anticipation of lower prices; conversely, on a violation of last week's high, be a buyer in anticipation of higher prices. However, for the move to be considered genuine, prices must *stay above* the previous week's high or *below* the previous week's low. For example, for the week September 6 - September 9 (September 5th was Labor Day), the high of September Standard & Poor's futures was 168.95 and the low was 166.45. The open on Monday, September 12th was 169.40—above the previous week's high. This would be a signal to buy. But prices soon traded lower and the signal was proven false. On the same day, prices violated the low of the previous week at 166.45 and prices declined by more than two points by week's end. This, by the way, shows why flexibility is so important to good trading. You should be willing to take losses quickly on the false breakout and double-up and go the other way on the subsequent decline since such price action occurs frequently in the stock index futures market. This price action, which caught many traders by surprise, is simply the floor's way of gunning the stops of those who thought they were safe in placing their stop-loss orders well above or below the market.

Shortcut #4. How to use Gann angles for buying and selling. When you have 45 degree angles drawn on your price charts, always buy as prices come down to the 45 degree line from above and sell against rallies to the 45 degree line from below. If prices cannot hold at these angles, reverse and go the other way. This is the well-known concept of the support becoming the resistance, and vice versa.

Figure 9
S&P INDEX Sept. '83

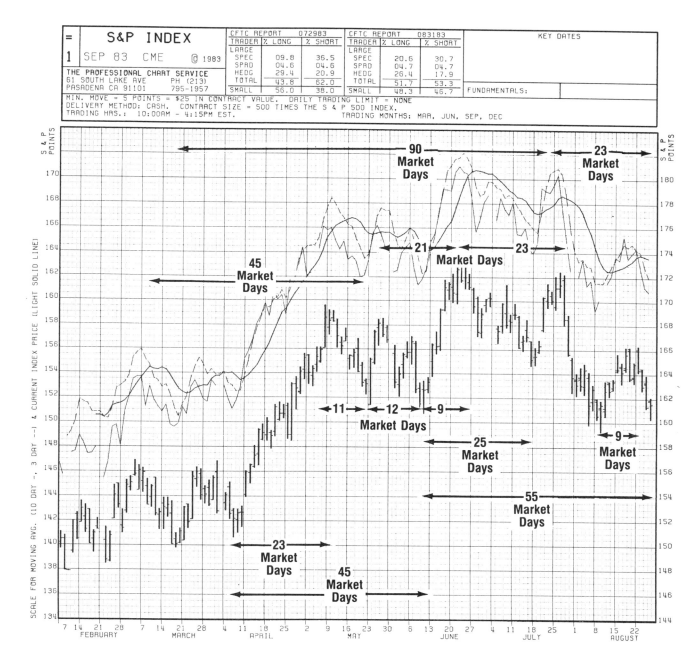

Part III

A POINT OF VIEW

LSS—A System for Consistent Profits

Chapter Seven

THE 3-DAY CYCLE
Pinpointing The Patterns
Of A Market

More than 30 years ago, a little-known grain trader on the Chicago Board of Trade published a work purporting to show how grain price fluctuations were "engineered from within." The "Book Method," as the self-published notebook later became known, presented a day-by-day trading strategy that, in the words of its author, George Douglas Taylor, was designed to capitalize on the misleading actions of the market insiders who frequently "put prices up" in an attempt to create buying—a strategy whose real purpose, of course, was to manufacture a selling opportunity for the market insiders. Similarly, an impression of declining prices was created in order to trap sellers at market bottoms. Moreover, according to Taylor, the pattern was repeated endlessly, in a variety of configurations, in a continuous three-day pattern.

At the heart of Taylor's Book Method was a three-day cycle consisting of a Buy Day, a Sell Day, and a Short Sell Day. The ideal pattern was to purchase grain contracts at the open on the Buy Day, when the low of the day was made first; these long positions were then liquidated on the second day, the Sell Day, at a price which was slightly below, at, or slightly above the Buy Day High; lastly, on the third day up, the Short Sell Day, short positions were to be taken at the open on the high made first. Ideally, prices would then fall and the cycle would begin all over again.

Taylor realized, of course, that the market was not always quite so cooperative as to provide the sequence called for in his cycle theory. Often, for instance, the high would occur first on the Buy Day, thus preventing the opportunity to place a profitable long position on the open. To deal with this situation, his method called for reversing positions and *selling* on the Buy Day—and, conversely, occasionally buying on the Short Sell Day. It is this flexibility which makes Taylor's work so attractive.

Before proceeding, I'd like to point out that this system is the nucleus for the LSS System which I currently trade. You may find it a little confusing at first, but read it carefully. This system, and the improvements I've incorporated in the LSS System, provide startling insight into the working of the markets.

You may find you have to reread these chapters, or study them slowly. Believe me, it's worthwhile. When you can correctly use this system you will be one of the 10% of commodity traders who make substantial profits.

"ENGINEERED FROM WITHIN"

You cannot spend a lot of time around a futures market without realizing that Taylor's contention—that the market was indeed "engineered from within"—contains an element of truth. When I first came in contact with the "Book Method," it was for a very simple reason. I was having difficulty in my own trading and I realized that someone knew something that I was most certainly unaware of. Why else were a handful of traders *always* selling market tops and buying market bottoms? What did they know about the pattern of prices that proved so elusive to me?

The more I read about the grain market in the nineteen-fifties, the more I began to see what was occurring in the futures markets of the nineteen-eighties. At first, I remained skeptical. If there did exist an identifiable pattern, why hadn't more traders already discovered it and used it to the point where it wouldn't occur anymore? What were the signs that a market was ready to move sharply higher or lower? How do you read the footprints of these market manipulators who were doing a pretty good job of disguising their activities—if indeed they existed at all? And did the grain markets of the fifties really have anything to do with the gyrations of the stock index futures markets of the eighties?

216

It wasn't long before I decided to test the theory in the market. Although the notion of a one-two-three pattern seemed overly simplistic, it was worth a try. At first, I limited my activities to paper trading. If it worked on paper, it would be worth a try in the market. My initial area of interest was the open, and how the opening prices were frequently out of line or in reverse of the day's ultimate price trajectory. Was there a way to read the "random" movements of the market?

Sure enough, a pattern, or really a series of patterns, emerged. On one day, the market would open higher on an optimistic note. After a few minutes of trading, however, prices would weaken and slowly retreat to the level where they threatened to take out the previous low. Then the low would indeed be broken and a flurry of activity would result. Soon thereafter, after the previous day's low had been violated by just a couple of ticks, the market would stage a rally, and, despite a series of selloffs during the day, the rally would continue and the market would close right at the high of the day, or a tick or two lower. What was happening, of course, was a classic case of the stops being gunned. Once the weak hands sold their contracts at the bottom of the day, just below the previous day's low (where, remember, the conventional wisdom calls for placing the stops), the strong hands took control and the market made a sustained and significant rise.

On other days, a reverse pattern would occur. Opening higher, the market would stage a nice rally in the first hour of trading. But then, inevitably, the rally would stop and the real trend of the market would become clear as prices started to descend, slowly at first, but then with greater force, until there was a virtual bloodbath of the longs on the close. Significantly, the bull trap at the top took out the previous day's high by just three or four ticks—again to get the stops.

There would be days when both the previous day's high and low would be taken out, the classic search-and-destroy mission. And, of course, there would be days when the market was just marking time, neither rising or falling with any decision. But there were relatively few of these days. The pattern that was emerging was one of calculated effort to frighten, scare, or intimidate traders out of would-be winning positions—if only they had held on, or waited to do their buying or selling at the proper moment, the losers would have indeed been winners.

Not only were there identifiable daily patterns, but there were

217

identifiable three-day patterns as well—Taylor's three-day cycle complete with a Buy, Sell, and Short Sell Day. But always, the pattern seemed purposely hidden behind a variety of misleading market moves. At one major bottom, the market opened higher and only then sold-off. Going into new life-of-contract low ground, the market made its low first and mounted a significant rally. On the next day (Taylor's sell day), the market opened lower and declined (again to fool the buyers) and once again surged higher. Finally, on the third day in the cycle (Taylor's Short Sell Day), the market opened higher and went higher—temporarily. But then, having trapped the buyers who had waited too long, it sold-off to its previous day's close. Then the pattern repeated itself over the next three days—and again on the three days following that.

The three-day pattern was quite consistent. But even more consistent was the misleading price movements, those that often moved against the trend and indeed seemed calculated to confuse. Why was the market so often made to look bullish or bearish when, in fact, the very opposite was about to occur? Obviously, this was contrary opinion in action. But was there hidden "engineering" at work?

PATTERNS THAT ARE NOT RANDOM

How and why the market is manipulated (if indeed it is), is secondary in importance to understanding the underlying reason why most market participants behave in a manner calculated to make the "engineering" work. Understandably, most people are not rational when it comes to a situation where they are about to lose a great deal of money. In the face of the unknown, the typical investor is apt to behave in a manner that benefits the less-emotional trader who understands the market. That is, the typical investor may turn to his broker (who may know less than he does) for advice; he may want to hold onto a position in the face of adversity despite the tenuousness of a thinly-financed, highly-leveraged position; he may, on the other hand, run at the first hint of adversity—indeed, he may engage in one of several actions, none of which will help him if he doesn't truly understand what is going on.

But if a trader can bring an idea to the market—call it "a point of view"—he is in a much better position to profit from his trading. The point of view that Taylor helps one to acquire is that price patterns are, in fact, discernible, that one can "read" the market if he knows what to look for.

In devising the notion of a three-day cycle theory, Taylor pinpointed *not only the day, but, significantly, the time and price at which one could be a buyer or a seller at very low risk.* By isolating these periods of optimal opportunity, Taylor's contribution becomes a significant one.

WHEN DO YOU BUY?
WHEN DO YOU SELL?

The Buying Day, as Taylor termed it, occurred on the first day of the three-day cycle. The cycle itself is determined by taking the *lowest low of ten market days* and counting ahead—buy, sell, short sell, and so on. Thus, the Buying Day occurs after the Short Sell Day and the cycle is continued in an endless pattern. The problem with this notion, of course, one which Taylor himself acknowledged, is that the three-day cycle often becomes a four- or five-day cycle. How, then, do you determine the next Buy Day? In the LSS Three-day Cycle Method, which is based squarely on Taylor's Book Method, the cycle is rephased to account for these out-of-synchronization cycles. But for now, let's concentrate on the theory as put forth by Taylor. Where do you buy—and when? Simply put, you buy at the Buy Day low when it occurs first. According to Taylor, the low should occur "at, through, or slightly above" the previous day's low—namely, the Short Sale Day low.

Before we examine this rule further, you should be aware that Taylor is speaking about simple support and resistance. In essence, he's saying you should buy contracts at yesterday's support level, or slightly above or below that support. Or, at the very least, you should buy every third day at that level—which, of course, will be changing from day to day. More importantly, he is saying you should buy the low made first—the old "make-your-money-early-in-the-day" rule. Unfortunately, this poses several problems. For one, how do you know when a price represents the low of the day? Or, for that matter, the high of the day? For another, what do you do if you misinterpret the market and find yourself buying prematurely? When do you run? Or reverse?

If there were a sure-fire answer to this one, he wasn't saying. But chances are, you have to do the best you can with what you have—and here's where he offered a truly innovative approach. Relying on probabilities, he concluded you would have the highest odds of buying near the low by *measuring* similar declines in the market. If, for instance, the market broke X points from the previous day's high in the last six cycles, chances are you should be looking to buy on an X-point decline on this one as well. This is the "magic" of Taylor—measuring rallies and declines—which is really no magic at all. In fact, this is precisely the kind of thing that technicians have been doing for years. Taylor simply ignored charts in favor of quantifying the numbers. These numbers he kept in his "Book."

When it came to selling, he also relied on his book. But for selling, you want to measure rallies—how far does a market tend to rally before a top is made? You'd be surprised how consistent certain range patterns can be. In the last ten trading days in the nearby S&P contract, for example, the largest one-day range was 2.10 points, while the smallest was .90 points and the average 1.50 points. Given this recent history, what do you think is the likelihood of having a 3.00 point range tomorrow? While possible, not too great. The trader who is looking for a one-to-two point range is more likely to find himself closer to selecting the top and bottom of tomorrow's market.

KEEPING THE BOOK

The "Book," which was Taylor's Bible when it came to trading, contained the key measurements of the market's recent past. On a daily basis, the Book recorded four key measurements: the rally, the decline, the buying under, and the buying high. These four measurements, respectively, provided an exact count of precisely how far the market had rallied from a previous low to the next day's high; how far it had declined from a previous high to the next day's low; how far under a previous low the current low had gone; and, finally, how far over a previous high a current high had carried. Moreover, Taylor believed in filling out only certain columns on certain days in the cycle. In modifying the system, however, and in creating the LSS Three-day Cycle Method from Taylor's work, I've made it a practice to take every measurement every day. The four key measurements can be summarized as follows:

1. The Rally or "R" Column. This column measures the distance from a previous day's low to the next day's high. It measures, of course, the greatest possible profit you could have made by buying at the low of one day and selling at the top of the next. It is used to measure how far the market tends to rally from day to day.

2. The Decline or "D" Column. The reverse of the R Column, the Decline Column measures the distance from a previous day's high to the next day's low.

3. The Buying Under or "BU" Column. This column measures the distance from one day's low to the next day's low. If the second day's low is lower, the BU Column will be filled with a positive number. If the second day's low is higher, on the other hand, the BU Column entry will be a negative number. It is derived by taking a current day's low and subtracting it from the previous day's low.

4. The Buying High or "BH" Column. This column measures how far over a previous day's high a market carried. For example, if today's high was one point over yesterday's, the BH Column entry would be one point. If it were one point under yesterday's high, the entry would be minus one.

How the numbers might be recorded in actual practice is shown in the table below.

Table 25
SEPTEMBER 1983 S&P 500

Date	Open	High	Low	Close	Decline D	Rally R	Buying High BH	Buying Under BU
Aug 16 T	164.60	164.95	163.20	164.15	—	—	—	—
Aug 17 W	164.45	166.25	164.25	165.65	.70	3.05	1.30	− 1.05
Aug 18 Th	166.05	166.25	163.50	163.65	2.75	2.00	0	.75

Taking Wednesday, August 17th as an example, you can see that the entry in the Decline Column for that day was .70 points. This is the difference between the previous day's high and the August 17th low. Thus:

$$164.95 \quad \text{August 16 high}$$
$$-\,164.25 \quad \text{August 17 low}$$
$$\overline{.70} \quad \text{D-Column entry}$$

In this case, the September Standard & Poor's 500 contract declined .70 points from Tuesday's high to Wednesday's low. Looking down one entry in the D-Column, you can see that the market's decline increased on the following day, August 18th to 2.75 points.

Moving over to the Rally Column, you can see that the market rallied a total of 3.05 points on Wednesday, August 17th, from 163.20 at the previous day's low to 166.25 at the next day's high. On Thursday, a day when prices were declining, the Rally only amounted to 2.00 points, the difference between 166.25 and 164.25. Thus:

$$166.25 \quad \text{August 18 high}$$
$$-\,164.25 \quad \text{August 17 low}$$
$$\overline{2.00} \quad \text{R-Column entry}$$

The Buying High Column entry on Wednesday, August 17 was 1.30, since that day's high exceeded the previous day's high by that amount. The entry is zero on the following day because the highs were identical.

Lastly, the Buying Under Column measures how far under yesterday's low you might have purchased S&P futures. On August 17, the entry is −1.05, a minus number since that day's low did not go under the previous day's low. It would have been impossible to purchase S&P futures below the previous day's close on Wednesday, August 17th, hence the negative 1.05. On August 18, however, the low was .75 points below the low on August 17. Hence, the positive number. An inference to be drawn from the Buying Under number is that in a rising market, the bottoms will be progressively higher, therefore the Buying Under entries will be negative numbers. During breaking markets, however, the Buying Under entries will be larger and larger positive numbers, as the market trades lower and lower with each successive number further below the previous day's low.

But what do these numbers mean to you in terms of trading the market on a daily basis? Well, first of all, you have to accumulate a sufficient number of entries to discern a pattern and to spot the three-day cycle. After that, there are a number of insights that can be derived from comparing different markets and different stages in a market with one that may have occurred some time ago. By themselves, a half-dozen entries are not particularly significant. But once you accumulate a couple of dozen entries, you'll be able to see the patterns much more clearly. One point needs to be stressed, however: you must maintain the book daily. Missed entries will only serve to confuse you.

THE 3-DAY CYCLE

How do you select the three-day cycle? As we've mentioned earlier, you take the *lowest low of the last 10 days and that becomes the Buy Day.* You then count ahead in a three-day pattern: Buy Day, Sell Day, Short Sell Day. Then the pattern repeats. After you identify the Buy Day, you count backwards as well until all the days are identified. *The low on the Buy Day is always circled. On Sell and Short Sell Days, the high is circled.* Let's take a representative sampling of 10 trading days and see how the three-day pattern might be identified.

Table 26
DECEMBER 1983 STANDARD & POOR'S

Day	Open	High	Low	Close	3-Day Cycle Day
1	166.65	169.20	(166.65)	168.95	Buy
2	169.55	(170.70)	169.00	170.15	Sell
3	170.75	(171.65)	170.60	171.25	Short Sell
4	171.20	171.65	(169.95)	170.75	Buy
5	170.35	(172.25)	170.15	171.90	Sell
6	172.00	(172.10)	170.95	171.40	Short Sell
7	171.85	172.60	(170.85)	171.50	Buy
8	171.20	(171.35)	169.50	170.40	Sell
9	170.20	(170.40)	169.50	170.00	Short Sell
10	169.70	170.15	(169.15)	169.40	Buy

In looking over the numbers, you can easily see that the *lowest low* occurred on Day 1 at 166.65. You then count ahead three days and again circle the low on Day 4, Day 7, and Day 10. The highs of the Sell Days and Short Sell Days are then circled as well.

Figure 10
FOUR MEASUREMENTS

1.   D measures High to Low

2.   R measures Low to High

3.   BH measurements High to High

4.   BU measures Low to Low

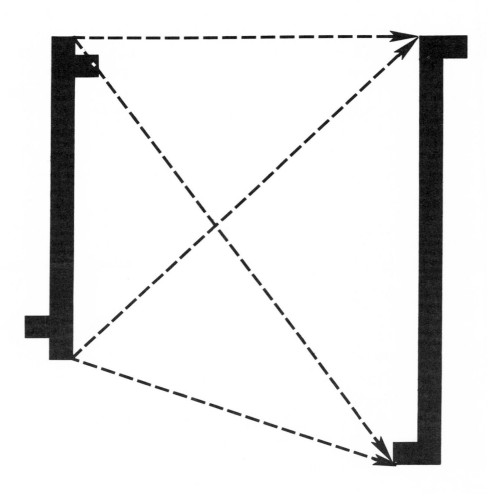

THE ORDER IN WHICH
THE HIGH AND LOW OCCURS

The order in which the high or low occurs is vitally important. On a Buy Day, you want the low to occur first, preferably right after the open. On a Short Sale Day, and, to a lesser extent, on a Sell Day, you want the high to occur first, preferably right after the open as well. To designate the occurrence of a circled high or low making its intended high or low *first* in the trading session, you insert an X (X) within the circle. Conversely, should the pattern not occur as planned—such as the low being made last on a Buy Day or a high being made last on a Short Sell Day—you insert a check mark (✓) within the circle. For example, using this same illustration of days 1-3 in the table above, the completed cycle pattern in the Book would appear as follows:

Table 27
DECEMBER 1983 STANDARD & POOR'S

Day	Open	High	Low	Close	3-Day Cycle Day
1	166.65	169.20	166.65 (X)	168.95	Buy
2	169.55	170.70 (✓)	169.00	170.15	Sell
3	170.75	171.65 (✓)	170.60	171.25	Short Sell

If you do not know for sure how the market traded on a given day, you can usually make an informed guess. Usually the market opens near one end of the range and closes near the other. For instance, in the example above, it is obvious that the low was made first on day 1, the Buy Day, because the open proved to be the low of the day. On day 2, the relationship is less clear, although it is likely that the high was made last—hence the check mark in the circle. On day 3, the open was just three ticks higher than the low of the day; as a result, one can safely assume that the high was indeed made last.

THE STRONGEST TRADING SIGNALS

The strongest trading signals occur at precise times during the three-day cycle under precise market conditions. Because not every trade contains the same degree of risk, it can often pay handsomely to wait for a strong signal when all factors favor the success of your trade. Unfortunately, relatively few people have the patience to wait for a really good trade—and fewer still know how to spot the trade in any case; so you can improve your odds by selecting your spot and waiting. If your trading is to be a success, it is important that you have the confidence to take a greater number of positions during periods when you are sure you are correct.

The strongest possible buy trade occurs on a Buy Day when the low is made first and the market is in an uptrend, or bull market. This is not to say that you can't make money buying in a bear market—you can—but that a bull market greatly improves the odds of your success. The strongest place to put on a long position will exist slightly above the previous day's low, a trade known as buying a higher bottom.

Ideally, the market will rally once you buy your stock index position and close strong in the upper quarter of the day's range. The long futures is then liquidated on the second day, the Sell Day, at a price which is slightly below, at, or above the previous day's (Buy Day) high.

On the third day of the three-day cycle, the strongest possible sell short signal occurs on the high made first. In addition, if the market is weak, the signal may be even stronger. This position is then liquidated on the following day (Buy Day) at the low made first, which will be slightly above, at, or below the previous day's (Short Sell Day) low.

You may find, of course, that the market is unwilling to cooperate and provide you with a Buy Day low right at the open. Indeed, based on the previous day's price action, the high may occur first and you must be flexible enough to sell these rallies even on a Buy Day if circumstances warrant the sale. Just remember, such a sale is not a strong trade and should be liquidated prior to the day's close. Conversely, the same might be said of a low occurring first on a Short Sell Day. You would want to buy such a low and liquidate the same day. But, again, you want to be more cautious in these counter-trend trades and save the substantial trades for the days when all factors are in your favor.

READING THE MARKET

In order to read the market correctly, you must realize that support and resistance are critical. For unless a market can penetrate prior tops and

Figure 11
THE TWO STRONGEST TRADING SIGNALS

Buying a Higher Bottom on A Buy Day in a Bull Market

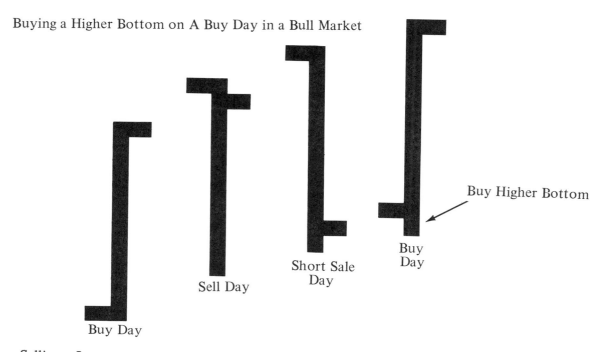

Selling a Lower Top on a Short Sale Day in a **Bear** Market

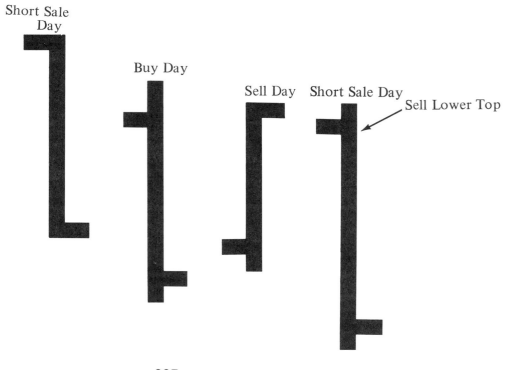

227

bottoms, there is an excellent chance it will rebound off former lows and react off former highs. We'll look at an actual example that occurred in the March 1983 Standard & Poor's contract. The target day is Tuesday, February 1, 1983, a Buy Day. The market had been rallying, going from a low made first of 143.05 on Thursday, January 27th to a high made last of 147.40 on Monday, January 31st. A rally of 4.35 points in just three days suggests a selloff is in order, despite the anticipation of the Buy Day scheduled for the target day. First, we'll list the key data for the previous day, the Short Sell Day, on Monday, January 31.

Table 28
MARCH 1983 STANDARD & POOR'S

Date	Open	High	Low	Close	D	R	BH	BU
Jan 31	145.00	147.40	144.50	147.30	2.45	2.80	.45	.10

On the day listed above, the Short Sell Day, the high occurred last near the close; or, you might say, the market opened near the low and traded higher. The high and low of the day pinpoint the support and resistance. If the market is to move higher on the next day, the Buy Day, it must clearly break the resistance at 147.40, the January 31 high. Looking at the Decline, Rally, Buying High, and Buying Low columns, you also know that if tomorrow's market is to parallel today's, it will decline no lower than 2.45 points off the high (144.95), nor rally more than 2.80 points off the low (147.30). In addition, the Buying High column suggests that the market will be fully extended at .45 points over the high (147.85) and should find support at .10 points below the low (144.30). Now, this is no guarantee that these numbers will prove to be the parameters of tomorrow's move—only that these are key support and resistance levels. As such, they deserve our attention. If the market can't stop at one, it may stop at another; if it fails to observe any of these parameters, it may be indeed a powerful new move into higher or lower ground.

If you've gotten through all the above, don't stop reading now, you're over the worst. But there are two other pertinent observations to be made.

One is the prior day's range and the other is how the market traded. The previous day's range was 2.90 points, call it 3 points. The market traded in an upward pattern, the low being made first, the high last—the reverse of the normal Short Sell Day pattern. This last observation is important since it suggests the normal Short Sell Day pattern—the high being made first, the low last—is a day late, and perhaps it will occur tomorrow, on the Buy Day. Very often when you push the cycle ahead a day, the pattern will again become normal—low to high on the Buy Day, high to low on the Short Sell Day, and so on. Moreover, in this example, the close near the high of the day suggests the high will be made first on the next day, and the selloff will occur from there. Remember, Taylor's rule calls for selling at, through, or slightly below the previous day's high, which is the resistance. Let's see what happened.

Table 29
MARCH 1983 STANDARD & POOR'S

Date	Open	High	Low	Close	D	R	BH	BU
Feb 1	147.25	147.25	143.15 ✓	143.20	4.25	2.75	− .15	1.35

The opening was at 147.25, down a tick from the previous close and just three ticks from the previous day's high. Significantly, the open proved to be the high of the day. It was just one tick lower than the previous day's Rally (R) number, which had been predicted at 147.30. On openings like this one, you pretty much have to start selling immediately—and then sell more when the previous low is taken out. The day's low was 143.15, well below the estimates. But the open near the prior day's high, the Rally number sell target, and three days of higher prices all pointed toward a selloff.

Notice that the close is almost on the low of the day. This is significant because it shows that the short sellers have little inclination to cover their short positions. How do we know this? By the absence of a rally on the close. If the selloff were indeed just a temporary intra-day decline, the short sellers would have covered and bid prices up in a short covering rally. But this didn't occur. Rather, more selling came in on the close and knocked the price lower. The significance of this close near the low, therefore, is to expect lower prices on the following day. Indeed, the price broke to 141.50 on the next day's open, a decline of 1.70 points, and only then found support—after the hapless longs had lost their money. It was a classic example of the spring effect in action.

Not only were the stops all hit on the open, but the open proved to be the low of the day as well. That makes two trading days consecutively when the open was either the high of the day or the low of the day. Perhaps surprisingly, the next day's open at 143.80 proved to be the low of that day as well, making three consecutive days when the open was at the extreme end of the range. Had you been placing your orders at the open and had you been correct, the adversity would have been very little. Moreover, had you been wrong, you would have had ample opportunity to realize your mistake and take the other side—in other words, the open proved to be the safest time of the day to put on a trade.

On the other hand, traders who had the misfortune to hold stop-loss orders overnight would have been in trouble had they been stopped out on the open. Not only would they have received a bad fill, but, since prices jumped back up due to the spring effect, they would have had the misfortune of seeing the trade go their way—long after they had exited the market at a loss!

AND NOW A SIMPLE RULE

Despite a varying number of reversals in the market, you want to find just one trend a day. You want to select your trade, make your money, and get out! The tendency to want to overstay the market, to make it both coming and going, and to catch the entire day's range is what makes for trouble. If the range, let's say, is three points, be happy with half that much in profit—or even less. There will be days when you will catch the lion's share of the range, but don't be greedy. At times, you can lose your entire day's profit trying to win that last half-point in profit. And then all you've got is a loss. So settle for consistent profits and take larger positions if necessary to reach your profit goals.

You must remember that flexibility is what counts. In the example above, the so-called Buy Day turned out to be an ideal selling day—so don't let the name throw you off. In fact, in the LSS 3-Day Cycle Method, I've changed the name of the days so that you won't be wedded to the notion that you must buy on a Buy Day and Sell on a Sell or Short Sell Day. As the market changes, you must change. This is the key to success. Your whole speculative philosophy must reflect this attitude. So always remember to keep your eye on what the market is doing—and be quick to change sides if you find yourself in a losing position.

WHICH IS THE BEST SIDE—
LONG OR SHORT?

I was asked this question in a seminar in Los Angeles several years ago. The answer is, of course, the best side is the winning side. But, without being flippant, the correct answer is: it depends. In a week's trading in Standard & Poor's futures not long ago, the market broke six points from Monday's high to Wednesday's low and then rebounded seven points to Friday's high. In the light of such volatility, how can you pick one side or the other? It clearly depends on where you are in the trading cycle—and that's where a system based on a cyclical method of trading can help.

The Taylor Method and the LSS 3-Day Cycle Method, which is based on Taylor, are flexible systems for a very good reason. The flexibility works. Most investors want to be told the market will go up or down regardless of changing technical or fundamental conditions. But it isn't that simple. First of all, no one has the answers to the proverbial question—namely, what will the market do? Second, knowing the short-term, and often even intra-day, trend is vital to your financial health if you trade stock index futures for any period of time. It is this short-term cycle that you want to master—not the reading of the Dow Jones Industrials six months from now. The swings in the market are often too steep for even the most well-financed trader to withstand market adversity. Hence, you pretty much have to concern yourself with learning how to trade on a short-term basis.

Let's look at another example where the resistance on the Short Sell Day provides the main clue for trading June 1983 S&P futures. The day was Tuesday, March 22, 1983, a Buy Day. The market had risen for three consecutive days, each with a higher high. The numbers for the previous day, the Short Sell Day, Monday, March 21, 1983 appear as follows:

Table 30
JUNE 1983 STANDARD & POOR'S

Date	Open	High	Low	Close	D	R	BH	BU
Mar 21	149.80	(152.40)	149.55	152.30	1.15	3.20	1.70	− .35

The market opened near its low and rallied on this Short Sell Day, setting up a possible short sale on the following day when the cycle was pushed ahead a day. The resistance is at the high of 152.40, as well as at 152.75 based on the previous day's rally number. If real bullishness sets in, one could expect resistance at 154.10—the number arrived at by adding the Buying High (BH) column number to the day's high.

The key to the next day's action, however, will be the open. An open near one of the resistance numbers, based on the three-day cycle, would indicate a short sale was in order. Here's what the subsequent Buy Day's numbers looked like:

Table 31
JUNE 1983 STANDARD & POOR'S

Date	Open	High	Low	Close	D	R	BH	BU
Mar 22	152.40	152.40	150.50	(151.10)	1.90	2.85	0	− .95

Once again, the open proved to be the high made first, providing an excellent opportunity for a short sale. The fact that the range was not as great, that the market held a higher bottom, suggests the market was headed higher—which, in time, it was. In two days, the market traded at 155.45, or almost three points higher than the day's low. But for a day trade, one needed only to sell against the previous day's high to gain an excellent entry price with virtually no risk. By using the Decline column number, you could have covered at 151.25—that's 1.15 points from the top at 152.40. Or you could have covered on the close. The BU column number, .35 points *over* the previous low, or 149.90, was never reached.

If this pattern sounds familiar (remember the last example?), you may have a clue to recognizing similar patterns by looking back in your Book for a similar-type day. You then "take the measurement" of the pattern day and transpose it to anticipate prices in the future. This technique is known as pattern recognition, which we'll cover next.

PATTERN RECOGNITION

Pattern recognition uses previous price experience to pinpoint future price action. To use this technique, you have to identify where you stand in the current cycle and then look back for a time when a similar pattern existed. Ideally, you should have as many similarities as possible. Among the important factors are: how the market traded (low made first, etc.); day in cycle (Buy, Sell, Sell Short); day-to-day price movements (higher highs, lower lows, inside days, etc.); and nature of overall market (rising, falling, stationary). Once you note the pattern of the previous trading day, you should look for more distant trading days where similar patterns existed. For example, let's say tomorrow is a Short Sell Day and the high today occurred last, suggesting a higher open tomorrow. Go back in time to find a similar day and then *measure* the relation of all the key numbers: previous close to open; high to high; low to low; and so on. Moreover, notice how the market traded. Was the high made first? Was the open the high of the day? Did the market open lower and then rally only to break at the close? And so on. This is the type of information that can prove very, very valuable.

Let's look at an example of pattern recognition. We'll list eight days of price data for the June 1983 Standard & Poor's 500 contract for the dates Wednesday, April 6 through Friday, April 15, 1983. The eight-day period contains two and two-thirds 3-day cycles, beginning with the Buy Day low on Wednesday, April 6, 1983.

233

Table 32
JUNE 1983 STANDARD & POOR'S

Date	Open	High	Low	Close	D	R	BH	BU
Apr 6	152.00	152.10	149.70	151.35	4.50	.75	− 2.10	1.65
Apr 7	151.10	152.05	150.20	151.80	1.90	1.95	− .05	.50
Apr 8	151.80	152.15	150.60	151.85	1.45	1.95	.10	− .40
Apr 11	153.10	155.20	153.05	155.10	− .90	4.60	3.05	− 2.45
Apr 12	154.95	155.70	154.15	155.60	1.05	2.65	.50	− 1.10
Apr 13	155.25	157.20	155.25	156.35	.45	3.05	1.50	− 1.10
Apr 14	156.70	158.50	155.60	158.40	1.60	3.25	1.30	− 3.55
Apr 15	157.70	158.90	157.50	158.20	1.00	3.30	.40	− 1.90

The target day, Monday April 18, is a Short Sell Day, being the third day in the three-day cycle. Note that despite progressively higher prices, every third day provided an opportunity to buy near the low of the day after the open—on the Buy Day low made first. In looking at the anticipated price action on Monday, April 18, the likelihood is that the high will be made *first* since the high was made *last* on Friday, April 15. But there is no certainty of this. Moreover, since the market has already carried more than nine points in eight trading days, one must be respectful of the bullish nature of the market—there is little reason to think the trend won't continue.

In order to select a good pattern recognition day, you must first eliminate the many patterns that it does *not* resemble. Your elimination process begins with the *type of day*. You have a Short Sell Day in a bull market. For the days that fall into this category, you must look back in your Book. In looking back (and you'll have a comprehensive list of prices once you begin to maintain your daily price data), Friday, February 11 and Monday, February 14 immediately suggest a similar pattern. First, February 11 is a Sell Day. Second, the pattern of a higher open, high and low coupled with a *lower* close is identical. Third, the market has just made a significant rally. The numbers for the two pattern recognition days are as follows:

Table 33
MARCH 1983 STANDARD & POOR'S

Date	Open	High	Low	Close	D	R	BH	BU
Feb 11	150.20	150.75	148.40	148.40	1.70	3.75	.65	− 1.40
Feb 14	148.95	151.70	148.90	150.95	1.85	3.30	1.00	− .50

By the way, in maintaining the price data, it helps to use two different color pens. I use black ink pens for higher prices and red ink pens for lower prices. And I compare open with open, high with high, and so on. In the example above, the open at 148.95 would be written in red ink, since it is lower than the previous open; the high at 151.70, however, would appear in black ink since it is higher than the previous day's high. By using different color pens, you can tell at a glance whether a market has been rallying (black ink) or declining (red ink).

Now let's compare open with open, high with high, low with low, close with close, and, finally, first day's close with second day's open, to establish an *anticipated* pattern for the target day, Monday, April 18. You might prepare a list as follows:

Table 34

	Pattern	Change
1.	Open-to-open	− .25
2.	High-to-High	+ .95
3.	Low-to-low	+ .50
4.	Close-to-close	+ 1.15
5.	Previous close-to-open	+ .55

Next, you want to transpose these numbers to the current day in order to help predict the price action on the target day. First, we'll again list the prices for the Sell Day, April 15, 1983.

Table 35

Date	Open	High	Low	Close
Apr 15	157.70	158.90	157.70	158.20

By adding the various pattern changes, you will form an anticipated price pattern as follows:

235

Table 36

Previous Day	Change	Target Day
Open @ 157.70	− .25	157.45
High @ 158.90	+ .95	159.85
Low @ 157.70	+ .50	158.20
Close @ 158.20	+ 1.15	159.35
Close-to-open	+ .55	158.75

Lastly, since the market opened near the low of the day on February 14, 1983, making the low first, one would expect the same pattern to occur on the target day. This is a clue that one will *not* sell the high first, but rather buy the low made first. Let's see what actually happened.

Table 37
JUNE 1983 STANDARD & POOR'S

Date	Open	High	Low	Close
Apr 18	158.00	159.40	157.45	159.05

As it turned out, the anticipated open (which should have been close to the low) proved to be the *exact* low tick of the day. The anticipated high at 159.85 was a bit ambitious since the actual high was at 159.40, and the anticipated low was too high. The anticipated close at 159.35 was just .30 points too high, a reasonable effort. The low was made first, as was anticipated by the pattern recognition method.

ADJUSTING THE RANGE AFTER THE OPEN

Using the pattern recognition method, you can often pinpoint the top or bottom of the day's range after the open. This has obvious advantages, since it can tell you where to take profits or expect resistance or support to enter the market. First, you take the anticipated range for the target day. In the example above, the anticipated range is 1.65 points, or the difference between the anticipated high at 159.85 and the anticipated low at 158.20. Once the market opens and a high or low is made, you then throw out the

236

anticipated numbers and forecast new ones on the basis of the low of the day or the high of the day. To do this effectively, you must make a judgment about whether an intra-day high or low will hold. For instance, in the above example, the market opened at 158.00 and traded lower until it found support at 157.45. Making a judgment that this price will indeed be the low of the day, you then take the anticipated range and add it to this number, as follows:

Intra-day low	=	157.45
Anticipated range	=	+1.65
predicted high of day	=	159.10

In fact, the actual high was 159.40, but 159.10 is clearly close enough. If you begin selling your long positions as that number is approached, you will have a very profitable day. This is a very useful tool to have since it is often the most accurate reading of the market you will find.

For this technique to work, you must be willing to own up to any mistakes in judgment that you make. For instance, let's say, for whatever reason, you decided the intra-day high of 158.00 formed on the open would hold and that you then *subtracted* the anticipated range of 1.65 points from this number. You would then have an anticipated bottom of 156.35. You may have even sold short in anticipation of lower prices. This is fine, as long as you are willing to correct your mistake as soon as the intra-day high is violated. On the first violation of the intra-day high, you must get out of any short positions and take long positions in order to ride the trend higher. Remember, being wrong is part of stock index futures trading; it is what you do to correct your mistakes that will decide whether you will be a success in the market, not the initial mistake.

PICKING THE WINNERS

So far, we've spent a lot of time concentrating on countertrend trades. But what about when everything seems poised for success? The strong trades, buying the low made first on the Buy Day or selling the high made first on the Short Sell Day, provide the real profits. What should you look for then?

Since you are really playing a percentage game, you want as many factors favorable to the trade as possible. Only then should you decide to back the position with a greater number of contracts than you normally trade. Moreover, you want the trade to go your way more or less right from the start.

In choosing the trade to plunge on, look for the one that has been developing for some time. The number of market days between bottoms might be coming up on a Gann or Fibonacci number, or an important anniversity date might be due. For those with the patience, August 9, 1983 proved the classic example. Not only was it an important anniversity date, but it was also the Buy Day in the three-day cycle! If you do your homework, you'll be better prepared for your opportunity when it comes. In addition, you'll need the confidence of having a reliable system if you are going to risk the kind of funds you need to risk to make substantial profits. As a rule, I try to make it a policy to always trade at the level where the money at risk—and the potential profit—is meaningful. If the money isn't meaningful, you won't watch it carefully; on the other hand, if it is *too* meaningful, you are going to make emotional mistakes. This is especially true on the big, important trades when you have to make the serious money that will see you through the periods of whipsawing prices, where it is almost certain you will get a little chewed up. In summary, you want to be at the point where you are perhaps a little nervous about the money but not panic-striken.

Next, you want to know exactly what you are going to do in reaction to adversity. In short, you want a contingency plan—one you can stand by. By this, I don't mean being foolish by hanging on when the market has already proved you wrong. Rather, I mean having the courage of your convictions.

I'll never forget the day all the signals were overwhelmingly bullish and I loaded up with contracts. Awaiting the market rise, I became concerned because the intra-day low (which was holding) was being threatened. The sellers were making significant attempts at the stops at, and below, the intra-day low. Lacking the courage of my own conviction, I sold out at a loss (which was significant because I held so many contracts). In less than an hour's time the market was soaring upward—and I wasn't aboard! Talk about disappointment. There is no excuse for this kind of a mistake except, perhaps, chickenheartedness. Having been shaken out of a good position, I should have been prepared to jump right back in—even at a higher price if need be. After all, at that stage, you want the market to hold a higher bottom.

One important clue that I had that the above position was a correct one was the existence of a Buy Day low made first near the previous day's low, or support. In looking back at a list of Buy Days, one can easily see the reason why Taylor suggests buying at, through, or slightly above the previous day's low. The following list shows where the support existed (the previous day's low). The range, from low to high, is also listed. In every case, the trader would have profited by buying the low made first. In the 14 Buy Days listed below, 10 buys would have been taken at a higher bottom, or about 70 percent of the trades.

Table 38
FOURTEEN REPRESENTATIVE BUY DAYS—
S&P 1983 NEARBY FUTURES

Date Date	Previous Day's Low	Buy Day Low	Rally from Low (range)
Mar 07	153.35	153.10	1.95
Mar 30	152.15	152.60	2.10
Apr 11	150.60	153.05	2.05
Apr 14	155.25	155.60	2.90
Jun 21	169.85	169.75	3.35
Jul 20	165.75	167.55	2.85
Jul 25	169.80	169.30	2.80
Aug 09	160.25	159.25	2.55
Aug 12	162.15	162.70	.90
Aug 17	163.20	164.25	2.00
Aug 30	161.10	162.40	1.55
Sep 02	164.20	164.50	.95
Sep 02	164.20	164.50	1.05
Oct 06	168.15	170.00	2.05

Note that the Buy Day low is not always near the previous day's low. April 11 is one such example. On that day, the low was considerably above the previous day's low. On days like this—July 20 and October 6 were other examples—the higher open constitutes a breakout to the upside and must be purchased, a case of the market never being too high for a buy to prove profitable. On October 6, for example, the open was right at the previous days high. You might have tried selling on that day, albeit a lesser number of contracts than you would have purchased, but once prices moved against you, you would have wanted to purchase contracts in keeping with the higher trend.

What about selling short? How do you find the best short sell trades? Short sales can often be the most profitable, even in a bull market, because the public has a natural bullish bias. If this suggests the breaks will be fast, it should. Because stop-loss orders are apt to be clustered together and because a certain herd instinct encourages panic selling, sharp market breaks are often real money-makers for the short sellers. And this applies to bull, as well as bear, markets; in fact, this latest bull market has been no exception.

Let's look at some examples. Take Thursday, March 10, 1983, a Short Sell Day in the three-day cycle. The previous day's high (resistance) was at 153.95 in the June '83 S&P 500 contract. The March 10 open was at 153.80, right under the resistance. Soon after the open, the market carried up to 154.50 on short-covering and then the decline got underway. The market then declined more than three points to 151.45, prior to closing at 151.60. It lost still another point on the following day prior to beginning the cycle over again. The three days culminating in the March 10th Short Sell Day appear as follows:

Table 39
JUNE 1983 STANDARD & POOR'S

Date	Open	High	Low	Close
Mar 08	154.00	154.25	152.10	152.35
Mar 09	152.60	153.95	152.10	153.80
Mar 10	153.80	154.50	151.45	151.60

Another good selling opportunity came a short time later, when the Sell Day high at 155.20 occurred last on Wednesday, March 23rd, setting up an opportunity for the high to be made first on the following day, Thursday, March 24th. Indeed, the market opened down that day, rallied over a point taking out the previous high, and then declined. The numbers for the three-day cycle appeared as follows:

Table 40
JUNE 1983 STANDARD & POOR'S

Date	Open	High	Low	Close
Mar 22	152.40	152.40	150.50	151.10
Mar 23	151.50	155.20	151.25	154.70
Mar 24	154.35	155.45	153.70	154.85

The strongest possible sell signal occurs on the Short Sell Day, when the high made first *fails* to penetrate the previous day's high. In this situation the selling is so strong as the market approaches the previous day's high that it can go no higher—and the subsequent decline is often substantial. Consider the July 27 Short Sell Day high made first in the table of prices listed below. The selloff that followed carried 10 points in four days.

Table 41
SEPTEMBER 1983 STANDARD & POOR'S

Date	Open	High	Low	Close
Jul 25	169.55	172.10	169.30	171.15
Jul 26	171.15	172.45	170.40	171.40
Jul 27	171.85	172.25	168.00	168.50
Jul 28	168.50	168.85	165.55	165.55
Jul 29	165.20	165.40	162.45	163.70
Aug 01	163.50	164.05	162.20	163.10

TAKING A POSITION OVERNIGHT

Taylor's original Book Method called for taking a long position, purchased at the Buy Day low made first, as an overnight trade. The rule was to then liquidate on the second day, the Sell Day, at, through, or slightly below the previous day's (Buy Day) high. Again, the reasoning was that the previous day's high constituted the resistance. In the table above, the long position acquired on the low made first on July 25 could have been liquidated on July 26 at, through, or slightly below the previous day's high. In fact, this proved to be an excellent selling area. In the second three-day cycle, the low was made last, meaning no long position would have been taken on July 28. As a result, the rule calling for liquidation on the Sell Day does not apply.

As for selling on the Short Sell Day high made first, the rule calls for covering at the Short Sell Day low on the following Buy Day. Thus, the position taken on July 27 could have been liquidated at 168.00 on July 28, the Buy Day.

What about the rest of the downward move? Taylor never claimed to have a system that would provide you with *all* the profits available in a given move. As long as you take profits consistently, you should not concern yourself with the profits you "leave on the table." Besides, there are other techniques you can use to forecast longer-term moves. Remember, more often than not, these longer-term moves won't exist. Instead, the market will stabilize after a down move and rally, providing profits to the percentage players. Obviously, this "Book Method" works best in a trading market not a trending market. The point is, trading markets are far more prevalent. If you can profit in the trading markets, you'll be way ahead of the game.

PUSHING THE CYCLE AHEAD A DAY

One shortcoming of the Taylor Book Method is that it doesn't tell you when to adjust the cycle. Taylor's method of determining the Buy Day is simplicity itself. Count back ten days and take the lowest low. But where you begin counting will determine which cycle you follow. Taylor admits that the 3-day cycle may become a 4-day or even 5-day cycle. So it is particularly frustrating not to know how to change the cycle.

One method that tends to work quite well is to disregard that day itself—Buy, Sell, or Short Sell Day—and concentrate on anticipating the pattern. Specifically, let's say you are anticipating the normal Buy Day pattern, with the high made last and the low made first. But instead the reverse pattern occurs—the Short Sell Day pattern; high first, low last. You must then *push the cycle ahead a day* and look for the normal Buy Day pattern on the *following day*. Very often this works. The fact that prices closed near the low suggests the support may hold prices tomorrow and they will be bid higher. Of course, if the market is "falling out of bed," the decline will continue—but you can usually tell this by how the market opens. And even if you can't spot the bear market on the open, you'll know soon enough by the price action. When prices break, you must be willing to get out of the longs and aggressively sell short. This rephasing of the cycle is shown in Figure 12.

In Figure 12, you'll notice that today's close often dictates tomorrow's open and subsequent price action. If the market opened near its high and more or less sold-off all day, closing near its low, chances are tomorrow's open (all other factors being equal; which they never are!) will be in the vicinity of the close. At that point, the market may very well stage the anticipated rally, albeit one day late. And the reverse, of course, is true for anticipated short sales. If you can't find the selling opportunity you anticipated today, the market may need another day. Save yourself some money by not trying to force the issue when the market may simply need another day.

EVERY DAY IS A COMPLETE CYCLE

A successful trade is often highlighted by a number of complimentary signals all coming together to form a comprehensive picture. The more indicators you follow, the more confirming signals you are likely to gather. In turn, the more signals you have, the greater your confidence and the better your ability to capitalize on your knowledge by taking a substantial position.

So far, we have hit upon a number of techniques used in selecting winning trades, but we haven't really put them together in order to fashion a comprehensive approach to the market. To show how such an approach can indeed result in significant profits we'll focus on a single trading day, using a sort of zoom-lens approach, to see some of the factors influencing prices. Granted, the day we will look at is not your typical day, but rather one on which a number of extraordinary influences all converged in order to set up an ideal trade.

The day in question is Monday, August 22, 1983. The market is the September 1983 Standard & Poor's 500 contract. We'll begin with a list of

243

Figure 12
WHEN TO PUSH THE CYCLE AHEAD A DAY

1. When low made last on Buy Day, look for low made first on following Sell Day

2. When high made last on Short Sale Day, look for high made first on following Buy Day

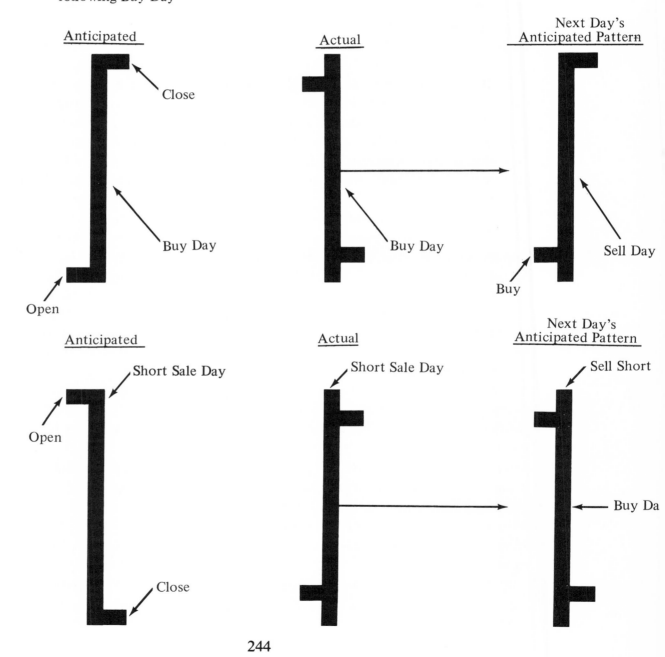

244

relevant factors to consider:

Fibonacci Days	Day of Cycle
Gann Days	Relation of Close to Open
Anniversity Dates	Spring Effect
Breakout Play	Opening Price
Psychological and	Stop Placement
Fundamental Factors	Recent Trend
Support and Resistance	Contrary Opinion

Even a casual glance at some of the factors influencing prices on this bright summer morning could have pinpointed a short-term selloff—one that would ultimately take the September 1983 S&P 500 contract down more than six points in four trading days. First and foremost, a new week was beginning. Mondays are particularly important in the stock index futures market because they are the first trading day following the release of Friday afternoon's Money Supply figures.* The Money Supply results are important to the Street, and hence stock prices, *not* because they can always pinpoint the direction of prices, but because of their *psychological* impact on the market. If the Money Supply numbers are "unexpected" by Street analysts, the market is likely to undergo an adjustment on Monday morning. Monday, August 22nd was to be no exception.

Friday's numbers were interpreted as bullish—the perfect excuse to take the market up on the open. The higher open, of course, caught a lot of bears on the wrong side of the market. After all, prices had been trending down off the June highs and had only recently made a low on the anniversity date of the beginning of the year earlier bull market. The previous high on the rally off the anniversity date lows was 166.25 for September S&P 500 futures. Guess where a lot of short sellers had placed their stops?

Sure enough, the market opened that Monday morning at 166.00, 1.15 points over Friday's close. It then rallied to 166.35 to take out the previous high—and the stops—and, after consolidating for a couple of hours, began to move down in earnest. It was a perfect illustration of the "spring effect." The market is taken higher on "news" only to collapse and fall apart.

Had you been cautious and not had a position on the open (again,

---

* Money supply figures are now available on Thursday afternoons, so Fridays should take on the importance formerly given to Mondays.

holding a position over a weekend trying to outguess the impact of the Money Supply numbers is never a good idea), you could have waited for the intra-day low, formed about an hour after the open, to be taken out. Violation of the intra-day low proved an excellent signal that the market was about to break.

Looking back in time, you would have found a number of good signals all pointing toward August 22nd as a top. It fell on the ninth market day (the square of 3) from the August 9th low at 159.25 in the September contract. Had you been following Fibonacci numbers, you might have also noticed that August 22nd was the 13th market day following a significant high and 34 market days from a significant low.

In terms of the three-day cycle, it was a Buy Day. But the previous Friday's price action, with the high made last, suggested Monday would see the high made first—which was indeed the case. Markets are often forgiving. This was no exception. Even if you had missed selling short and watched the break from the sidelines, you had another opportunity late in the day. Using the 61.8 percent rule, you could have taken the intra-day high and low and arrived at 165.50 as a likely intra-day rally top. The market, in fact, carried about four or five ticks higher before collapsing. Three days later it traded as low as 160.30.

Like many market days, August 22nd had a number of identifiable patterns. It had a high opening, presenting an excellent selling opportunity. Remember, the open is often near one end of the range. It had three sets of double tops and an equal number of double bottoms. Moreover, the sharp break was followed by a sharp rally, driven, no doubt, by panic buying on behalf on the hapless short sellers who waited a little too long to take profits. In the end, the downward trend prevailed and the market closed down near the low, a sign that the shorts were still in command. The subsequent selloff confirmed this analysis.

THE FUTURE OF THE 3-DAY CYCLE

One need only glance at a table of daily futures prices to see that index futures are among the most popular short-term, day-trading contracts ever introduced. Unlike more traditional futures contracts, the daily volume on index contracts typically exceeds the number of outstanding contracts held,

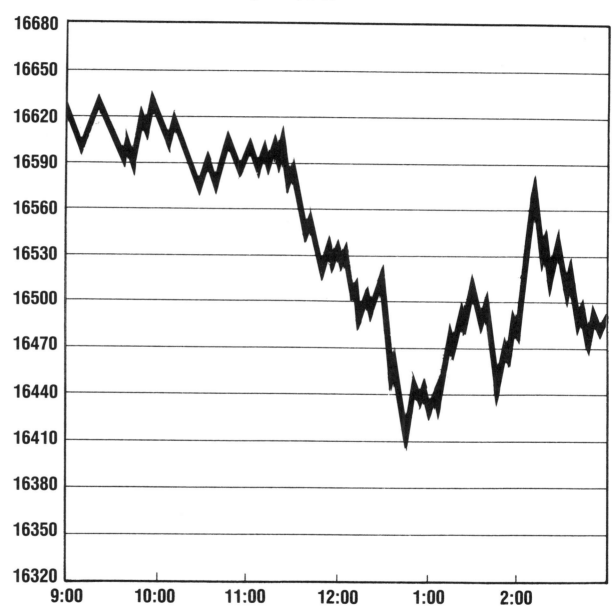

Figure 13
SEPTEMBER '83 S&P 500
August 22, 1983

as measured by the open interest. On a recent trading day, the nearby S&P futures contract reported daily volume as 57 percent higher than the open interest, and the popular NYSE Composite Index futures traded at a rate twice as high as the longer-held contracts as measured by the open interest. This compares with a volume level 27 percent below the open interest in the once-popular pork belly contract and a volume level 25 percent below the open interest in U. S. Treasury Bond futures—both known for their popularity among day traders.

One inference that can be drawn from these statistics is that stock index futures traders are extremely biased in favor of the short-term. This stands to reason, since the gyrations of the index markets are legendary, and traders, seeking to capitalize on these short-term movements, have, understandably, focused their attention on capturing small moves. After all, given the typical two-point range, a trader who can earn just a single point, or half of that range, on five or six contracts can make $2,500 to $3,000 a day. In such a potentially lucrative environment, it shouldn't be too surprising that more and more traders are seeking to understand shorter-term cycles that exist in the marketplace.

George Douglas Taylor developed a theory of price movements based on the grain market more than thirty years ago. That this theory today is applicable to stock index futures shouldn't come as a surprise. Human nature hasn't changed in the past three decades, nor has the leveraging effect of futures contracts. But the real proof rests with the market itself. Market rallies and reactions are as much a feature of the financial markets as waves lapping against our North Atlantic shores. And, despite an occasional tidal wave, the likelihood of rhythmic rallies and declines continuing to influence markets is strong indeed.

Taylor was an expert in "reading" the market, and that's where the three-day cycle can stand you in good stead. By helping to pinpoint the precise time and conditions of a good trade, the three-day cycle can improve your odds of winning immeasurably—and that's what profitable stock index trading is all about. Our task now is to develop *specific* rules for buying and selling. And for that we'll turn to the LSS Three-day Cycle Method.

Chapter Eight

THE LSS 3-DAY CYCLE METHOD
The Stock Index Trading System For The Eighties

After more than three years of careful testing in actual and hypothetical trading conditions, the LSS 3-Day Cycle Method has finally reached the point where the results measure up to its original promise. LSS owes its origins to Taylor's Book Method. After all, the three-day cycle notion is at the heart of the system. But it goes beyond Taylor's pioneering work, incorporating added flexibility and responsiveness, and adding a much needed money management formula to Taylor's calculations.

Tested on a variety of futures—including gold, U. S. Treasury bonds, soybeans, and pork bellies among others—LSS has been extremely profitable. It's been particularly effective in the stock index futures market, where the volatility and liquidity are tailor-made for a system such as LSS.

COMPUTER-PROVEN AND MECHANICAL

LSS—the letters stand for "long," "sell," and "short sell"—is an entirely mechanical day-trading system that has been programmed for computer testing and found to be consistently profitable under a variety of market conditions. (Complete results can be obtained by writing the publisher, Windsor Books). In order to develop the system, however, a number of revisions had to be made in Taylor's original theory. As a result, Book Method "purists" may find the system only slightly resembling Taylor's work—a criticism I'm quite willing to acknowledge. Moreover, although much is borrowed from Taylor, there were a number of areas in which his suggestions didn't seem to work in practice—at least not in the stock index futures market—and I've changed these to make the system more profitable.

CAN YOU BEAT THE MARKET?

In 1980, when I first encountered Taylor's work, I was looking for something that would help me select tops and bottoms on a daily basis—in short, a system suitable for day-trading. In addition, as a short-term trader, I wanted a system that was *consistently* profitable. It wasn't enough that the system could capture the trend of the week, or even the day. It had to tell me *when* to enter the market at low risk; otherwise, what was its use? You don't have to trade futures for long to know that you can be right about the market and still lose money. More importantly, I needed a system that told me when and where the time had come to cash in my chips. It seemed that when I was losing (a common enough event in the futures market), I was naturally afraid of losing more; and, conversely, but not really surprising, when I was winning, I was afraid they were going to take away my hard-won profits. If only I had a system, I thought.

Finding that system became an obsession. Fortunately, I had an opportunity to observe first-hand some of the best—and, occasionally, the worst—traders in the world. By pulling together these experiences and talking to a number of traders both on and off the floor, I began to see a pattern. While the number of approaches varied, the winners tended to share common characteristics. The more inexperienced traders, on the other hand, shared a number of mistaken ideas that seemed somehow fostered by the notion that the market *had* to behave in some preordained pattern. Since obtaining maturity as a futures trader is a truly relative concept, I began to see my own first signs of growth when I finally accepted and embraced the realization that I really didn't have any idea where the market would go. Indeed, did anyone? One novice trader told me he bought silver limit-down one day after a sharp break because it

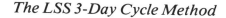

appeared to be a bargain. He was wiped out after it broke lower and locked limit on two subsequent days. More telling, the guys who were always offering abundant advice on their fantastic profits were inevitably suddenly quiet when they took a "hit." But the real winners, who won day after day, never had opinions—just positions—and they churned out the profits in a consistent, albeit hard-won, flow of dollars.

Yes, the good news is that the market can be beat. And not just on an occasional trade either. On a consistent basis. Certainly, not everyone can win; it is, after all, a zero sum game. The bad news is that the market can only be beat by the informed minority—the few who are willing to really learn *how to trade.* But is this really bad? It depends. Fortunately, for the winners, there is no lack of uninformed traders.

This realization occurred during a time when I was trying to be perfect about every trade. It seemed sensible then. If I lost money on a trade, I'd quit for the day. It wasn't long, however, before I was repeating the old lament, "if only I'd gone the other way." If only...the losses would have been winners. By observing others, I soon found that the real winners wouldn't call it a day simply because one trade had gone sour. On the contrary, if they found themselves on the wrong side of the market, they'd close out their positions and go with the trend. The point is, the system had to embrace this philosophy.

Now it so happens that the conventional wisdom doesn't include this kind of concept; it is simply contrary to generally accepted practice. Market letter writers rarely advise switching from side to side. They are paid to be one-sided. The same is true of brokers. Basing their analysis soundly on the side of the fundamentals, it would be inconsistent to advise switching sides. Besides, what about commissions? Couldn't a broker get in trouble by advising a client to switch from side to side? Too risky. No, you won't find a lot of enthusiasm for this approach. But this is precisely the approach that works.

Unfortunately, when you first start out trading stock index futures, there usually isn't someone to tell you these things. Now you've been forewarned. Unless you are prepared to be aggressive about your trading activities, you had better look elsewhere. Stock index futures is too competitive an arena to casually await profits.

The LSS 3-Day Cycle Method is designed to provide you with flexibility coupled with maximum profitability. Using the method, you won't have a winner with every trade, no one can guarantee such a record. In the end, you should have profits, however. After all, the bottom line is the final measure of any trading system. What else is more important?

SAFETY FIRST—THE REST IS SECONDARY

If you are going to reach your profit goal, you are going to have to concern yourself with safety; for unless you know how to protect yourself from the vagaries of the marketplace, you won't be around to enjoy the benefits. The market is too unforgiving. And this is the plight of most novice traders; they know they can earn incredible profits, but they don't know the risks—and hence, rarely see the profits. The professionals know the risks and protect themselves accordingly. There are simply too many things that can go wrong with a trade to allow fate to play an important role. This is why LSS is strictly a day-trading system. Forget the overnight stuff; speculation in the index futures markets is enough of a gamble as it is. You needn't make it riskier. Hence, the rule: no positions overnight. And, if you are determined to hold a position longer, you might as well adhere to this rule: *no losses overnight*. Winners, yes; losses, never. For some reason, unlike wine, losing trades never seem to improve with age.

WHERE TAYLOR CAME UP SHORT

Paradoxically, Taylor's main shortcoming rested squarely in the area where he was strongest—flexibility. The 3-day cycle, he maintained, repeated itself over and over again—which it does. But isn't it logical to assume the cycle will occasionally skip a day or two, or get out of phase? To take a major low and count forward in an endless 3-day pattern seems overly simplified. To overcome this drawback, the LSS 3-Day Cycle Method employs a short-term *Momentum Trend* indicator that signals when the cycle should be rephased.

In keeping with this notion that a so-called Buy Day need not be a day when buying is called for, I've changed the name of the days to: L-day (Buy), S-day (Sell), and SS-day (Short Sell). And this is where the system can get a little tricky. Today's L-day, due to rephasing, may be tomorrow's

S-day. Each time the 3-day cycle is rephased, the label on the days may be changed. The point is, *you* are frequently operating with incomplete information; why not let *the market* be the ultimate arbiter of the cycle?

Then there is the question of only taking certain measurements on certain days. In practice, since this is an inexact art, not a science, you need all the information you can gather. Why limit yourself to only measuring some rallies and some selloffs? Especially since you aren't sure at the time you take the measurement of which day you are in fact measuring! LSS takes into account all four key Book Method measurements (Taylor actually had more than four, but they were really the same measurements with different names on different days). Finally, where Taylor used zeros for negative numbers, LSS employs the actual negative number. For example, if the market fails to rally from an SS-day low to an L-day high (that is, the next day's high is *below* the previous day's low), don't you want to know how far under the low the high occurred? Where Taylor would call that a "zero rally," LSS calls it a minus one point (or whatever) rally.

As with Taylor's Book Method, the order in which the high or the low occurs is at the heart of the system. LSS attempts to *quantify* rallies and declines in order to provide trading envelopes within which prices are likely to stabilize. These key trading ranges are pivotal areas within which support and resistance should hold; when they can't, you should follow the move out of the envelope, either higher or lower. Moreover, the relation of the open to the target range dictates trading objectives. By having all the eventualities covered, the system immediately signals entry points, stop-and-reverse areas, and target objectives—all in response to current market action. (The system is currently being programmed to provide these real-time signals on a low-cost, real-time basis to users of the system throughout the country).

In Figure 14, the buy and sell envelopes are placed over the actual trading range of the September '83 Standard & Poor's 500 contract for August 31, 1983. You can see that the safest place to take a long position would have been right on the open on the low made first. Moreover, a move out of the buy envelope also presented another buying opportunity. The move into the sell envelope presented a good selling opportunity. Even with modest luck, you could have gained at least a point in profit ($500 per contract) during the first two hours of trading, using the LSS trading envelopes. And, had you held the position until the close, you could have made more than twice that amount!

Figure 14
SEPTEMBER '83 S&P 500—August 31, '83

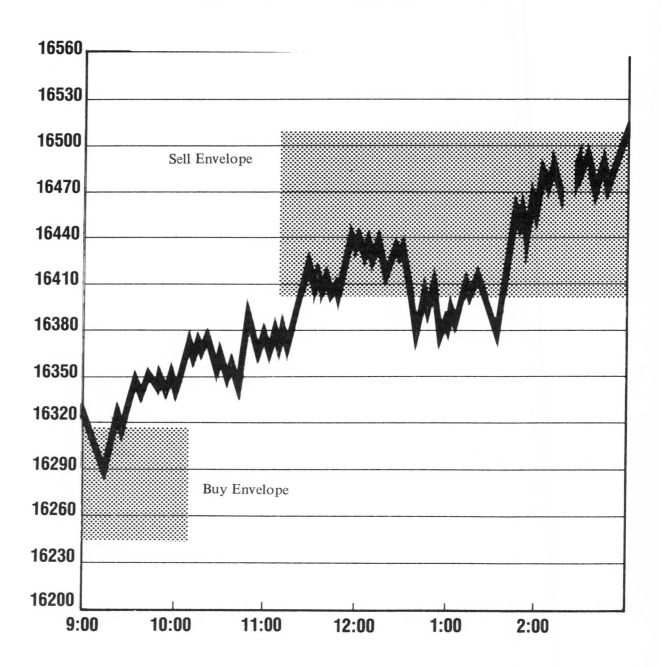

WILL THE SYSTEM SELF-DESTRUCT?

The most common criticism of trading systems, apart from whether they work at all, is that they will not continue to work once they become widely known. This is a misconception for several reasons.

Although a large number of users can put pressure on prices, the assumption is that everyone will want to buy or sell at the same prices. First of all, differences of opinion make the market. No matter how good a trading system, there will always be those doubters who won't follow its rules. Moreover, a consensus rarely exists, and, ironically, when there is a wide consensus on the general direction of prices, the next move is highly likely to be in the *opposite* direction. Second, the LSS 3-Day Cycle Method, while providing daily buy and sell numbers, also pinpoints areas of support and resistance—suggesting that followers of the system will place their orders at *different* prices. If anything, this is apt to make the system self-fulfilling—just as the number of Gann indicators are now. Third, fear and greed still move the market. The thinly-financed, small traders who routinely panic and generate price breaks in the process, will continue to do so, providing profits for the unintimidated. Finally, and this is the key point, the market is bigger—much bigger—than any one group of investors, no matter how well financed. The market will continue to do what it wants to do in response to the hopes and fears of millions of investors—not the few following this or any other trading system.

Even were a great many influential traders able to capitalize on seemingly "sure-thing" moves, the system remains flexible enough to "fade" even this majority. For as one trade didn't work and prices reversed, the system would automatically move your money to the other side. Timing, after all, is everything.

TIME AND PRICE

Did you ever sit in the back of a taxi in a traffic-clogged street with the meter running? Then you understand that you were paying not only for miles traveled, but minutes spent as well. This notion of time as a commodity is an important one for investors to understand. For unless a trading system can move you into the market at the correct time, you will surely find yourself in more risky trades with the meter running.

By quantifying, as well as qualifying, trading situations, the LSS 3-Day Cycle Method can improve your results. For instance, let's say a signal calls for selling short at a price of 162.50. If the market reaches that price only five minutes before the close, chances are it isn't going to make a very good day trade. The time of the day is vitally important to the success of a trade—especially a day trade. The LSS system, in order to deal with this question of time, calls for taking a trade within specific time parameters.

Moreover, once established, a trade must perform within a reasonable time limit, or the trade should be liquidated. The market is not always willing to oblige the system, however, in which case you must get out—or, perhaps, take the other side. It depends on the price action.

By creating a series of price zones, which we call buy and sell envelopes, the system pinpoints areas where the market should be purchased, sold, or left alone. Averaging, or the stock market technique of purchasing more on market declines or selling more into rallies, can be accomplished profitably in the stock index futures markets *within specific price zones.* But close attention must be paid to the subsequent price action. And, as always, if your trading is going to be consistently profitable, you are going to have to reverse and go the other way on occasion.

The conventional wisdom, such as you always want to buy low and sell high, is completely ignored by the system, since (although technically correct) it is often misleading. What, precisely, is low—or high? On a memorable Monday morning in April 1983, following the release of bullish Money Supply figures, the Standard & Poor's stock index futures market opened *above* the selling envelope—a sign of extreme bullishness. The point is, prices *seemed high* at that level; but the breakout on the open proved to be the *low of the day.* The system called for a buy up there, although the open was almost a point higher than the previous Friday's high. The rally was good for two points.

At other times, however, such a breakout will prove false, and the market will collapse. In such an event, the system is flexible enough to cause you to reverse and double-up positions. How will you know? Time. Time will pass and the rally won't come. At that stage, prices will fall of their own weight. Flexibility. It's the secret of market success.

Despite this type of information, investors will persist in asking, "Should I buy stock index futures?" If that's the question, the answer is no. For someone willing to withstand the uncertainty of the situation, the probable answer is, "It depends." For you, the crucial importance of a trading system is in helping you decide not *whether* you should buy or sell, but *when* to buy or sell. That's timing.

So we'd better talk about timing techniques.

THE TIMING DILEMMA

Timing is everything in the stock index futures game—or, at least, 99 percent of the game. But most trading systems rely on a reactive approach, in which case they are late in getting in the market, or an anticipatory one, in which case they are often simply wrong. What is needed for success is a system that is both reaction *and* anticipation. Let me explain.

If you rely on any trend-following method—moving averages are the classic example—you are, by definition, late in getting into the market. Trend-following techniques only signal a trend once the trend is, understandably, underway. A short-term trading method relying on such an indicator will invariably get you in the market at the worst possible time—typically, right when the market is about to go the other way.

Now suppose you have a system that anticipates price action but relies on recent trading history to pinpoint specific trades. What you would have is a system based on both anticipation of future events and reaction to past events. Such a system is the LSS 3-Day Cycle Method. It anticipates before an event occurs, yet it is flexible enough to shift direction in response to market activity. Why is this important? Because most of us, being human, want some reasoning for taking a position. Unfortunately, the evidence is often lacking at the time the trade is most appropriate. As a result, the best trades are missed, and often the worst are taken. Why? Because the market rarely *seems* to be headed higher when it is sitting on its lows or headed lower when sitting on its highs. This is the paradox of the market. Remember, the market is always the most bullish at the top and the most bearish at the bottom.

The LSS system removes the timing dilemma by providing you with the best possible estimate of where the support and resistance, based on recent price history, should exist. Moreover, it is flexible enough to update your analysis of the market during the trading day.

When most trend-followers are still watching the market—at the open,

257

which is often the statistically-proven safest point of entry—the trader following the LSS 3-Day Cycle Method is busy taking positions. Later, following the move of the trend away from the open, the LSS follower is already taking profits. Once the trend is underway, the trend may *seem* intact, encouraging traders to take positions. But, in fact, such trades are indeed precarious since profit-taking will probably create a short-term, if not a longer-term, reversal. You'd be surprised how often this precise scenario occurs.

PUTTING THE LSS SYSTEM TO WORK FOR YOU

Traditional stock market analysis involves such factors as price-earnings ratios, measurements of corporate sales, net earnings and debt, projected growth, market share, and the like. These factors remain at the heart of fundamental analysis in the securities market. But from a trading standpoint, stock index futures don't lend themselves to such an analysis, because an index contract is based on hundreds of stocks and because razor-thin margins make the volatility of index futures far too unstable to trust long-term indicators.

What is needed to trade index futures is a short-term technical indicator—one that measures immediate values and churns out instant analysis. Which is exactly where the LSS system proves so valuable. The trading system sets up two or three possible scenarios. It is the task of the trader to respond based on which one is actually played out.

Being anticipatory in nature, the system does the basic footwork for you. It identifies the day in the cycle, establishes the likelihood of the high or the low occurring first, provides the buying and selling zones—even tells you where to take losses and establish new positions on the other side of the market. You have to supply the money and the courage.

Let's look at an example. On any given trading day, the system provides a list of prices and other important data that can tell you where prices *should* encounter support and resistance; no system, of course, can tell you in advance precisely what the market will do. Because this information is drawn from immediate past price history, it is among the best available at the time. But the real task rests with applying the signals to the market.

At the close of trading on Tuesday, March 15, 1983, June '83 Standard & Poor's 500 futures had just completed a three-day cycle with the SS-day high being made last, having risen 2.75 points in three days. The next day in the cycle was the L-day (or Taylor's Buy Day). The strong signal, normally, would have been the low made first on the L-day. But because of the price action on the preceding trading day, the SS-day saw the *high made last*, the likelihood of the high being made first on the following day was a good one. The sell envelope numbers ranged from 152.50 on the low end to 153.20 on the high end, with the average right at the previous day's high, 153.00. An opening within this area on the following day would have generated a sell signal. Taking a clue from the previous L-day, three days previous, the rally from the open to the high of the day measured .60 points. The stage was set for a good selling opportunity.

On Wednesday, March 16, 1983, June Standard & Poor's futures opened down .55 points from the close at 151.90. Since the open was below the sell envelope, no action was immediately indicated, although a possible rally would indicate a sell and a possible decline would indicate a buy. The open was between the buy and sell envelopes. By adding the last rally from the open to the high on the previous L-day (.60 points) to the opening price, a possible sell target could be established. The target number became 152.50, right at the bottom of the sell envelope. Indeed, within a short period of time, prices traded up and through that target sell number—all the way to 152.80. It was early in the day, prices had rallied off a lower opening, and the trend of the day was about to get underway. The system called for taking short positions within the sell area—namely 152.50 to 153.80, 1.30 points higher. As the selloff began, prices soon slipped below the sell envelope and the move was underway.

Based on recent price history, the average day's range was about 2 points (2.15 over the past five trading days). Assuming the intra-day high made shortly after the open at 152.80 would hold, therefore, one could project that 150.80 would be the low. Moreover, the buy envelope consisted of numbers that ranged from 151.55 on the high end to 150.50 on the low end. The average was 151.20 and, again assuming the two point range, the projected low at 150.80 would be a viable buy (cover) area. Chances are reasonably good that profits could be taken in that area. But first, the trader has to assume the worst. What if the open proved to be the low of the day? Indeed, in that case, and assuming a two point range, prices would likely top out around 153.90. Thus, one had to be prepared to take losses and go long at the top of the sell range at 153.30. Fortunately, prices never went that high.

Instead, panic selling drove prices close to 4 points lower. As a result, the follower of the LSS system had an opportunity not only to cover and take profits in the buy envelope, but to sell short additional contracts as prices slipped *below* the buy envelope at 150.50. The low of the day was 149.10 and the close was 149.20.

Several important points should be made here. First, the safest time to take a position is generally shortly after the open. Although the open was somewhat below the target sell area, patience would have enabled a trader to sell short at very low risk. Second, never, never attempt to pick a bottom (or top), by purchasing (selling) contracts late in the day. Instead, go with the trend if it breaks out of the buy or sell envelopes. As you can see here, selling additional contracts late in the day would have resulted in additional profits. A cautionary note is called for here. These late inning sales should never be greater than the initial number of short positions. After the market has already sold off 2 points, chances are greater that you will see a rally—hence the risk is higher. Lastly, don't be upset with yourself if you only made 2 points on the initial short sale and called it quits on the day. You are trying to make consistent profits, not grab the whole range. Based on recent price history, the 4 point range was unanticipated.

TESTING THE WATERS

Ideally, you want to put on your positions in varying increments in the specific buy and sell areas. There is no rule that you have to put on all, or any, positions at a single price. Conversely, you should look to take off positions at different levels as well—just in case. In the example above, you might have sold on the first entry into the sell area and continued selling until prices slipped out of the sell area. Covering could have been done in the same manner, except you could have held onto one or two positions in the event prices indeed "fell out of bed"—as they most certainly did. This is just another way of saying, "I'd rather be safe than sorry."

You have to remember the psychology at work here. So many traders, having missed the initial move down, would have been saying, "Well, as soon as prices sell off a couple of points, I'll step in and buy the bottom." This is dangerous thinking, of course, but these late-in-the-day bottom-pickers, who, by the way, are very often locals looking for a quick bounce upward, think they have a very safe buy. But once proven wrong, the buyers provide a potent source of downward price momentum. By waiting, by watching their positions too long, these buyers often become panic sellers and drive prices to unrealistic levels. For the short-sellers, of course, this is an ideal situation. Just make sure you are on the right side!

Returning to the testing-the-waters concept, let's look at a day when the system doesn't really select the numbers too well. We'll look at Friday, March 18, 1983, a day I remember because I was visiting California and trading from the Los Angeles office of a broker-friend. The day was an SS-day, but the recent trend had been down and I expected the previous day's high of 150.15 in the June '83 S&P 500 contract to hold. The sell envelope ranged from 150.45 on the high end to 149.25 on the low end. The average target sell price was 150.00. I managed to sell a couple of contracts using market orders at 150.05. The intra-day high at the time had been 150.25 and I regretted not selling sooner, but I resolved to sell more if the high was again approached. It wasn't, at least not then. Instead, prices sold off about a point and then things went dead. A couple of very minor rallies followed. But prices didn't seem to want to go up or down. Instead, they stabilized in the 149.25 to 149.50 area. My target cover area, however, was another point lower—148.20—and I wasn't about to abandon ship simply because the market found temporary support. So I waited.

But soon a modest rally began, and then quickened. As prices soared back upward, I realized the time had come to bail out of my short position. No sense in giving back a profit—at least, what was left of the profit. So I took my profits and stood aside. And a good thing, too. June S&P futures sailed into new high ground, closing a point higher on the day!

At times like these, you have to be thankful with what you can salvage. Having overstayed the market to the downside (the initial deadness should have been a clue), I had to accept the reality of the situation; prices were headed higher—I had to run. Why didn't I go long? Looking back, I should have; but it was late in the day, and it was hard to believe the rally would continue with such power. As it was, I came out ahead a few hundred on the day.

WHEN EVERYTHING GOES RIGHT...

All this is just a way of saying, the LSS 3-Day Cycle Method, or any other system, is not always 100 percent on the money. But you do have those days, thankfully, when all the signals converge and a strong trade develops. One such day occurred on Monday, July 25, 1983, when the market had been rallying with some strength. It was an L-day in a bull market and the recent price action suggested the 3-day pattern was intact. During the previous cycle, the L-day low occurred first and the market had rallied, and subsequently taken out the highs on the following S-day. On the SS-day that followed, the high had occurred first and then prices had declined. One couldn't have asked for a smoother, more cooperative, cycle. So looking toward that Monday, one had a sense of a strong buy trade—the low made first and then up, up, up.

On the open, the market traded at 169.55, right at the bottom of the buy envelope. The time was ripe for buying. The market then traded down five ticks to 169.30 and held. No need for worry. Just hold on. Sure enough, the rally began. The target sell was at 171.75. The actual high was 172.10, just .35 points higher. It was a classic buy day in every respect. There was relatively little adversity and the numbers were hit in the proper order.

...OR WRONG!

Taking the same example, let's assume you mis-interpreted the open and sold contracts in anticipation of lower prices. After all, differences of opinions being what they are, the lower open might have appeared as the beginning of a sharp break. For whatever reason, we'll assume you sold S&P contracts. In time, the error of your ways would have been evident. What would you have done? Stayed with the position? Sold more contracts? Switched sides?

The first rule is, don't panic! Check the buying envelope and look for a breakout from the *top of the envelope* to justify becoming bullish. Typically, the breakout to the upside from the buy envelope is a confirming signal that prices will trend higher. Second, any penetration of new intra-day highs is a signal the shorts are wrong. Once the decision is made to take the other side, you must exit your short positions and undertake long positions. If at all possible, avoid buying on the sharp short-covering rallies. Wait for a selloff. This is the time to cover and go long. But don't expect prices to trade down to the old intra-day lows. They won't. Nor, for that matter, do you want them to; in fact, you want to buy a higher bottom, a sign that new buyers are coming into the market on the dips and supporting the higher bottoms. Keeping your wits about you, quickly calculate where the high of the day may occur. There are several ways to do this: establish the average range and add it to the intra-day low; take the anticipated range and add it to the intra-day low; or use a pattern recognition method. Then be prepared to sell into rallies as this number is reached. Having been wrong once, you want to take *more positions* on this second venture into the market and, as a result, you only need half the distance to recoup your losses.

HOW THE MOMENTUM TREND INDICATOR WORKS

No cycle will repeat endlessly, which brings us back to the Momentum Trend Indicator we spoke of earlier. When a market begins to rise, it will slowly shift direction from down to up, pick up momentum, begin to top out, and gradually shift direction to the downside—all in an endless, albeit sometimes confusing, pattern. The reason is simple enough. As the market rises, buying picks up and pushes the market higher. At some point, the balance between buyers and sellers shifts in favor of the sellers. The buyers are now prepared to take profits, and the cycle begins over again. Now suppose you had an indicator that told you, in effect, the downward slide is coming to an end, it is time to start buying; and vice versa. And then suppose the same indicator helped you select the right time to do your buying and selling? This would be a pretty useful tool, wouldn't it?

Exactly! And that's why I've incorporated the Momentum Trend Indicator into the LSS 3-Day Cycle Method.

The basic rule of thumb here is that *the momentum of a market is the key to price reversals.* When the momentum rises, up or down, the market will continue in the direction of the trend. When the momentum falls off, the trend will change.

Each day's Momentum Indicator consists of a single number generated after the close of trading. The formula for generating the number is as follows:

Today's close − close two days' prior = Momentum Indicator

The calculation will result in a plus or minus number. *When compared with the Momentum Indicator of the two previous days, the Momentum Trend will be established as one of the following: UP, DOWN, or SIDEWAYS.* Simply put, when today's Momentum Indicator is more positive than that of the two previous days, the Momentum Trend is UP; when today's Momentum Indicator is more negative than that of the two previous days, the Momentum Trend is DOWN; and when the Momentum Indicator is more positive than one day's and more negative than the other day's, the Momentum Trend is SIDEWAYS.

First, we'll look at an example involving the simple calculation of the Momentum Indicator. Remember, you use only closing prices in the calculation. A list of six representative closing prices and their Momentum Indicator numbers appears below:

Table 42
NEARBY S&P 500

Day	Closing Price	Momentum Indicator
1	152.45	—
2	149.20	—
3	149.35	− 3.10
4	150.35	+ 1.15
5	152.30	+ 2.95
6	151.10	+ .75

To make sure we are together, you should see that you understand how each number was established. For instance, the close on day 3 minus the close on day 1 (two previous days back) results in a negative number, − 3.10. On day 4, you subtract the close on day 2, to arrive at + 1.15, and so on. Once you have the current Momentum Indicator and two previous Momentum Indicator numbers, you can establish the Momentum Trend as follows:

Table 43
NEARBY S&P 500

Day	Closing Price	Momentum Indicator	Momentum Trend
1	152.45	—	—
2	149.20	—	—
3	149.35	− 3.10	—
4	150.35	+ 1.15	—
5	152.30	+ 2.95	UP
6	151.10	+ .75	DOWN

As you can see, day 5 received the UP Momentum Trend designation because the Momentum Indicator was *more positive* than the previous two indicators. But day 6 received a DOWN designation, because the Momentum Indicator was more negative—*even though the trend was still rising*. The point is, the *rate of the rise* was slowing.

Because this is a short-term indicator, the changes in the Momentum Trend can get quite choppy. In fact, as a general rule, no matter how bullish or bearish the market, you will rarely get more than four or five days without a change in the Momentum Trend.

The Momentum Trend Indicator has three important uses. First, it is used to rephase the cycle after a sharp rise or break in the market (or, for that matter, even after a period of considerable choppiness); second, it serves as a daily forecasting tool; and third, it provides a confirmation role for your other indicators. Let's start with the first use and treat them in order.

Rephasing the cycle. Because it is a measurement of the rate or speed of a decline or rally, the Momentum Trend Indicator is extremely valuable when deciding to rephase the cycle. In fact, the rule calls for rephasing the cycle *each time the Momentum Trend changes*. It doesn't matter whether the change is from UP to DOWN, DOWN to UP, SIDEWAYS to DOWN, UP to SIDEWAYS, or whatever. Each time the Momentum Trend changes, go back ten days and begin the count over again, starting with the lowest low and moving forward. The purpose of this is to insure that you regularly pick out the lowest low as the beginning of the three-day cycle.

Not to rephase the cycle, in this manner or another, only results in the possibility that a low made six months ago is still being used to pinpoint the current cycle. And, as we know, the likelihood of the cycle remaining intact over such a long period of time is extremely slim. Let's look at an example of how the Momentum Trend might help us to select a new cycle through rephasing.

Table 44
JUNE 1983 STANDARD & POOR'S

Date	Open	High	Low	Close	Momentum Indicator	Momentum Trend
April						
04 M	152.50	153.40	151.85	153.20	− 1.35	DOWN
05 T	153.70	154.20	151.35	151.75	− .15	UP
06 W	152.00	152.10	149.70	151.35	− 1.85	DOWN
07 Th	151.10	152.05	150.20	151.80	− .05	UP
08 F	151.80	152.15	150.60	151.85	+ .50	UP
11 M	153.10	155.20	153.05	155.10	+ 3.30	UP
12 T	154.95	155.70	154.15	155.60	+ 3.75	UP
13 W	155.25	157.20	155.25	156.35	+ 1.25	DOWN
14 Th	156.70	158.50	155.60	158.40	+ 2.80	SIDEWAYS
15 F	157.70	158.90	157.50	158.20	+ 1.85	SIDEWAYS

You should notice in the table above that there are three consecutive L-days. This is because each time the Momentum Trend change, the cycle is rephased and, based on the previous ten days' price data, the lowest low changed, thus influencing the three-day cycle. For example, starting with Monday, April 4 as an L-day, the following day should be the S-day. Instead, because the Momentum Trend changes, the cycle is rephased at the close on Tuesday April 5. Tuesday then becomes the L-day, because it made the lowest low of the ten days prior. The cycle then counts ahead in the three-day pattern—L-day, S-day, SS-day, and repeats. As the pattern develops, the Momentum Trend Indicator changes once again on Wednesday, April 6 from UP to DOWN. Taking the count back ten days

266

shows that the April 6 low is indeed now the lowest low. Hence, the L-day designation is given for Wednesday, April 6. If you look carefully at the numbers, you'll see why it is important to find this true trend. The third day up is indeed the high of the cycle: on Friday, April 9, the high was 152.15; on Wednesday, April 13, the high was 157.20; and, though it doesn't appear in the ten-day table, the third day up in the last cycle occurred on Monday, April 18 at 158.90. Since the market was rallying during this period, it is understandable that the 6-day lows were progressively higher. These were powerful buy signals, since you would have been buying higher bottoms.

There are times when the three-day cycle doesn't appear to work. For instance, when the market is breaking you are apt to have progressively lower bottoms, which may be accompanied by changes in the Momentum Trend Indicator. At times like these, you will have one L-day after another. Sooner or later, however, the market will stabilize and you will have an opportunity to again trade the cycle. Obviously, the system works better during normal trading ranges. But due to the stop-and-reverse money management strategy, you should have no difficulty profiting during times of quick rallies or declines.

Forecasting. We know how the Momentum Trend Indicator is calculated after each day's close. We know how to compare today's Momentum Indicator with the previous two days' in order to determine the current Momentum Trend. All this data is based on price history, on available price data. But what about forecasting tomorrow's trend? Would it not be possible to calculate where the market must close in order for the Momentum Trend to change? Certainly. By looking for a close within or close to a given range, we can see whether the Momentum Trend is about to change—and take appropriate action. In general, the assumption is made that tomorrow's Momentum Trend will be the same as today's. For example, if the Momentum Trend is SIDEWAYS today, we'll assume it is SIDEWAYS tomorrow. Obviously, this presents difficulties, since we know that the Momentum Trend can, and will, change frequently. But the assumption is the best we can make.

Now assume that we would like to know where the market must close in order to maintain today's momentum? The arithmetic is relatively straightforward. For the Momentum Trend to remain UP, today's number must be more positive than the previous two numbers; conversely, for the Momentum Trend to be DOWN, today's number must be more negative. And, of course, a SIDEWAYS Momentum Trend would have to fall within the past two numbers.

Let's take an example. In the table above, the Momentum Indicator number is +3.30 on Monday, April 11. This compares with a +.50 on Friday, April 8 and −.05 on Thursday, April 7. Hence, the UP designation. But assume it is now Monday afternoon and we are trying to decide whether the market has run out of steam. After all, nothing lasts forever, and the market has just had three consecutive UP designations. Very simply, we add one tick onto the +3.30 Momentum Indicator number and we add this number to the close on Friday, April 8. Why? Because by tomorrow's close (Tuesday, April 12), the Friday close will be two days previous. Thus, 151.85 plus 3.35 (one tick higher than the highest of the last two Momentum Indicator numbers) equals 155.20. What does this mean? That on Tuesday, April 12, a close above 155.20 will mean the Momentum Trend Indicator is still UP and that the market is still going up at a greater rate. In other words, look for higher prices still.

As you can see, not only did the market close above 155.20, gaining another UP designation in the process, but the close right at the high meant that the bulls were in command—or, at the very least, the shorts panicked on the close and covered.

The day would have gained a DOWN designation if the close were 152.30 or below (.45 plus Friday's close of 151.85). The .45 points were one tick below the most negative of the last two Momentum Indicator numbers. Lastly, a close between 152.40 and 155.10 would have seen the Momentum Indicator number fall between the two previous numbers, thus gaining a SIDEWAYS designation.

Confirmation. The Momentum Trend Indicator also serves as a confirmation tool by pinpointing the strongest possible trades. For instance, let's say you are looking for a place to buy stock index futures. You know the strongest possible trade will exist at the L-day low made first; the Momentum Trend Indicator will confirm that the market is still gaining ground at a faster pace, and hence provide you with the go-ahead signal. The strongest trades will occur on the *L-day low made first when the Momentum Trend is UP.* Looking back at our two weeks of representative prices, you'll notice in the first complete three-day cycle, from Wednesday, April 6 through Friday, April 8, the L-day Momentum Trend was DOWN and the market rose a total of 2.45 points over the three-day period. During the second three-day cycle, from Monday, April 11 to Wednesday, April 13, the L-day Momentum Trend was UP and the market rose a total of 4.15 points over the three-day period, an increase of 69 percent. Finally, during the third three-day period, prices were still rising, but at a slower rate. The L-day Momentum Trend Indicator for Thursday, April 14 was SIDEWAYS and the market rose only 3.80 points over the three-day period.

From a selling standpoint, the reverse is true. The strongest selling signal is the *SS-day high made first when the Momentum Trend is DOWN.* Comparing the SS-day high on Friday, April 8 with the one made on Wednesday, April 13, you'll see that in the first instance, when the Momentum Trend was UP, the market did not even decline from Friday's high to Monday's low. Indeed, Monday's low was higher. When the Momentum Trend Indicator was DOWN, however, on the following Wednesday, the market sold-off a total of 1.60 points from the SS-day high at 157.20 to the L-day low at 155.60; and, the daily range was even higher, 1.95 points. However, in neither instance was a strong short sale trade indicated since the highs occurred last on both days. But the use of the Momentum Trend Indicator as a confirmation tool does illustrate which was the better trade.

Taking a representative sample of SS-days when the high occurred first and comparing the results of the average daily ranges (from high to low) reveals that when the Momentum Trend Indicator was DOWN the selloff averaged 2.80 points compared to an average selloff of only 1.65 points when the Momentum Trend Indicator was UP, a decrease in profitability for the short sellers of more than 40 percent. As you can see, the Momentum Trend Indicator can help you select the most profitable trades.

MONEY MANAGEMENT

Stock index futures trading is a money game above all else. In almost every instance, the trader who has more money and is willing to risk it intelligently in the pursuit of profits is going to win *no matter how good the*

269

under-financed traders. Unfortunately, the implications of this statement are not very encouraging. "You mean the rich get richer?", you might ask. Precisely. Having said that, however, I'd also bet money that the trader who knows what he is doing, no matter what the size of his bankroll, is at an advantage over the uninformed—no matter what the latter's resources. So you indeed can win. The problem is, it won't come easy.

Now we hit upon the idea of being a selective plunger, as mentioned in Chapter 5, without spelling out any rules. Since then we've covered a lot of ground, much of it about finding those "sure-thing" trades when the probabilities are highest in your favor. But first we have to reiterate a few things about the nature of the game of stock index futures trading. Remember, it's a zero sum game. For you to win, someone else has to lose. On every trade, you can count on giving up the "edge," paying a commission, and, if history is of any value, ultimately losing on more than fifty percent of your trades. Sound grim? Cheer up. You only need to win on a relatively small percentage of your trades in order to make money.

To make sure the percentages work in your favor, *you must be willing to take positions of varying sizes.* If you trade just one contract each time, you are almost guaranteed a loss. I suppose it has been done, but I've never known anyone who made money trading the same number of contracts on each trade. Check with your broker on this score, and see if he can show you the actual P&L statements of someone who made money over time trading the same number contracts on every trade. The experience of most who've tried is to get their money slowly, but inexorably, ground-up. Remember, the futures industry supports an enormous working force—and it is all paid for by commissions, a little paid out on every trade.

If your bankroll is short, you have to start small at first; as you'll see in a moment, the margin kept in reserve may be needed. Moreover, even if you don't have substantial resources—and this is important—*you must be willing to trade as if you did!* What do I mean by this? Simply that you must be willing to do the folowing: one, take a larger number of positions when you think you are right; and, two, be prepared at all times to close out a losing trade and take the other side with a position twice as large. This is very, very difficult to do. But it is what will win you the gold ring. In a word, what is required is *courage.* Even a system as powerful as LSS just can't function without it.

Now, how do you acquire the courage it takes to trade aggressively? By doing it. You must understand that you won't be correct about every trade. The novice trader, especially, thinks he can somehow get into the market at the perfect time and sell at a profit. In practice, it doesn't work that way. Even the best traders have loss after loss; it is how you deal with the losses that will make you a winner. A loss is only a temporary setback; learn to love your losses and take them quickly and you will never find yourself in trouble.

Rather than recommend the number of contracts to take on specific trades, the LSS 3-Day Cycle Method calls for taking multiples of your minimum trading unit. Thus, if you are a 4-lot trader, you will take 8 contracts when you double up and 12 contracts on initiating the most attractive trades. For a 1-lot trader, the stop and reverse would call for first closing out the trade and then taking two contracts in the opposite direction. Three would be the maximum initial position for a 1-lot trader. Occasionally, however, the 1-lot trader might want to take on a more sizable position. But if you want to do it right, be willing to admit when you're wrong—and back your judgment with cash. Remember, we are talking about consistent day-to-day profits here. By using this approach, you shouldn't have more than one losing day in twenty, if that.

It is possible to make money on either side of the market virtually every day—*if* your timing is right. This is not to say that all trades are equally promising. They're not. In general, the idea is to test the market by putting on the minimum number of contracts on S-days, and any short positions on L-days or long positions on SS-days. The reason? These are all low-quality trades. The time to plunge is on the long side on L-days and on the short side on SS-days; taken a step further, these trades become even more promising if the Momentum Trend is UP on the L-day and DOWN on the SS-day. And if it is a known bull market on an L-day and the Momentum Trend is UP—well, that's better yet. The more confirmation, the stronger the trade. The stronger the trade, the more willing you should be to commit yourself. But remember: more often than not, you are going to have to commit yourself *before* the move gets underway. Buying or selling after the trend is underway will be much more risky, with a much greater likelihood of a reversal. Hopefully, I don't have to stress the importance of the open, catching the first move out of the opening range, and so on. The importance of these factors has already been stressed.

What about averaging, or buying more when prices decline? That's fine within reason. The conventional wisdom among futures traders, of course, says never, never average. But positions should be put on in steps until you reach the numbers you want. The important point is, the market must be within the buying or selling range and *holding* when you average on these positions. And, once you decide you are wrong, you must be willing to get out of the entire position without hesitating. Don't dwell on the losses. The market doesn't know—or care—about your position. Once the trend is clear, you must make sure you are on the right side.

Don't be unrealistic when it comes to profits. There are some days when you may be lucky to make a couple of hundred dollars; on others, there will be opportunity to make thousands. Give yourself an opportunity to make an important amount of money every day, but if it isn't there, get out of the market and wait for another day. Never try to force the market to move. But be prepared yourself to move if the signals come up strong. It may be weeks, or even months, before such an opportunity comes again.

Finally, remember your initial commitment dictates your ultimate level of trading. If you start out buying three contracts, your double-up-and-reverse strategy calls for taking six contracts (nine contracts, if you consider the three it takes to offset the longs). And, if this second trade doesn't work out, you may find yourself having to take twice as many again—or 12 contracts. Rarely, if ever, would you reverse more than twice.

Let's take an actual example of how this money management strategy might work in practice from the list of prices shown in the table below:

Table 45
SEPTEMBER 1983 STANDARD & POOR'S

Date	Open	High	Low	Close	Momentum Indicator	Momentum Trend
June						
22 W	172.90	173.85	171.60	171.75	—	—
23 Th	172.00	172.80	171.05	172.00	—	—
24 F	171.60	172.30	171.00	171.20	−.55	SIDEWAYS

272

I've purposely picked a difficult example. From the three days shown, you would assume the following Monday would see the low made first on the S-day and a rally. Based on the declines and rallies, one would look for support in the 170.75 to 170.95 area and for resistance in the 171.90 to 172.40 area—essentially, a retracement of Friday's price action. But this was not to be the case.

On Monday, June 27, the September S&P 500 opened at 171.00, just above the buy area. But before long, prices traded down and a contract (the minimum unit number) could have been purchased at, say, 170.85. After a brief rally to 171.15, prices broke lower and the purchaser of S&P contracts soon found himself in trouble. Assuming the worst, you might have given the contract ample room to swing—say, one point. Having purchased a contract at 170.85, you would then take the loss of one point at 169.85. At the same time, you would have sold two September S&P contracts short. Having lost one point on one contract, you would have sustained a loss of $500 plus commissions on the first trade. By doubling up and going the other way, your new breakeven point on the short sale was .50 points lower, or 169.35. Since the market traded all the way down to 169.00, you could at the very least have recouped all losses and commissions by covering in the 169.00 to 169.25 area. As you can see, this was hardly a great trade. But it does illustrate how you can protect yourself by taking losses quickly and going with the trend. With the low made last and the Momentum Trend changing from SIDEWAYS to DOWN, the market was ripe for further decline into the 167.00 area. The prices are shown below.

Table 46
SEPTEMBER 1983 STANDARD & POOR'S

Date	Open	High	Low	Close	Momentum Indicator	Momentum Trend
June						
27 M	171.00	171.15	169.00	169.55	− 2.45	DOWN
28 T	170.25	170.40	167.10	167.45	− 3.75	DOWN
29 W	167.40	169.40	167.00	168.90	− .65	UP
30 Th	169.65	170.20	169.10	170.15	+ 2.70	UP
July						
01 F	170.30	170.75	169.55	170.25	+ 1.35	SIDEWAYS

273

Tuesday, June 28. Having experienced one sharp decline below a support area on Monday, June 27, the pattern was set up for a repeat performance on Tuesday, June 28. This time the Momentum Trend was signalling lower prices, as was the Decline column. Because of the change in Momentum Trend from SIDEWAYS to DOWN on the previous day, the cycle was rephased and 169.00, Monday's low, became the new L-day. As a result, Tuesday was scheduled to be the S-day and a close below 168.70 (171.20 − 2.50) would signal another DOWN designation. The open at 170.25 presented an excellent sell opportunity and one could have easily covered a point lower for a $500 profit on the day. The rather brisk selloff toward the close presented additional opportunity. But the important point is to make the initial profit.

Wednesday, June 29. Looking back now, we can see that due to rephasing of the cycle, this was an excellent buying opportunity. The Momentum Trend turned UP, the low was made first—in short, an excellent buying opportunity. Unfortunately, we didn't know this at the time. Instead we anticipated (albeit incorrectly) an SS-day. But there were warning flags flying. First, Tuesday's close near the low suggested the *low would be made first.* In the absence of news, there was little to suggest the market would open much changed. Indeed, the open was practically identical with the close and some early selling left over from the previous day at first suggested the selloff would resume. Here was a perfect example of the market being taken lower in order to be taken higher as soon as the buying entered into the market. And where did it stabilize? Right at the previous low—right at the support where Taylor said it should stabilize. After all, in six days the market had lost almost seven points. It was time for a rally. The anticipated range was about 2.80 points. By taking the intra-day low of 167.00 and adding the 2.80 points, the new adjusted range showed a high of 169.80. In fact, it topped out at 169.40, just .40 points off that high. Even assuming bad fills and a complete missing of the bottom and the top, there was plenty of room to take out a point in the market.

Thursday, June 30. With the Momentum Trend UP, the reversal seemed complete but the higher open was deceptive, since the market would first have to close the gap on the open. Unless there is a drastic breakout to the upside, such opening gaps (the difference between the open and the previous day's high) are almost always retraced. On this day, the market sold-off following the open. The breakout also showed the "spring effect" in action; having been pulled apart, the spring had to first close or resume its normal shape. Moreover, the price action on this day illustrates the resistance becoming the support. With the open outside the sell or resistance area, the price action called for standing aside until the market reached some support near the previous high (resistance now became support). Because it is an S-day and because no strong trade appears, one should have only purchased the minimum unit near the previous high at 169.40. With any luck, the trade was good for .65 points.

Friday, July 1. After more than a week of waiting, the first really strong trade presents itself. With the bulls in control once again and a relatively fast rise off the bottom, the third day up usually presents a pretty good selling opportunity. With the market up, one should anticipate a new high being made first right after the open. Moreover, due to the previous day's close near the high of the day, you can expect the next day's high to be made first. Multiple units should be sold because the high made first on the SS-day is a strong signal. The system calls for selling short three units. With the open at 170.30—well within the selling range—you should start putting on short positions on any rally. An ideal way to do it would be to sell at 170.40, 170.45, 170.50, and so on; with any luck, you'll have a nice average selling price. Once the intra-day top is made and then holds, you have reason to believe you are in good shape. Because the range on the day was less than expected and because the market did mount another rally toward the close, the profits weren't everything they could have been. But you did make money—say, .50 points on one, .55 points on another, and .60 points on another for $825 in profits before commissions. With a three-day holiday ahead and prices closing near the high, there was just no way to predict the sharp break that would come on Tuesday morning, when the market opened 2.50 points down and declined another 1.25 points before the day was over.

Summary. From this brief glance at a week's trading, you can see there was really only one incidence were you would have been required to reverse and double-up. Every day yielded profits, if only relatively small ones, yet overall the small profits amounted to a couple of thousand dollars with only minimum risk.

THE MOST FREQUENTLY-ASKED QUESTIONS ABOUT LSS

In developing the LSS 3-Day Cycle Method, I gave a preliminary 1½ -day seminar in Los Angeles last year in order to detect investor reaction. For some, the daily calculations, while requiring less than five to ten minutes of time, proved a stumbling block. While the calculations are simple math, a number of traders prefer an instant analysis—one which is now available with the computerization of the program. For others, used to longer-term trades, the day-trading aspects of the system proved a drawback. While the LSS system can be used to pinpoint the best day to place longer-term trades, it is a short-term system by design. Frankly, the index markets, which are often up today and down tomorrow, seem ideally suited for precisely such a system. Commission costs were another concern. While I gave the seminar in cooperation with a discount brokerage house, my message was the same. *Keep your commission costs low. And trade like the professionals.* If the floor-trader population finds overnight positions too risky to handle, why should a novice trader with no experience in the market think long-term trading is the way to beat the market? It just seems so unwise to let a paper profit slip away because of the reluctance to pay a commission. Better to shop around and find a commission structure you can live with.

Ironically, the precise criticisms of the system seemed to rest with risk. The system is short-term in nature in order to minimize risk. But as soon as I impressed upon some individuals how important it was to control and manage risk, they seemed upset that such risk existed at all; why can't stock index futures trade like a blue-chip?

Finally, among a small minority, I found a reluctance to want to work for the money. They wanted an overly simple solution, a sure-thing approach, but most of all they wanted to, in what a friend of mine describes as a common phenomenon, ''believe''—believe, primarily, in an easy solution to a very difficult problem. I don't know anyone who works harder for the money than professional futures traders. Stock index futures trading is so competitive and so demanding that relatively few individuals are any good at it. Yet some investors want to be told they can make several thousand dollars a day without working!

Apart from these criticisms, I found a widespread acceptance of the ideas behind the system. After all, if the best minds in the country can't agree on the direction of the stock market, how can a trading system? It can't. But it can incorporate the sound trading strategies that you need to win. Despite advertisements to the contrary, do you really think anyone *knows in advance* what the market will do? A professional floor trader, who makes his living trading stock index futures, would be the first to scoff at such an idea. Indeed, these "true believers" are welcome down on the exchange floor precisely because their inflexibility makes them so easy to beat. *Knowing how to trade is the key to profits.*

Now, for the questions. There are a number of questions that come up over and over again, so it is probably best that I answer a few of them now to clear things up a little. Some are more technical than others, some are merely questioning the approach. But among the investors who have been exposed to the system, I find that the following are the most common.

Why Can't You Take A Position Overnight? Wasn't That Taylor's Original Idea Anyway?

"Of course you can" is the answer. It's your money, you can do what you want. You can even hold a position for a month-and-a-half if you wish. And, indeed, there will be times when this is the most profitable approach to the market. But for day-in and day-out trading, the LSS system is short-term in approach. Why? *Because it works!* Almost without exception, everyone I ever met who ever made a killing by taking a position and holding on, ended up, in the long run, losing. The reason? You have to withstand a lot of risk to trade long-term, and have a lot of capital behind you. And even this sometimes doesn't work. Stanley Kroll, who made a ton of money trading long-term, once answered the question, "What do you do when wrong?" as follows: "You go down with the ship." To avoid this fate, you should take short-term trades.

Why Is It Important To Double-Up And Go The Other Way?
Shouldn't You Bet Less When You Are Losing?

You want to make money *every day*. No exceptions. Since more than half of your positions will be wrong, you have to take action that will make you "right" even when wrong. Moreover, the stock index market, being quite volatile, tends to move one or two points virtually every day. Since there are only two directions the market can take, why not recoup your losses before the day's end? You'll feel better about yourself for winning, and your account will be far healthier as well. As for betting less when losing, yes, that is the general idea. But the percentages favor one side or the other, and, if you have selected the wrong side, the task is to reverse positions. One's ego should not play a role in these decisions. The idea is to make the money and get out. Lastly, by doubling up, you only need half the distance to make back the loss.

How Do I Know When My Position Is Wrong?
Sometimes You Just Can't Readily Tell
Whether Your Position Is Right Or Wrong.

There are several ways. First, a position must maintain a certain level—for instance, it must hold the envelope within which it is trading—for a trade to be considered viable. Second, unless you have a favorable movement within a certain period of time, you are usually better off getting out of the position, although this specific period isn't always easy to judge. Finally, let the market tell you what to do. If you don't have profits within a reasonable length of time, you are probably wrong.

Where's The Best Place To Sell Short?

On the SS-day, or third day up in the three-day cycle, on the high made first when the Momentum Trend is DOWN.

Can You Sell Short At Other Times?

Of course, you can sell short virtually at any time. But, remember, not all short sales have an equal percentage probability of proving profitable.

Does The LSS System Work Better With
One Stock Index Contract Than Another?
What About Options On Indexes?
Is The LSS System An Options Trading System?

The LSS system should work equally well with all three of the major stock index futures contracts. It is not intended as an index options trading system, although options may be used with the system to offset risk.

If The High Is Made Last On The SS-Day, When Do You Sell Short?

You should look to sell short on the following day, the L-day, on the high if it's made first. In this case, the cycle may be pushed forward a day. If the Momentum Trend Indicator changes, rephase the cycle and you'll see that it's changed.

What Are The Four Key Measurements Of The LSS System?

There are four measurements of rallies and declines. They are as follows:

1. D measures previous high to current low;
2. R measures previous low to current high;
3. BH measures previous high to current high;
4. BU measures previous low to current low.

How Often Do You Rephase The Cycle?
What Is The Procedure?

The cycle is rephased each time the Momentum Trend changes. Count back ten days and find the lowest low and then count ahead: L-day, S-day, SS-day, L-day, S-day, SS-day, and so on.

How Do You Tell Whether The High Is Occurring First On The Open?

You can't tell for sure. Rather, you have to make a judgment concerning the intra-day high at that point. If, after a trading range is established, the market seems to hold under the resistance, there's a good chance you have seen the high of the day. If the high is violated, however, look for higher prices and get out of short positions.

In Using The Pattern Recognition Method, How Do I Select An Appropriate Day To Use As A Pattern?

You look for as many similarities as possible. For instance, if you are trying to predict a pattern for an L-day when the Momentum Trend is, say, DOWN, you will look back in time for a similar day. Then you will measure the changes from the previous day...i.e. close to open, open to high, high to low...and try to predict tomorrow's price action. It is especially important to follow the predicted price pattern once you see that pattern unfolding similar to the pattern recognition day. Let's take an example. Assume we are trying to predict the price action on Thursday, September 29, in the December Standard & Poor's 500 futures contract. The prior day is an SS-day with DOWN Momentum Trend and price action as follows:

Table 47
DECEMBER 1983 S&P
SS-Day—Wednesday, September 28

Open:	170.20
High:	170.40
Low:	169.50
Close:	170.00

280

The pattern recognition day we'll select occurred on Thursday, June 23 in the September S&P 500 contract. On that day, the relationship of the SS-day to the following L-day pattern was as follows:

Table 48

SEPTEMBER 1983 S&P SS-day Thursday, June 23		SEPTEMBER 1983 S&P L-day Friday, June 24	
Open:	172.00	Open:	171.60
High:	172.80	High:	172.30
Low:	171.05	Low:	171.00
Close:	172.00	Close:	171.20

Taking the pattern recognition day, we develop the following relationship between prices on the SS-day and the L-day:

Table 49

Close to open:	− .40
Open to high:	+ .70
High to low:	− 1.80
Low to close:	+ .20

Now, going back to the current day, we can construct a possible price pattern for tomorrow's price action as follows:

Table 50

Current Day		Pattern Recognition Change			Predicted Price		Actual Price	
Close:	170.00	minus	.40	=	160.60	open	169.70	open
Open:	170.20	plus	.70	=	170.90	high	170.15	high
High:	170.40	minus	1.80	=	168.60	low	169.15	low
Low:	169.50	plus	.20	=	169.70	close	169.40	close

While the actual price fell short of the predicted price, you get the idea how pattern recognition works.

281

The LSS 3-Day Cycle Method

What Should You Do With Paper Losses?

Take them quickly. Never take a loss overnight. You must, of course, allow the market room to swing around the point you initially identify as a buying or selling objective. But once the market proves you wrong, you should take the loss. Never try to fight a market. While the system is not always right, the market is always right.

When Do You Take Profits?

When the selling and buying objectives are met. Following an L-day, you look to take profits slightly below, at, or through the L-day high on the S-day *if* you hold the trade overnight. As a general rule, however, you want to take day-trading profits at the buy and sell objectives. Once your objective is met, you should not hesitate to take profits on at least a portion of your positions. Remember, the system is based on taking "realistic" profits.

When Do You Take Profits On An L-Day?

When you have a rally up through the previous (SS-day) day's high. Speed is essential when the market rallies fast, because sharp selloffs frequently follow.

What Does The Decline (D) Column Measure?

The decline from one day's high to the next day's low. When there is no decline, a negative number will be entered into the column to indicate the extent of the rally from one day's high to the next day's low.

Should You Buy A Low Made Last On An L-Day?

No. Wait until the next day to buy the low made first. Typically, in this instance, the cycle will be pushed ahead a day.

On An L-Day High Made First,
Should You Sell Short After The Decline Begins?

You can, but it is a risky trade. Typically, you want to sell into a rally. If you already have profitable positions on, however, it is acceptable to later sell additional contracts as the market declines.

What Is The Typical Relationship Between
The Numbers In The Rally (R) And Decline (D) Columns?

When one is large, the other is usually small. In a sideways market, of course, the two will tend to be comparable, signifying what was gained in a rally was lost in a subsequent decline.

Why Are Market Objectives Placed At, Through Or
Slightly Above Or Below Previous High And Low Points?

Because previous highs and lows signify near-term support and resistance. The most recent support and resistance points, of course, are the most useful since the system is based on generating short-term profits. In addition, intra-day highs and lows are significant in selecting buy and sell objectives, since a new high signifies strength that the market didn't have when it made the last high—and the reverse is true for intra-day lows. Since the market constantly fluctuates, a preponderance of buying or selling can be anticipated at specific areas in the trading cycle. Since markets are apt to turn after making a new low or new high, this is precisely the spot where the trader must be cautious.

Assuming The Low Is Made First On An L-Day,
What's The Best Place For It To Hold?

Above the previous day's low. The reason is that this constitutes a higher bottom. And higher bottoms, by definition, are characteristic of bull moves. As a result, you are unable to buy a low made at the previous day's low when the market is in an uptrend. By buying a higher bottom, you often buy into a decline just prior to a sharp upward move.

What Does The Rally (R) Column Measure?

The gain in profits from one day's low to the next day's high. When there is a down move, the entry will be a negative number.

At What Times During The Trading Day Do The Big Moves Occur?

A significant move can occur at any time, although the open and the close tend to be among the most volatile periods of the the day. At times, on an up day, a market may hover around the low of the day for the entire trading session and rally only on the close. And on a down day, the market may bounce around the high throughout the session and only break lower on the close. Look for the previous day's low and high to be the key areas where support and resistance will occur.

What Do You Do If Your Buying And Selling Objectives Are Not Hit?

Stand aside. You don't have to trade every day in order to earn consistent profits. In fact, it is often better not to trade every day. The trades with the highest percentage probability of profits are apt to occur only about one day in three.

Does It Help To Watch The Tape?

Yes, if you know what to look for. You can often distinguish between a genuine rally and a short-covering rally by correctly reading the tape. You can also tell if a market is weak by knowing how to read the tape. Try to determine how the market takes new buying. Are the bids progressively higher? Or is each gain immediately followed by a lower low? A market will always rally and react. But the genius of tape reading is understanding what a particular rally or decline signifies.

What Is The Significance Of A "Flat" Or Weak Closing?

That the shorts are in no hurry to cover. Anticipate additional weakness the following day when you see a flat closing. If you see a flat closing about to occur, liquidate your position if you are long.

BEWARE THE PSYCHOLOGICAL PITFALLS

The most important aspect of any trading system is the person using it. Many systems work fine on paper, but once it comes time to take the trade, one's emotions often get the upper hand. Now, let's say you've done your homework and you're prepared to take the plunge once your numbers start coming up. The average trader is apt to stand aside and watch the trade slip away. Or worse yet, chase the market after the move is underway—and, inevitably, get whipsawed in the process. Don't let this happen to you. If you are going to give yourself a fair chance to win, make sure you are willing to do what you must.

Because the LSS 3-Day Cycle Method requires split-second decisions—often reversing one's position in the process—you are particularly liable to do the wrong thing by listening to your emotions. Don't. Just because you have a short-term loss, you shouldn't think of giving up. On the contrary, resolve to get back your losses, but do so in an intelligent way. Just as fear tends to rule when you have losses, euphoria tends to set in when you are on a winning streak. Chances are they will both be short-lived. For some reason, we tend to be most bold when we should be cautious and most cautious when we should be bold. Remember this: a trading system can provide you with signals, but you have to be the one to take the trade.

You've read this far and you may be slightly overwhelmed by the complexity of it all. But stock index futures trading isn't as complex as it may seem at the outset. My recommendation is to trade on paper for a while until you've gained the necessary confidence to try some of the suggestions in this book. Keep a running record of your trades. You'll be amazed at how easy it seems. Once you decide to commit your funds, however, be prepared for some difficulties to set in. It takes courage to be a good stock index futures trader. So if you win, rest assured, you've gone up against the best. Only then will you know that it has been worth the effort.

The LSS system is a viable, profitable system for profiting in the Stock Index Futures market. I've shown you a number of helpful tools and advantages. And what you've learned will be very helpful to your trading. However, you've only learned the basics of the system—the tip of the iceberg. I'm using the system in the markets now and certainly don't want to reveal the complete system to thousands of traders.

I will be teaching it to a select few interested traders. If you would like more information about the system, please contact my publisher, Windsor Books. The address is:

Mr. George Angell
c/o Windsor Books
P. O. Box 280
Brightwaters, N. Y. 11718

I'll only teach a few traders. But if you're even remotely interested you can send for free information on how to learn it. I wish you success with your trading.

APPENDICES

Appendix I
GLOSSARY

Aggregate Exercise Price—The index multiplier times the exercise price. For example, since the S&P 100 (traded on the CBOE) has a multiplier of $100, the aggregate exercise price at a strike of 170 is $17,000, or $100 times the quoted price.

Amex—American Stock Exchange. The Amex currently trades four index options: The Major Market Index, the Amex Market Value Index, the Computer Technology Index, and the Oil and Gas Index.

Anniversity Dates—Significant market dates occurring one year, or multiples of one year, following a major high or low in the market. Followers of W. D. Gann place special emphasis on these dates and look for new highs or lows to occur there.

Arbitrage—The simultaneous purchase and sale of the same or related futures contracts or index options in one or more markets in anticipation of making a profit through the price difference between the markets.

Asked—The price at which an index future or option is offered for sale. Also known as the *offer.*

At-The-Money—An option with an exercise price equal to or near the current underlying futures price or underlying cash index.

Basis—The difference between the price of the nearby futures contract and the price of the underlying cash, or spot, index price. For example, when the NYSE Composite Index nearby futures is trading at 94.35 and the underlying NYSE Composite Index spot price is 93.35, the basis is one point.

Basis Risk—The risk resulting from a change in basis while one is hedged in the index futures market while holding stocks. This risk cannot be hedged against.

Bear—One who expects lower prices.

Bear Spread—The purchase of higher-strike options and sale of lower-strike options on the same index in anticipation of declining prices. When done with calls, the spread is always put on with a net credit since the lower-strike options, trading at a greater cash value than the higher-strike options, are worth more than the options which are purchased. For the spread to prove profitable, the market must stabilize or move lower.

Bear Trap—A market phenomenon in which the market appears to be declining, prompting sellers to sell contracts, only to rally, trapping the unwary sellers.

Beta—A figure which measures the ratio by which a particular stock is likely to change price relative to a given move by the stock market as a whole. A beta measurement of one suggests the stock is likely to move in tandem with the market as a whole. Higher-volatility stocks will have a Beta in excess of one and lower-volatility stocks will have a Beta less than one.

BH Column—In the LSS 3-Day Cycle Method, the difference between one day's high and the following day's high. A positive number denotes a rising market; a negative number a lower top and declining market.

Bid—The current price at which buyers are willing to purchase index futures or options subject to immediate acceptance by a seller. A market will typically have a bid and an asked price at any moment of time.

Book Method—A trading system developed by George Douglas Taylor upon which the LSS 3-Day Cycle Method is based. The name is derived from the "book" in which Taylor made entries concerning market rallies and declines.

Breakout—The point at which prices penetrate a previous high or low on an intra-day or inter-day basis. Breakouts frequently accompany important market action to new high or low ground. Occasionally, however, the penetration creating the breakout is only temporary, in which case it is known as a "false breakout."

BU Column—In the LSS 3-Day Cycle Method, the difference between one day's low and the following day's low. It measures how far one can "Buy Under" the previous day's low. Positive BU entry numbers indicate lower lows; negative BU entry numbers indicate lows which hold above the previous day's low.

Bull—One who expects higher prices.

Bull Spread—The purchase of lower-strike options and sale of higher-strike options in the same index in anticipation of rising prices. When done with calls, the spread is always put on with a net debit since the lower-strike calls are more expensive. For the spread to prove profitable, the market must move higher. Often used as a proxy for an outright "long" call option position.

Bull Trap—A market phenomenon in which the market appears to be rising, prompting buyers to purchase contracts, only to decline, trapping the unwary buyers.

Butterfly Spread—A bull spread and a bear spread together, in which two options share a common strike price with a single option one strike higher and another single option one strike lower. Sometimes called a *sandwich spread*.

Buy Day—The first day in the three-day cycle in Taylor's Book Method. When the low is made first on this day, one has the strongest possible buy trade in the cycle. Corresponds to the L-day in the LSS 3-Day Cycle Method trading system.

Buying Hedge—Buying index futures to "lock-in" today's prices, while awaiting an inflow of investment funds or until stock selection decisions are made, to hedge against a rise in prices.

Call—An option giving the buyer the right to purchase the underlying index at the stated strike price within a given period of time.

Cash Settlement—A provision, unique to stock index futures and some stock index options, by which the buyer or seller simply pays or receives a cash payment. This cash payment would equal the cash difference in market value between the futures settlement price on the next to the last day of trading of the settlement month and the value of the *actual* underlying stock index at the close of the last trading day. All other gains or losses prior to the final trading day have already been credited to or debited against accounts under the daily mark-to-the-market procedure.

CBOE—Chicago Board Options Exchange. The leading listed stock options exchange in the country. In addition to listed stock options, the CBOE currently trades the popular S&P 100 and S&P 500 index options.

CFTC—Commodity Futures Trading Commission, which regulates the futures industry.

Class—All put and call options on the same underlying futures contract.

Clearing House—A non-profit, centralized division of a trading exchange which serves as a party to every transaction. The Clearing House settles all transactions through its clearing members, who must post substantial sums with the clearing fund in order to insure the integrity of every trade.

Close—The last one minute of the trading session, in which the settlement price is established.

Closing Purchase Transaction—A transaction in which an investor who is obligated as a writer of an option intends to terminate his obligation as a writer.

Closing Sale Transaction—A transaction in which an investor who is the holder of an unexpired option intends to liquidate his position as a holder. This is accomplished by selling an option of the same series as the option previously purchased. Such a transaction has the effect of liquidating the investor's pre-existing position as a holder of the option, instead of resulting in the investor's assuming the obligation of the writer.

Computer Technology Index—A new Amex index, having a multiple of $100, that tracks the performance of 30 leading firms in the computer industry.

Continuous Auction Market—A marketplace which provides a continuous process for holders and writers of options to liquidate their positions.

Contrary Opinion—A market theory based on the notion of doing the opposite of what the majority of the participants in a market are doing. Contrary opinion is particularly useful in pinpointing market reversals when prices become oversold and overbought, as measured by taking a consensus of traders.

Covered Writing—The sale of an option against a position in the underlying futures contract.

Credit Spread—A spread in which the value of the option sold exceeds the value of the option purchased.

Crescendo Effect—Momentary buying or selling resulting from a triggering of stops, usually just after the open. This phenomenon usually occurs just prior to a trend reversal.

Cycle—The months in which options expire. Can also refer to the time interval, as in three-day cycle, in which a futures contract or option index completes a repeated event.

Day Trading—Establishing and offsetting the same futures market position within a single trading session.

D Column—In the LSS 3-Day Cycle Method, the difference between today's low and the previous day's high. The column entry measures how far the market declined, from one day's high to the following day's low.

Debit Spread—A spread in which the value of the option purchased exceeds the value of the option sold.

Deep-In-The-Money—An option which has a large value because the stock index is substantially beyond the strike price.

Delivery—The process by which funds and the physical commodity change hands in the futures market upon expiration. In the stock index futures market, there is no *physical delivery,* only *cash delivery* since no real stock changes hands.

Delivery Month—The month in which settlement is to be made in accordance with a futures contract.

Discount—The excess in price that the actual index is over an index future.

Exercise Price—The price at which a call buyer can purchase an index option or the price at which a put buyer can sell an index option. Same as *strike price.* Exercise prices are standardized in order to provide liquidity. They usually bracket the cash index price, and new exercise prices are added as the underlying cash index rises or falls.

Expiration Date—The last day that an option may be exercised.

ast Market—When transactions in the pit or ring take place in such volume and with such rapidity that price reporters are behind with price quotations.

Fibonacci—Italian mathematician who formulated a series of numbers based on adding the previous two numbers, starting with one. Market days, based on taking the market count from previous highs and lows, are widely followed in the futures market by technical analysts.

Fill-Or-Kill Order—An order that must be filled immediately or cancelled.

Fundamental Analysis—Study of basic, underlying factors which will affect the supply and demand of the index being traded in the futures market.

Fungibility—The characteristic of total interchangeability.

Futures Contract—A standardized, transferable, legal agreement to make or take delivery of a special amount of a certain commodity or financial instrument of a certain grade or type at a specific point in the future, at a price determined at the time the agreement is made.

Gann—Brilliant, early 20th-century theoretician and analyst who formulated market rules based on laws of the universe.

Hedge—The limitation of risk by taking an equal and opposite position in another or similar market designed to offset losses. The most common type of hedge in the stock index futures market is the *short hedge* against a long stock position.

High-Balling—Bidding up the price of a futures contract in an attempt to generate stop-loss buy orders.

Initial Margin—The minimum margin required when an option is written or a futures contract is purchased or sold.

In-The-Money—When the market price of a futures contract is higher than the exercise price of a call, or lower than the exercise price of a put. For example, a call option with an exercise price of 155 would be in-the-money when the underlying futures or underlying cash index was trading higher (for example, at 160).

Intrinsic Value—That portion of an option's premium that represents the amount an option is in-the-money. Same as *cash value.*

IOM—Index and Option Market. The Chicago Mercantile Exchange's division set up to trade stock index futures and options.

Kansas City Board Of Trade—First futures exchange to offer stock index futures. Home of the Value Line Index futures contract which commenced trading in February, 1982. Prior to that time, it was known primarily as a grain exchange.

L-Day—The first day in the LSS 3-Day Cycle Method. Corresponds to Taylor's Buy Day.

Leverage—The use of a relatively small amount of money or an asset of nominal value to control an asset worth many times as much. In the futures market the leverage is often as high as 20-to-1, since a modest margin deposit enables an investor to trade a stock index futures contract worth 20 times as much.

Limited Risk—When applied to options trading, it means that the option holder can lose only the amount of his investment and no more.

Locals—Floor traders who trade for their own accounts.

Long—A position in which an investor, hedger, or speculator agrees to purchase the underlying stock index futures at the purchase price and stands to profit from an increase in value or lose from a decrease in value. Also, in the options market it applies to an investor who purchased a put or a call.

LSS—Long, short, short sell. The 3-Day Cycle Method trading system roughly based on Taylor's Book Method.

Major Market Index—A new index, traded on the Amex, that measures stock market performance through changes in the share prices of 20 leading ''blue chip'' corporations.

Margin Call—The request for the customer to deposit additional funds in order to restore the margin account balance to the initial margin level.

Margin—Funds deposited with a commission house to insure the integrity of every contract traded. Margin requirements may be changed to reflect an increasing or lessening degree of volatility, and hence market risk. An investor is required to post an *initial margin* which is larger than the *maintenance margin* he is required to maintain after a trade is opened.

Market Value Index—A new index based on the collective performance of over 800 issues traded on the Amex. The index is market weighted, which means the total value of the shares outstanding is taken into account when calculating the average.

Mark-To-The-Market—A process of crediting and debiting underlying gains and losses accruing from changes in the prices of futures contracts.

Mini Contracts—Smaller-sized index futures contracts. The most popular mini-contracts are the mini-Value Line futures traded at the Kansas City Board of Trade and the new S&P 100 futures contract traded at the Chicago Mercantile Exchange.

Multiplier—The number by which the index contract quoted value must be multiplied by in order to establish its total value. Typically, the multiplier is $100 for index options and $500 for an index futures. Thus, a NYSE Composite Index November 90 call quoted at

164.20 would be worth $82,100, or $500 times its quoted value.

Naked Writer—One who sells a put or call option without having a position in the underlying index futures.

Narrow Indexes—Sub-indexes which measure specific market segments. The Amex's Computer Technology Index would be an example.

Net Position—The net total number of contracts either bought or sold which have not been offset by opposite trades.

New York Futures Exchange—The NYFE (pronounced "knife") is a subsidiary of the New York Stock Exchange and the first exchange to trade index options and index futures side-by-side.

New York Stock Exchange Composite Index—A market-weighted average of the value of all the stocks traded on the New York Stock Exchange. The New York Futures Exchange trades options and futures on the NYSE Composite Index and the New York Stock Exchange trades options on the index.

Offset—Closing out or covering an open futures or options position by making an equal but opposite futures or options transaction.

Open Interest—Those contracts that had been bought or sold and are still outstanding.

Open—The period at the beginning of the trading session officially designated by the exchange, during which all transactions are considered made "at the opening."

Opening Purchase Transaction—A transaction in which the investor intends to become the holder of an option.

Opening Range—Price range of trades made during the opening of the trading session.

Opening Sale Transaction—A transaction in which the investor intends to become the writer of an option.

Option—A legal document allowing the owner to buy or sell a fixed number of shares of stock or a stock index at a stated price during a specified amount of time.

Overbought—A technical opinion that the market price has risen too steeply and too fast in relation to underlying fundamental factors.

Oversold—A technical opinion that the market price has declined too steeply and too fast in relation to underlying fundamental factors.

Parity—The point at which the market price of an option is exactly equal to its intrinsic value.

Pattern Recognition—A technical method of forecasting future prices by superimposing similar price patterns from the past onto future price action.

Pit—A specially constructed arena on the trading floor of the exchange where trading in a futures contract is conducted.

Premium—The cost of a put or call option. Also, the amount by which an index futures contract exceeds the price of the actual index.

Put Option—An option that gives the holder the right to sell the underlying contract at the strike price. The buyer of a put expects the market to decline.

Put Spread—Long and short positions in puts.

Ratio Write—An advanced option spreading strategy in which you sell more options than you buy.

R Column—In the LSS 3-Day Cycle Method, a measurement of the difference between one day's low and the following day's high. It measures the extremes of the range of two consecutive days, from low to high.

Reverse Conversion—A position consisting of a short futures contract, a long call and a short put.

Reverse Hedge—A strategy in which you purchase calls on more shares than you have sold short. Also known as *simulated straddle*.

Reverse Strategy—Any strategy which is the reverse of a better known strategy. For example, a ratio spread consists of buying calls at a lower strike and selling more calls at a higher strike. A reverse ratio spread consists of selling the calls at the lower strike and buying more calls at the higher strike.

Rolling Down—Buying a particular option and selling one with the same expiration but a lower strike price.

Rolling Out—A strategy in which you buy in the option you previously sold and sell another option at the same strike price with a longer duration. Also known as *rolling over*.

Rolling Up—Buying in an option you previously sold and selling one with the same expiration date but a higher strike price. This is typically done when the market has risen in price.

Round-Turn—Refers to both a purchase and a sale, although not necessarily in that order, when you trade index options or futures. Usually refers to a *round-turn commission*, meaning you pay just one price to buy and sell.

Rule Of Three—A general rule that places the breakout point prior to the resumption of a trend at the third attempt to penetrate support or resistance.

Scalper—One who trades the market for very small profits. Usually a floor trader, also known as a *local*.

S-Day—In the LSS 3-Day Cycle Method, the second day of the three-day cycle.

SEC—Securities & Exchange Commission, which regulates the securities industry.

Sell Day—In Taylor's Book Method, the second day of the three-day cycle. Taylor maintained that long positions that had been initiated on the previous day, the Buy Day, and held overnight should be liquidated on the Sell Day and no new positions taken. The target sell area was at, through, or slightly below the previous day's high. Same as the S-day in the LSS system.

Selling A Spread—A spread transaction that begins with a net receipt of money by the spreader. Also known as a *credit spread* or *bear spread*.

Series—Options of the same class, having the same exercise price and expiration month.

Settlement—The official final closing price of the day. Also refers to how a futures contract is delivered. All index futures have a cash settlement provision.

Short—The selling of an open option or futures contract. To be short an option, futures contract or stock means to owe it to someone else. Whereas the investor who is long buys a security and then sells it, hopefully for a higher price, the short seller sells the security first, and then buys it back later, hopefully for a lower price.

Short Sell Day—In Taylor's Book Method, the third day of the three-day cycle.

Specific Stock Risk—Risk resulting from changes in fundamental factors affecting a particular company or industry.

Speculator—One who is willing to assume greater than normal risks in pursuit of a capital gain.

Spot Price—The current market price of the cash index. Also known as *cash price*.

Spread—Being both long and short one or more futures or options of the same index or related indexes. A popular *inter-market spread* would be long one March S&P 500 futures and short one March Value Line Index futures. *Inter-delivery spreads* consist of long and short futures of the same index, but in different trading months. For example, long one March NYSE Composite Index futures and short one June NYSE Composite Index futures would be an *inter-delivery spread*. Spreads are popular because they often serve to limit risk and can be traded with lower margin requirements.

SS-Day—In the LSS 3-Day Cycle Method, the third day of the three-day cycle.

Standard & Poor's 500 Stock Index—A market value weighted stock index, first introduced in 1957. Since April 1982, a futures contract based on the S&P 500 has been traded on the Chicago Mercantile Exchange. The S&P futures is currently the most popular index ever traded.

Stock Index Future—A futures contract pegged to a stock market average.

Stock Market Index—A measure of either price level or the average change in prices of the stocks included in a particular index, measured from some base period values.

Straddle—The purchase or sale of both a put and a call having the same exercise price and expiration date.

Strike or Striking Price—The price at which an option may be exercised. Also known as *exercise price.*

Sub-Indexes—Indexes which measure specific market segments, such as financial, utility, transportation and energy stocks. The Amex's Computer Technology Index is a sub-index. Same as *narrow index.*

Systematic Risk—Pertains to risks associated with the stock market as a whole, such as those risks associated with a decline in the broad market averages. It is this type of risk that stock index futures can hedge against.

Taylor, George Douglas—The originator of the "Book Method," upon which the LSS 3-Day Cycle Method is based.

Technical Analysis—An approach to analysis of futures and stock markets which examines patterns of price change, rates of change, and changes in volume of trading and open interest.

Theoretical Value—The price of an option, or a spread, as computed by a mathematical model.

Time Spread—The purchase and sale of two options covering the same futures contract with the same exercise price, but different expiration dates.

Time Value—Value remaining in an option due only to the remaining time to expiration. An out-of-the-money option only has time value. This compares with in-the-money options, whose premiums' reflect both time and cash value.

Trading Range—A narrow band within which prices trade, characterized by resistance at the top of the range and support at the bottom of the range. Prices usually make substantial moves once they break out of a trading range.

Transaction Costs—Consists primarily of commission costs, but may include margin and interest costs under certain circumstances.

Underlying Security—The security which one has the right to buy or sell according to the terms of a listed option contract.

Value Line Stock Index Futures—The first stock index futures introduced. Traded at the Kansas City Board of Trade, the Value Line Index futures, based on the Value Line Index, is comprised of both second-tier and blue-chip stocks. The Kansas City Board of Trade offers both the large Value Line Index futures contract, currently valued at close to $100,000, and a smaller mini-contract which is one-fifth the size of the larger one, or about $20,000. The Value Line contract enjoys the reputation as the most volatile of the three major stock index futures.

Vertical Spread—A spread between options with different strikes but the same maturity dates. The vertical spread can be a bullish or bearish spread, depending upon which strike-priced option is purchased and which is sold.

Writer—The grantor or seller of an option.

Appendix II
TRADING INFORMATION

STOCK INDEX FUTURES

VALUE LINE INDEX

Exchange—Kansas City Board of Trade (KCBT)

Trading Hours—10:00 AM to 4:15 PM (NYT)

Index—Equally weighted average of 1683 NYSE, AMEX, OTC and regional stock prices

Trading Symbol—KV MV (mini)

Contract Size and Value—$500 x the Value Line Index

Contract Months—March, June, September, December

Fluctuations (Tick size & value)—Minimum .05 = $25 or 1.00 = $500 (mini) .05 = $5 or 1.00 = $100

Daily Price Limits—None

Last Day of Trading—Last business day in settlement month

Settlement Day—Business day after last trading day in settlement month

Settlement—Cash settlement mark-to-market based on the Value Line Index at the close of the last day of trading.

NYSE COMPOSITE INDEX

Exchange—New York Futures Exchange (NYFE) of the New York Stock Exchange

Trading Hours—10:00 AM to 4:15 PM (NYT)

Index—Total value of NYSE Market: 1505 listed common stocks weighted to reflect market value of issues

Trading Symbol—YX

Contract Size and Value—$500 x the NYSE Composite Index

Contract Months—March, June, September, December

Fluctuations (Tick size & value)—Minimum .05 = $25 or 1.00 = $500

Daily Price Limits—None

Last Day of Trading—Business day prior to last business day in settlement month

Settlement Day—Last business day in settlement month

Settlement—Cash settlement is based on the difference between the settlement price on the next to last day of trading and the value of the NYSE Composite Index at the close of trading of the New York Stock Exchange on the last day of trading (to the nearest .01).

STOCK INDEX FUTURES

S&P 500 INDEX

Exchange—Index and Options Market (IOM)

Trading Hours—10:00 AM to 4:15 PM (NYT)

Index—Value of 500 selected stocks

Trading Symbol—SP

Contract Size and Value—$500 x the S&P 500 Index

Contract Months—March, June, September, December

Fluctuations (Tick size & value)—Minimum .05 = $25 or 1.00 = $500

Daily Price Limits—None

Last Day of Trading—Third Friday of settlement month

Settlement Day—Business day after last trading day in settlement month

Settlement—Cash settlement mark-to-market at closing value of the actual S&P 500 Index on settlement day.

S&P 100 INDEX

Exchange—Chicago Mercantile Exchange (CME)

Trading Hours—Same as S&P 500

Index—Value of 100 selected stocks

Trading Symbol—SX

Contract Size and Value—$200 x the S&P 100 Index

Contract Months—Same as S&P 500

Fluctuations (Tick size & value)—Minimum .05 = $10 or 1.00 = $200

Daily Price Limits—None

Last Day of Trading—Third Friday of settlement month

Settlement Day—Business day after last trading day in settlement month

Settlement—Cash settlement. Marked to the actual closing value of S&P 100.

FUTURES OPTIONS

NYSE COMPOSITE INDEX

Contract—Call and put options on one NYSE Composite Index Futures Contract

Price Quotation—Same as NYSE Composite Index; .05 = $25, or 1.00 = $500

Contract Months—March, June, September, December

Trading Hours—10:00 AM to 4:15 PM (NYT)

Price Fluctuations (Tick size)—.05

Strike Price Intervals—Integers evenly divided by two (e. g. 82.00, 84.00)

Price Limits—None

Last Day of Trading—The last day of the underlying NYSE Composite Index Futures Contract (business day prior to last business day in contract month)

Expiration Day and Time—4:00 PM on the last day of trading

Exercise—Open puts and calls in index options may be exercised on any Exchange business day during the life of the contract by notifying the New York Futures Clearing Corporation by 6:00 PM EST on that day. A long call (put) that is exercised receives a long (short) position in the underlying futures contract, whereas a short call (put) receives a short position (long) position in the underlying futures contract, both at the strike price of the options contract. (Exercises on the final day of trading result in cash settlement rather than assignment on the futures position). All in-the-money options are automatically exercised on the last day of trading.

Margin—The purchase of long option positions requires the full payment of the premium in cash. Consult your broker for details on margin requirements for short option positions.

S&P 500 INDEX

Contract—Call and put options on one S&P 500 Index Contract

Price Quotation—Same as S&P 500 Index; .05 = $25, or 1.00 = $500

Contract Months—March, June, September, December

Trading Hours—10:00 AM to 4:15 PM

Price Fluctuations (Tick Size)—.05

Strike Price Intervals—5.00-point intervals in integral multiples of 5.00 (e. g., 100.00, 105.00, 110.00, 115.00)

Price Limits—None

Last Day of Trading—Third Thursday of settlement month

FUTURES OPTIONS

S&P 500 INDEX (CONT'D.)

Expiration Day and Time—4:00 PM on the last day of trading

Exercise—Any Exchange business day during life of contract by notifying CME Clearing Corporation.

Margin—Payment in cash for all long positions. Consult broker for margin on short positions.

S&P 100 INDEX

Contract—Call and put on S&P 100

Price Quotation—Same as S&P 100 Index; .05 = $10 or 1.00 = $200

Contract Months—Same as S&P 500

Trading Hours—Same as S&P 500

Price Fluctuations (Tick size)—.05

Strike price Intervals—Same as S&P 500 options

Price Limits—Same as S&P 500 Index

Last Day of Trading—Same as S&P 500 Index

Expiration Day and Time—Same as S&P 500 Index

Exercise—Same as S&P 500 Index

Margin—Same as S&P 500 Index

INDEX OPTIONS

THE MAJOR MARKET INDEX

Contract—Major Market Index—based on 20 leading blue-chip stocks

Price Quotation—Same as stock option premiums; a quote of 1 represents $100; a quote of 1¾ represents $175; and so on

Contract Months—MMI options are traded on a January-April-July-October cycle with 3 of the expiration months available at any one time

INDEX OPTIONS

THE MAJOR MARKET INDEX (CONT'D.)

Trading Hours—10:00 AM to 4:10 PM

Price Fluctuations (Tick size)—MMI options trading at prices up to 3 will trade in sixteenths; over 3, they'll trade in eighths

Strike Price Intervals—At 5-point intervals bracketing the current index level. New strike prices are added as the Index moves

Price Limits—None

Last Day of Trading—The third Friday of the expiration month

Expiration Day and Time—The Saturday following the third Friday of the expiration month. Options must be exercised by 4:10 PM on the third Friday of the expiration month.

Exercise—The call or put holder who exercises is entitled to receive the difference between the option's aggregate exercise price (exercise price x $100) and the closing index value (index number x $100) as of the day the exercise notice is tendered. Settlement occurs on the following day.

Margin—Payment in cash for all long positions.

THE AMEX MARKET VALUE INDEX

Contract—Amex Market Value Index—based on the collective performance of over 800 issues traded on the Amex

Price Quotation—Same as stock option premiums (see above)

Contract Months—March, June, September and December

Trading Hours—10:00 AM to 4:10 PM

Price Fluctuations (Tick size)—In sixteenths up to 3; over 3, in eighths

Strike Price Intervals—Strike prices are 10 points apart. New strikes will be added as the Index moves.

Price Limits—None

Last Day of Trading—The third Friday of the expiration month

Expiration Day and Time—The Saturday following the third Friday of the expiration month. Instructions to exercise must be given no later than 4:10 PM (Eastern time), and a time-stamped record of the instructions must be kept. Exercise settlement occurs the business day after the exercise notice is tendered.

INDEX OPTIONS

THE AMEX MARKET VALUE INDEX (CONT'D.)

Exercise—Settlement is based on the difference between the strike price and the closing value of the index on the day the exercise notice is submitted to The Options Clearing Corporation.

Margin—Payment in cash for all long positions. Margin requirements for put and call writers is based on whether the option is in-or-out-of-the-money at the time the option is written. Margin, in general, is based on the current premium plus 10% of the current Index value.

THE COMPUTER TECHNOLOGY INDEX

Contract—Computer Technology Index—based on a cross-section of 30 widely-held computer stocks

Price Quotation—Dollars per equivalent "share"

Contract Months—March, June, September and December[*]

Trading Hours—10:00 AM to 4:10 PM

Price Fluctuations (Tick size)—In sixteenths up to 3; over 3, in eighths

Strike Price Intervals—At 5-point intervals bracketing the current value of the Computer Technology Index. New exercise prices will be added when the current value of the Index touches an existing strike.

Price Limits—None

Last Day of Trading—The third Friday of the expiration month

Expiration Day and Time—The Saturday following the third Friday of the expiration month. Options must be exercised by 4:10 PM on the third Friday of the expiration month.

Exercise—Settlement is based on the difference between the strike price and the closing value of the Index on the day the exercise notice is submitted to The Options Clearing Corporation.

Margin—Payment in cash for all long positions. For writers, the margin is the same as it is for "uncovered" stock options writers—30% of the current Index value (Index number x 100) plus or minus the amount by which the option is in- or out-of-the-money, with a minimum of $250 per contract.

---

*A current proposal would change the expiration cycles of all Amex Index options to monthly expirations.

INDEX OPTIONS

THE OIL AND GAS INDEX

Contract—Oil and Gas Index—based on a cross-section of 30 widely-held oil and gas stocks

Price Quotation—Dollars per equivalent "share"

Contract Months—March, June, September and December

Price Fluctuations (Tick size)—In sixteenths up to 3; over 3, in eighths

Strike Price Intervals—At 5-point intervals bracketing the current value of the Oil and Gas Index. New exercise prices will be added when the current value of the Index touches an existing strike

Price Limits—None

Last Day of Trading—The third Friday of the expiration month

Expiration Day and Time—The Saturday following the third Friday of the expiration month. Options must be exercised by 4:10 PM on the third Friday of the expiration month.

Exercise—Settlement is based on the difference between the strike price and the closing value of the Index on the day the exercise notice is submitted to The Options Clearing Corporation.

Margin—Payment in cash for all long positions. For writers, same as requirements for The Computer Technology Index.

Appendix III
THE 30 STOCKS THAT COMPRISE
THE COMPUTER TECHNOLOGY INDEX

Amdahl
Automatic Data Processing
Burroughs
Commodore International
Computer Sciences
Control Data
Cray Research
Data General
Datapoint
Digital Equipment
Electronic Data Systems
Hewlett-Packard
IBM
Lanier Business Products

Mohawk Data Sciences
Motorola
National Semiconductor
NBI, Inc.
NRC Corporation
Paradyne
Prime Computer
Sperry Corporation
Storage Technology
Tandy
Telex
Texas Instruments
Wang Laboratories, Cl. B
Xerox

Appendix IV
THE 30 STOCKS THAT COMPRISE
THE OIL AND GAS INDEX

Amerada Hess
Apache Corporation
Atlantic Richfield
Dorchester Gas
Exxon Corporation
Getty Oil
Gulf Oil
Inexco Oil
Kerr McGee
Louisiana Land
Mesa Petroleum
Mobil Corporation
Natomas
Noble Affiliates
Occidental Petroleum

Pennzoil
Phillips Petroleum
Pogo Producing
Royal Dutch Petroleum
Sabina Corporation
Shell Oil
Standard Oil of California
Standard Oil of Indiana
Standard Oil of Ohio
Sun Company
Superior Oil
Texaco
Texas Oil and Gas
Tosco Corporation
Unocal Corporation

Granada

Ruby of Al-Andalus

susaeta

Intricate and delicate, marquetrywork is one of the greatest expressions of Granada artisan decorative art.

Edited by:
Thema, Equipo Editorial, S.A.

Photography by:
Marc Llimargas

Translated by:
Carole Patton

© SUSAETA EDICIONES, S.A.
Campezo, s/n - 28022 Madrid
Tel. 913 009 100 - Fax 913 009 118

S. MIGUEL ARCANGEL

Light and colour, wrought iron and ferns, form the spirit of a city full of history and life.

Contents

Granada

Ruby of Al-Andalus

"Give him alms, lady,
Since there cannot be anything
worse in life than to be blind
in Granada"

Francisco de Icaza (inscription on a tile of the Pólvora Tower, the Alhambra)

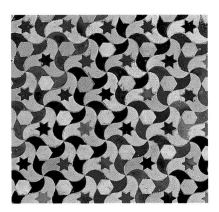

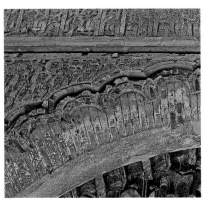

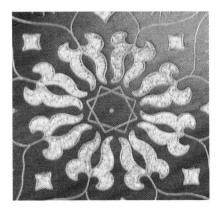

Colours
Colours sustaining figures which softly evoke the firmament.

Lines
Lines and squares are a testimony of spiritual harmony.

Writings
Cufic writing on the walls reminds us of God's omnipresence.

Strokes
Repeated strokes may depict Infinity as a representation of the Creator.

Motifs
Plant ornamentation is only an aesthetical interpretation of Nature.

Composition
The composition of ornamental motifs refers to the order of the Universe.

Belfries towering above the trees
in the Darro district.

Granada

Ruby of Al-Andalus

CITY OF LEGEND
Elvira

Granada, enclaved in the red-coloured foothills of the *Sierra Nevada* mountain range, appears shimmering like a precious stone amid the intense greenery of the fertile plain, at the point where the rivers Genil and Darro meet. Towards the 6th century BC, an ancient Iberian settlement called *Ilbyr* already existed in the hills where the Albaicín is today. Its inhabitants traded with Greeks and Phoenicians, who, at that time had already established factories along the Mediterranean coast. In time, the ambition of the Phoenicians from Carthage extended throughout the Iberian Peninsula and *Ilbyr* fell to them.

Paseo de los tristes

Looming up out of the wooded riverbank of the Darro is the *Alhambra*, the other side leading uphill to the *Sacromonte* district.

Calle Madrasa

This multicoloured street of the lower part bears the name of the universality created in the 14th century by Yusuf I, the Nasrite king who fought many battles against the Castilian king Alfonso XI. The *Madrasa* of Granada was the first centre of advanced Muslim studies in the West.

The Generalife

This is a splendid palace from the beginning of the 14th century. Its builder, Aben Walid Ismaíl, delighted Nasrite sovereigns and their court with this delicious blend of shade and water.

The Alhambra

The shape of the arches and their ornamentation bear the mark of Nasrite master builders.

This was how this little mountain village got involved in the terrible Punic Wars between Carthaginians and Romans. The victory of the imperial legions led to the fortification of the settlement, which was now called *Iliberis* or *Elvira*, name which appears on coins belonging to that period of the first century of the Christian era, when it now showed signs of becoming a city. Though it was administratively dependent on *Astigi*, Écija, the Christians chose *Iliberis* as the place to hold their first Council in Hispania in the 4th century. On the fall of the Roman Empire, the Visigoths occupied the foothills where the city stood and built new walls, some of which would later be used by the Arabs to build the *Alcazaba*, the primitive nucleus of the *Alhambra*. However, the city that developed with the Moors did not keep this name, but took that of a neighbouring village with which it ended up joining.

The Rich Legacy of the Jews

When the Moors invaded the Peninsula in the 8th century, the settlement was occupied for a long time, during which it appeared that nothing was going to change its destiny. However, in 1009, the *fitna* broke out, an Arabic term meaning "civil war", and the Berber rising against the Caliph of Cordoba made the inhabitants of *Iliberis* move to a nearby Jewish settlement on

Patio de los leones
This emblematic space of the *Alhambra* palace formed the most private part of the royal apartments. Built during the reign of Muhammad V al-Gani, who sought peace and solace here, a place which helped him bear his long and troubled reign, between 1354 and 1391.

The Alhambra
The *Sala del Mexuar*, finished in 1365, is where the Nasrite king met his advisers and listened to his subjects' petitions.

the other side of the River Darro, called *Garnatha Alyejud*. From the point where the current district of *San Matías* is located, at the foot of *Torres Bermejas*, the Jewish settlement occupied by the Moors began to extend rapidly, and within a few years ended up joining the old city and imposing its name: Granada. And this was where, in 1013, after the fall of the Caliphate of Cordoba, the Berber Zawí ben Zirí established the capital of a *taifa* kingdom, whose territory included the current provinces of Granada and Málaga.

Ziries, Almoravides and Almohades ruled the kingdom until 1237, when Muhammad ibn Yusuf ibn Ahmad Nasr seized the throne and founded the Nasrite Dynasty, which was going to turn Granada into the most beautiful and populous city of Al-Andalus. Under the reign of Muhammad al-Ahmad, name by which the first Nasrite monarch was also known, the kingdom of Granada extended its domains as far as what today is Almería, and became refuge to Muslims who fled from the progressive advance of Christian armies.

These Moors contributed decisively to the magnificence of the kingdom through their farming techniques, which they applied to the rich fertile plains of the River Genil, wisely using its waters for irrigation, as well as artisan and trading methods, the *Alcaicería* soon becoming a busy centre of trade. The silk and textile industries, which included those of cotton, linen, goat hair and woollen cloth, and a prosperous trade of exquisite and costly products, to which the intense traffic of gold between Sudan and Europe also contributed decisively, were the main sources of a long period of prosperity. During this age of splendour, the Nasrites promoted arts and sciences and built splendid palaces such as *La Alhambra* and *El Generalife*.

The Moor's Sigh

The decadence of the Nasrite kingdom began at the beginning of the 15th century, when court intrigues started to undermine sovereign power and the pressure of Christian armies became

Albaicín

The steep, narrow streets of the *Albaicin* take the eye towards the walls of the *Alhambra*, extending downhill. Some historians claim that this was where the primitive *Ilbyr* was located, later known as *Iliberis*, after the Romans took it from the Carthaginians.

Albaicín

This district is a splendid *mirador* over the fertile plain watered by the rivers Darro and Genil. Also from here, superb views can be seen of the white peaks of *Sierra Nevada*.

increasingly more evident. The situation got even worse during the reign of Muley-Hacén, who ruled between 1464 and 1482. The sovereign made the mistake of harassing frontier villages to the detriment of the interests of merchants and artisans. But an even greater mistake was made, which the ambitions of his family made even worse. Muley-Hacén fell in love with a Christian, Isabel de Solís, whom he kept in the tower known today as the *Torre de la Cautiva* ("The Captive's Tower"), near the *Puerta del Arrabal*. Muley-Hacén repudiated the Sultana Aisa al-Hurra and married the Christian, who converted to Islam, taking the name of Zoraya. Prince Boabdil, perhaps instigated by his mother, Aisa,

overthrew him and so became the last Muslim king of Granada. Pursued by one of his uncles and the Christians, who took Málaga in 1488 and Almería in 1489, and lay siege to Granada in 1490, Boabdil was finally defeated. After two years of siege, the last Nasrite's situation became unbearable and he was forced to capitulate to the Catholic Monarchs, who entered Granada on 2nd January, 1492.

Where Faith Put an End to the Silk Industry

It is said that "faith moves mountains", but in the case of Granada, it could also be said that it put an end to the city's silk industry. Now under Christian rule, Granada was main-

Chapel
The ceilings of the Chapel reflect the powerful ornamental influence of the Alhambra.

Gardens
The geometrical whiteness of the Albaicín contrasts with the equally geometrical greenness of the Patio de Machuca gardens.

tained by the Catholic Monarchs as an important centre of culture to which Carlos V contributed by building inside the *Alhambra* the circular palace that bears the name of this king.

Six years after the city was taken, Granada found itself divided into two sectors: one Christian and the other Muslim. The latter, located in the *Albaicín*, was made up mainly of rich merchants related to the silk industry. Tensions with the Muslim community reached their height when, after a royal decree was proclaimed forbidding Islam and Arabic, in 1568 a violent uprising occurred in *Las Alpujarras*, as a consequence of which the Muslims were expelled from the district of the *Albaicín*.

Fernando de Válor, leader of the rebellion, proclaimed himself king under the name of Abén Humeya. For four years the Moors resisted the attacks of the Christian armies until Juan de Austria, Felipe II's half-brother, managed to defeat them. The following expulsion of the Moors brought the economic decadence of the old kingdom and the end of the silk industry, and, consequently, the impoverishment of the inhabitants of Granada.

Romantic Days

Whilst faith, on the one hand, fought against the Muslims, it also gave the city a more Christian aspect. During the early days after its conquest, many mosques in the city were demolished or

turned into Christian temples. The Moorish city gradually started to be reshaped. The typical blind alleys were opened up and new buildings erected. New districts were added to the old city, such as *Hospital Real*, *La Virgen*, *La Magdalena* and *San Jerónimo*, whose reticular layouts extended as far as the flat, fertile plain. So, when the 19th century arrived, Granada had a markedly Christian aspect, although its Moorish character could still be felt in its streets, along with the spiritual greatness of a culture that built the *Alhambra*, whose walls covered with verses were witnesses to luxuries and excesses, and tales of court intrigues and love.

Liberals and Absolutists were two irreconcilable parties for a

Alhambra
A characteristic element of Moorish architecture is the use of *mocárabes* as a decorative element on friezes, cornices and capitals.

Royal Chapel
The solid Renaissance façade of this building attached to the Cathedral contrasts with the apparent fragility of Moorish palaces. This way, two different religious and cultural conceptions of the world were expressed.

or ivory pieces following a drawing previously done on paper in an object of fine wood, mahogany, ebony, cedar or walnut, the final result being an item which is a real work of art.

great part of the 19th century. Their differences were the cause of many an injustice, such as the execution of María de Pineda in 1831, accused of embroidering "the flag of liberty". Today a square reminds us of this heroine, on whose life Federico García Lorca, also from Granada, based his unforgettable play, and who would also be a victim of political intolerance.

Artisan Tradition
The main crafts of Granada come from Arab tradition, the most renowned ones being ceramics and marquetry. Today's potters have known how to maintain the prestige of their predecessors, especially those making *fajalauza*, a name which evokes the part of the *Albaicin* where the first Moorish workshops were established. This glazed earthenware is used for making ornamental and everyday items, beautifully decorated with blue, yellow or green vegetable motifs.

Marquetry is an intricate art consisting of inlaying wooden

Festivities in Granada
The religious nature of the war imposed some festivities and determined the solemnity and demonstrations of faith of others. In this way, the 2nd January is celebrated as the *Día de la Toma* ("Day of the Capture"), where there are parades of people dressed in period costumes and other events which commemorate the Catholic Monarchs entering Granada and the end of the War of Reconquest. Unmarried women follow the belief that if

Palace of Carlos V
The ornamental detail of the Palace of Carlos V, which reproduces a Greco-Latin mythological scene, sanctions the ideology of power and the validity of the new order implemented in Al-Andalus at the end of the War of Reconquest.

Carrera del Darro
Beside the river of the same name, stand many buildings with Renaissance façades alongside others of equal beauty, where balconies are adorned with delightful touches of vegetation.

they ring the bell of the *Torre de la Vela* on that day they will be married by the end of the year. Without any doubt, the greatest demonstrations of faith take place during Holy Week, without forgetting the colours, wit and charm of the people of Granada. Solemn processions take place one after the other from Palm Sunday to Easter Saturday.

The most emotive moments, full of religious sentiment, take place on Holy Wednesday, when the *Cristo de los Gitanos* ("The Christ of the Gypsies") procession goes to the *Sacromonte* abbey; on Maundy Thursday, with the *Cristo del Perdón* and *María Santísima de la Aurora* processions which end in *San Miguel del Albaicín*,

and, at midnight, with the *Procesión del Silencio*, which comes out of the Church of San Pedro on *Carrera del Darro*, and on Easter Saturday, when the procession of *Santa María de la Alhambra* comes out of the *Puerta de la Justicia*.

Shortly afterwards, we have the *Fiesta de las Cruces* ("Festivity of the Crosses"), a Christian celebration, which is, nevertheless, linked to an ancient tradition by which the primitive inhabitants of the city celebrated the arrival of Spring. During these days, squares, corners and balconies are decked with pots of flowers, copper vessels, and embroidered silk shawls, as well as beautiful crosses made of flowers, around which people sing, dance and drink until dawn, especially in

the picturesque district of *El Albaicín*.

After this joyful event, comes the festivity of *Corpus Christi*, which begins on a Wednesday of the second fortnight of May or the first week in June. Celebrations commence with *La Pública*, a parade of *gigantes y cabezudos* that goes through the streets of the city headed by *La Tarasca*, a woman riding on a dragon. In contrast to this, the solemn procession of the Monstrance takes place the following day.

Other examples of religious festivities are the patronal ones of *Nuestra Señora de las Angustias*, whose image is carried in procession on the last Sunday of September, and the 1st of February, the festivity of *San*

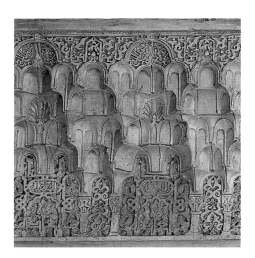

Cecilio, first bishop and Patron Saint of Granada, in the district of *Sacromonte*.

The *Abbey* of *San Cecilio* was a Christian centre of pilgrimage and *Via Crucis*. In time, the gypsies who had come to Granada, established their homes in caves. Nowadays, on the Day of St. Cecil, the City Council gives out beans, *salaíllas* and wine to the people who enjoy themselves singing and dancing.

The Pleasure of Good Food

The inhabitants of Granada love good food and drink. They consequently have a very rich gastronomy, which is a blend of Muslim, Jewish and Christian cooking traditions.

For example, we have the delicious *olla podrida*, a dish of Jewish origin, which, however, also contains pork, veal, lamb, chicken, ham, bacon, black pudding and spicy red sausage along with many vegetables. Other typical dishes are: *olla de San Antón*, a variation of the previous stew, which is eaten on the Day of St. Anton; rich stews of fennel and pork ribs, or of cardoon, green beans and eggs; *guisaíllo cateto*, consisting of veal, lamb and chicken cooked with pinenuts and almonds.

Lamb is a frequently-used meat in dishes such as *albóndigas de cordero* ("lamb meatballs"), lamb with pomegranate and the well-famed *tortilla sacromonte* ("Sacromonte omelette") filled with sheep brains. Equally popular is

hare, in dishes such as *andrajos de liebre* or *arroz liberal*, and chicken in *gallinita granadina*, of Arab origin, which is cooked with spinach, sweet potatoes and bananas.

We cannot forget the various kinds of *gazpachos* of Granada, for example, *gazpacho caliente* ("hot gazpacho"), which includes toast and orange juice, or the popular *salmorejo*, or the other typical starter, *ajo blanco* ("white garlic"), made with ground beans. Typical desserts are, to name just a couple, *compota de membrillo* (stewed quince) or *piononos*.

In short, Granada is a place where history is poetry in writing and the city, a throbbing *joie de vivre*. A real gem in the heart of Andalusia.

The Alhambra

The Red Fortress. The first Nasrite sovereign, Muhammad al-Ahmad, ordered this palace-fortress to be built in 1238 on the top of Sabika, one of the hills overlooking the fertile plain of the Genil, naming it Alqal'a al-Hambra or "The Red Fortress" due to the colour of the stone used. This was the beginning of a profound transformation of the capital of the kingdom of Granada, which later became known as the "Damascus of the West".

Patio de los Leones. Surrounded by the most private apartments of the Royal Palace, this space is a wonderfully harmonious blend of light, colour and the sound of water. Built in the days of Muhammad V, this was the place where the king met with his harem and surrendered to sensual pleasures. Of a rectangular shape, it is crossed by intersecting channels of water with four small fountains at each end and a large dodecagonal fountain, also made of marble, in the middle, supported by twelve lion statues, which, supposedly, represent the twelve bulls of Solomon's temple.

The Alhambra

The Alhambra

Palace of Comares. Through the beautiful arch of the *Cuarto Dorado* ("Golden Room"), the windows of the *Comares Palace* can be seen. *Comares* comes from the Arabic term *qamariyya*, meaning "stained-glass windows", which would have originally been here. This palace, in whose tower we find the largest rooms of the *Alhambra*, such as *Sala de los Embajadores*, was the place where public and government matters were dealt with.

Cuarto Dorado. ("The Golden Room"). The southern side of this chamber, which is in fact a small courtyard, leads onto the *Patio de Machuca or Mexuar*. Its most outstanding feature are the three stilted arches on the ground floor, the middle one higher than the other two, supported by slender columns. These arches open up the space of a narrow and shady gallery of chromatic and geometrical tiles in front of the doors.

The Alhambra

Patio de los Arrayanes. ("The Patio of Myrtles"). This patio marks the central point of the *Palacio de Comares*. Reflected in the still waters of the rectangular pool are the seven splendid stilted arches (of which the middle one is higher than the rest) of the surrounding arcades, together with the greenness of myrtle hedges and the light that illuminates the rooms, such as the *Sala de la Barca*. This was where luxurious official receptions would take place.

The Alhambra

Nasrite Arches. The master builders of the Nasrite kingdom of Granada showed their virtuosity in their building techniques, for example, in their mastery of arches, as well as their ways of decoration, such as their plasterwork, delicately carving the walls with epigraphical and plant motifs, achieving an extremely original emotional and visual impact.

Sala de los Mocárabes. Located between the *Patio de los Arrayanes* and the *Patio de los Leones*, this room is one of the most exquisite examples of Nasrite decorative art. The splendour of this hypostyle chamber is enhanced by the use of fine decorative elements such as *mocárabes*. These were a design of geometrical interlaced prisms carved in plaster, arranged in various ways achieving marvellous results.

Palacio del Partal. Located on the northern side, this palace is one of the oldest buildings in *La Alhambra*. Preceded by beautiful terraced gardens, all that is left of the original construction are a pavilion with arcades and several of the most popular towers, such as *Las Damas*, *Las Infantas* and *La Cautiva*. The latter ("The Captive's Tower") is where Zoraya lived, the Christian for whom Muley-Hacén lost the throne.

The Alhambra

Baths. Nasrite master builders made the baths beautiful tiled chambers where peace prevailed, illuminated by soft zenithal light shining through lanterns in the ceiling. There were rooms of cold, warm and hot water and one called *Sala de las Camas* ("The Room of the Beds"), lavishly decorated, where the harem would gather and listen to the music of blind players.

"The Ambassadors Room" and "The Boat Room". The plasterwork in these rooms is a copy of the refinement of the Nasrite court. The first, whose ceiling represents the seven heavens of Islamic cosmogony, as well as the second were used as government chambers. In the latter there is an inscription which reads, "Contemplate the splendour established herein to impart justice, and, when they can no longer see it, his subjects are filled with sorrow".

Entrance to the Patio del Mexuar. Also known as *Machuca*, a marble-floored, square courtyard with an arcade of nine semicircular arches and a small fountain in the centre. The original floor was of green-coloured glazed bricks. The patio leads into the *Sala del Mexuar*, or the Audience Chamber, which is where the Nasrite sovereign, surrounded by his closest advisers and relatives, would receive his subjects every Monday and Thursday morning, listen to their petitions and impart justice. There are also inscriptions on the walls transcribing Koranic verses, pious phrases or *qasidas*, a poetical form which also passed into Castilian literature. "Let your sight become static and your understanding absorbed", reads one. Ibn-al Yayyab and Ibn al-Jatib are two of the poets whose verses are reflected at the entrance of the *Palacio de Comares*.

The Alhambra

Oratory. The Nasrite dynasty ruled for 250 years under the motto, "*Wa-lâ gâliba illa-Llâh*, meaning "the only victor is Allah", basing their inspiration of the great red fortress on this belief, since, as one poet wrote, "Allah created the Alhambra in case one day he were to leave his heavenly abode". That is why this ensemble of palaces, where light, water and space blend and harmonise like a divine blessing, has spaces and rooms for prayer. Some are peaceful *mirhabs*, where light shines through finely sculpted windows, and others, spacious rooms with windows from where the eye can scan the roofs of the *Albaicín* and the various shades of green of the valley, going as far as the horizon and the mountains of *Sierra Nevada* and even further beyond, where the heart and faith may carry it as far as the Mecca.

The Alhambra

The Generalife

The Architect's Garden.
Muhammad II al-Faqih, Nasrite king of Granada between 1272 and 1301, ordered a summer residence to be built on the *Cerro del Sol* hill. This was the origin of *El Generalife*, the Spanish form of *Yennat al-Arif*, which means "the architect's garden" and probably refers to Paradise. Around 1319, Abu-l-Walid Isma'il applied the ideal described in the Koran to these gardens through an intelligent blend of shade and water.

El patio de las Acequias. ("The Patio of the Water Channels"). Between two beautiful pavilions, flanked by a gallery and court chambers, this patio is an exuberant garden where the water of the rectangular pond, its fountains and flowers represent Nature as a divine blessing. Here, Muhammad II al-Faqih could think only of peace for his kingdom, finally reaching an agreement with the Christian king Alfonso X, "The Wise One".

The Triumph of Water. The splendid arcades at each end of the *Patio de las Acequias* seem to harmonise with the water spurting from the twelve spouts on each side of the rectangular pond. Water springing like the essential liquid of life, evoking perfection in constant movement as an expression and symbol of the Creator. *El Generalife* is understood to be the replica of the gardens of Paradise.

Puerta del Vino. ("The Wine Gate"). This splendid gate is located in front of the *Alcazaba*, the oldest part of the fortress built in the 11th century by the founder of the kingdom, Zawi Ibn Zirí. The double-arched gate was built during the reign of Muhammad II, its name coming from the fact that the residents of the *Alhambra* used to buy tax-free wine beside the gate, in spite of the Koranic prohibition of drinking wine.

The Generalife

Palace of Carlos V

Palace of Carlos V. Pedro Machuca, a Toledan architect and painter formed in Italy, where his master was Michelangelo, started work on this building within the walls of the *Alhambra* in 1520, on the orders of the Christian emperor. In order to do so, various Moorish palaces were demolished. The final result was an original Renaissance-style building which is completely out of tune with the Moorish citadel.

Palace of Carlos V. Though the palace was not completed during the almost thirty years that its architect dedicated to its construction, nor was it ever inhabited by the monarch or his family, this huge, sturdy building synthesises the models of harmony and beauty laid down in Classicistic canons on which Renaissance Humanist ideas were based.

Palace of Carlos V

The Ionic Order. Evoking Greco-Roman architecture as a model of harmony and beauty, symbolising the implementation of a new social and political order that appeared as a result of the rediscovery of Man as an individual.

Inner Courtyard. The Palace of Carlos V was designed on a square ground plan with an original circular courtyard inside. This harmonic hypostyle space is 30 metres in diameter and has two floors, the upper one being open. The first floor is supported by sturdy Tuscan columns and the second by Ionic ones.

*Museo de Bellas Artes. The Madonna by Pedro de Mena.*The Palace of Carlos V houses the *Museum of Fine Arts*, where a splendid *Madonna* by the sculptor from Granada, Pedro de Mena, can be admired, amongst other items.

Museo de Bellas Artes. Pedro de Mena's *Ecce Homo* is a fine example of the intense dramatism given by the 17th –century artist to all his Baroque works.

Staircase. Access to the upper floor of the large Palace of Carlos V is gained by climbing a wide, stately marble staircase which follows the circular contour of the inner part of the building. It is flanked on one ide by a balustrade with carved elements, giving it that simple and sturdy aspect, considered by some to be stylistically obscure.

Museum of Hispano-Moorish Art. Jarrón de las Gacelas ("The Gazelle Vase"). This museum, which is also housed in the *Palace of Carlos V*, has numerous items discovered during the excavations of *La Alhambra* on display, such as different types of tiles, pottery and plasterwork. To be highlighted is the "Gazelle Vase", a fine sample of 16th –century Hispano-Moorish art, painted in fine bluish tones, with plant and animal motifs and a band of Cufic writing.

Palace of
Carlos V

The Lower City

Alcaicería. Lively and intense, Granada is that "silver goblet full of emeralds and rubies" as Yusuf I wrote. At the foot of the hill, the lower city bustled with activity as it still does today throughout the streets of the old Moorish market place. People from Granada called the market place *Alcaicería*, from the Arabic term *al-quaysaiyya* or "House of Caesar", in commemoration of Justinian I, the emperor who granted privileges to trade.

Plaza de Isabel la Católica. This square bearing the name of the Catholic Queen Isabella of Castile is the neuralgic point of the city. Not very far from here was the primitive Jewish settlement of *Garnatha Alyejud*, occupied by the Moors at the beginning of the 11th century after the Berber uprising. After its conquest by the Christians in 1492, the aspect of the city began to change, names were Christianised and the architecture was modified in a Renaissance style. The statue of Isabella I of Castile constantly reminds us of one of the protagonists of such a decisive change.

The Lower City

Monument to Carlos V. The strong white light typical of Granada shines on the figure of the emperor on whose domains "the sun never set". Legend has it that on his arrival in Granada he was told how Boabdil had wept when having to abandon the city and of his mother's reproach. The emperor did not say anything at the time, but, when he entered the Alhambra, is said to have exclaimed, "Woe is him who lost such a thing! How right was the king's mother! If I had been him, I'd have preferred to have been buried in the Alhambra than to live in the Alpujarras without it!" However, he never lived there.

Monument to Carlos V at the University Rectorate. Ferdinand of Aragón and Isabella of Castile, the conquerors of Granada, turned the city into an important centre of culture. Their grandson, Emperor Carlos V, followed their example and founded the University of Granada in 1526. The latter is in the square of the same name, beside the *Church of Santos Justo y Pastor*, which belonged to the Jesuit school, and the *College of San Bartolomé y Santiago*, both temples built during the 16th century.

Casa del Moro ("The Moor's House"). A magnificent vestige of the Moorish town with its sturdy, yet delicate, arches. The thick walls are transformed into a subtle architectural dream, where non-figurative decoration is the result of skilled craftsmen, who organised the elements evoking at all times the greatest of abstractions. The walls of this palace are a real exaltation of ornamental preciosity.

Corral del Carbón. A splendid example of 14th –century Moorish civil architecture, this building was once an inn for caravans of merchants coming to the city and also a corn exchange, where the king's officials controlled trade and collected taxes. After the Christian conquest, in 1531 the building was auctioned and became a warehouse for coal, from which it takes its name. Some time afterwards it was turned into a playhouse and flats.

The Lower City

Royal Chapel and Cathedral

Christian Architecture. After its conquest by the Catholic Monarchs in 1492 and the expulsion of the Moors, Granada was refurbished with sumptuous Christian constructions. Buildings such as the *Royal Chapel* ("*Capilla Real*") and the Cathedral were signs of a new order of construction and the seed of a universalist aspiration supported by the empire that Carlos V would take to its highest point of expression.

Royal Chapel. The royal coat-of-arms forms part of the splendid Plateresque grille made by Bartolomé de Jaén in 1520. The Royal Chapel, begun in 1504 by order of the Catholic Monarchs, was the last flamboyant Gothic style temple built in Spain. Its architect was Enrique Egas, who did not finish it until 1526. For many, this chapel is the symbol of the union between the crowns of Castile and Aragón.

Royal Chapel. Designed by Enrique Egas following the Gothic canon for a Latin cross plan and thickly ribbed vaults. Between the ribs are numerous pinnacles and heraldic symbols, which enhance the grandeur of the temple. In the Sacristy of the Royal Chapel, the Catholic Monarchs' mausoleum, there are some superb paintings by Boticelli, Van der Weyden, Berruguete, Bermejo, Memling, among others, which belonged to Queen Isabella's private collection.

Royal Chapel and Cathedral

Royal Chapel. A splendid wrought-iron grille separates the transept and mausoleum, where the remains of the Catholic Monarchs lie. This magnificent gilded grille, dating from 1520, is the work of Bartolomé de Jaén, and is considered a masterpiece of Spanish Plateresque forged ironwork. This magnificence is in line with that of the Carrara marble tombs sculpted by Domenico Fancelli.

Tomb of Juana la Loca and Felipe el Hermoso. ("Joan the Mad" and "Philip the Handsome"). Also to be found in the crypt of the *Capilla Real* are the marble sarcophagi of Carlos V's parents. They are next to those of the Catholic Monarchs, who wished to be buried in the place where they had achieved their final victory over the Moors. This explains the inscription over the entrance, which reads, "Here lie the monarchs who expelled the Muslim infidels..."

Royal Chapel and Cathedral

Main Retable. This exquisite Manneristic masterpiece forming part of the altar was carved in 1520 by Philippe de Bigarny, master sculptor and painter of French origin. Its Renaissance style, still rather influenced by the Gothic, features the grandeur and dramatism characteristic of the liturgical scenario. Other artists who also took part in the sculptural works of the Royal Chapel were Jacobo Florentino "El Indaco" and Pedro Machuca.

Royal Chapel
and Cathedral

Cathedral. Emblematic monument of Christian art in Granada, it is one of the most important buildings of the Hispanic Renaissance preceding the construction of El Escorial. The façade was carried out in the 17th century by Alonso Cano, with sculptures by Verdiguier, Duque Cornejo and José Risueño.

Cathedral. A masterpiece of the Spanish Renaissance, its monumentality is reflected by its dimensions, 115 m long x 67 m wide, and its enormous height. Designed by Enrique Egas, the works were undertaken by Diego de Siloé, the cathedral consists of five naves with an apsidal chapel, the outside part giving the building that solemn air. Work on the Cathedral, begun by order of the Catholic Monarchs, did not finish until 180 years later.

Cathedral Dome and Columns. The harmonious vault of the dome located above the High Altar has 16th —century stained-glass windows by Theodore of Holland and Juan del Campo. Corinthian columns support the ceilings of the five naves with large semicircular arches, which, owing to their design, become successive vaults.

Royal Chapel and Cathedral

Royal Chapel and Cathedral

Central Nave. The Cathedral was built on the orders of the Catholic Monarchs. Initially designed by Enrique Egas, Diego de Siloé later designed the northern façade and the round *Capilla Mayor*, and Alonso Cano, who is buried in the Cathedral, the main façade. From the central nave there is a splendid perspective of the building. Through the arches supporting the transept, we can perceive the harmonious balance obtained in the great circular funerary chapel, 22 metres in diameter. The seven arches of the vault which lead to the apse aisle are supported by Corinthian columns.

Organ. The sumptuousness of the organ case and pipes, built in the 18th century, is another outstanding feature of Granada Cathedral, which may be considered a masterpiece of the imperial Spain of Carlos V. The complex sound of the organ helps to eliminate limits of space.

The Albaicín

Heart of the Zirí Kingdom. It was in the 11th century, after the Berber revolt against the Caliph of Córdoba, when the Moors came to settle in the old Roman enclave. It was here that the *Zirí* Zawi Ibn Zirí established his court and founded the taifa kingdom of Granada. Only a few remains are left of the primitive *alcazaba* (fortress), which include some parts of the walls surrounding the latter and those in the area near the *Monaita* and *Elvira* Gates, and the *Arco de las Pesas*. According to some, this was the site of the ancient Iberian settlement of *Ilbyr*.

Streets and Doorways. Between the *Carretera del Darro* and the hill of San Miguel, the streets of the *Albaicín* become narrower or are interrupted by Christian-style portals or Moorish-style balconies. And always trees, the fragrance of flowers wafting through the air, the fresh mountain breeze and that peculiar white light shaping everything. At one time, there were up to 30 mosques here and a population of 30,000 inhabitants, who lived in small houses, with water tanks, beautiful patios full of plants and fruit trees, and flat roofs from where they could scan the horizon as far as the impressive fortress of the *Alhambra* on one side and the fertile plains of the River Genil and Sierra Nevada on the other. Even today, the *Albaicín* is still much more than just another typical district of Al-Andalus.

Towers and Rooftops. The eye which scans the rooftops of the houses always ends up encountering the solid, cubic Moorish tower, with its indented battlements standing out against the blue sky, or the domes and bell towers of a Christian temple. The person who once compared Granada with Damascus, surely had been captivated by the oriental air running through streets, alleys and squares of the old Moorish town, the district chosen by the surly *Zirí* aristocrats as their place of residence.

The Albaicín

Flowerpots. The typical Andalusian adornment of pots of flowers and ornamental plants on balconies, rooftops and patios is an Arab tradition. But the picture also has another meaning: that of craftsmanship and the liking for vividly-coloured pottery, especially blue. We must not forget that the *Albaicín* was also a neighbourhood of artisans, above all, potters and ceramists. Granada ceramics are well-famed for their quality and beauty, in particular, that known as *fajalauza*, coming from the name of the street where the best workshops were and where today we can find some of the most popular shops. The most striking features of this pottery are its plant motifs and its blue or green colouring.

The Albaicín

Streets and Origin of the Name El Albaicín. A characteristic of this district are its steep, narrow, winding streets, many denominated *cuesta*, meaning "slope", which altogether make up a real labyrinth. Labyrinthine too, is the name of the district, which today is still a topic of discussion. The most widespread version is that it comes from *albaezan*, Arabic name for the inhabitants of the city of Baeza, who took massive refuge here in 1227, when the Christian armies took over their city. Some believe that it comes from *al-bayyasin*, meaning "falconers", and others from the Arabic word for "on a slope", referring to the hillside on which it stands. Those who defend the latter, link it to the name of *Iliberis*, meaning "settlement on the hillside".

The Albaicín

Mirador de San Nicolás. The highest point of the *Albaicín* is the Mirador de *San Nicolás*. From here one can get a splendid panoramic view of the city and fertile surrounding countryside. For many, there is nothing comparable to watching the sun set over Granada from this vantage point.

Inherited Charm. Artists, intellectuals and gypsies have taken over this neighbourhood where the Moors took refuge after the city had been conquered by the Catholic Monarchs. However, after the 1568 uprising, Christian repression made them flee to the mountains.

The Past. Donkeys still form part of the landscape, just like the man cleaning the window grilles and whitewashing the walls.

Guitar Shop. Music in Granada is like the light illuminating whitewashed walls or the fragrance of orange blossom filling the night air. Granada's guitars are well-famed, along with its lutes, a tradition inherited from Muslim musicians and which hang today in shop windows.

The Albaicín

The Albaicín

Carrera del Darro. Starting at *Plaza Nueva*, this street gradually starts a steep climb following the bank of the River Darro, whose waters run shallow. The noble houses and mansions along the riverbank were once inhabited by *hidalgos* who settled here after the Christian conquest of Granada. This explains the Renaissance-style, aristocratic design of the houses along the street, a style that Carlos V was so fond of.

Bridges Over the Darro. Small stone bridges span the narrow riverbed, on the other side of which the Jewish settlement of *Garnatha Alyejud* was built. Later occupied by Moors, the settlement grew until it ended up joining *Iliberis*, and finally gave its name to the heavily-populated and bustling town that had been born. Not very far from this bridge, is *El Bañuelo*, 11th –century Moorish baths, whose interior is lit by natural light coming through numerous star-shaped lanterns in the ceiling, and which are reflected in the water.

Church of Santa Ana. Situated at the beginning of *Carrera del Darro*, between the squares of *Plaza Nueva* and *Plaza de Santa Ana*, stands this 16th –century Gothic-Mudéjar brick church, with an outstanding and elegant bell tower. Inside, it is worth seeing its fine coffered ceiling, typical of the Moorish artisans who, still faithful to Islam, used traditional Muslim decoration in Christian temples.

The Albaicín

Portal of the Church of Santa Ana. This Gothic-Mudéjar style church standing on the riverside was built in 1548. It also has some Renaissance features as we can see on its main façade. The Plateresque design of this portal contrasts with the typical *Mudéjar* brickwork, representing the harmonious blend of styles existing at the time in a city that had been recently taken over by Christians. It is important to remember that, in spite of the Capitulations of Santa Fe, the Muslims ended up being expelled from Granada.

Along the Banks of the River Darro. The elm trees and lush vegetation along the riverbank mark the natural boundary of the *Albaicín*, the traditional heart of Granada.

The Albaicín

The Albaicín

Islands of Tranquillity. In the maze of alleyways and slopes of the *Albaicín*, the district stretching from the bank of the River Darro and the hill of *San Miguel El Alto*, one can find islands of peace and tranquillity, mansions with wells and patios where old grapevines give shade to ponds, filtering the strong sunlight and allowing the scent of orange blossom to fill the night air. These places are known as *cármenes*, a kind of orchard-garden which the Arabs created in order to enjoy summer solace, surrounded by Nature, and get away from the bustling city full of artisan workshops.

The Albaicín

Carmen de los Mártires. One of the most beautiful mansions in the *Albaicín*. Its garden is full of trees, ponds and statues of mythological gods which blend in with the shades of the vegetation. The poet Luis de Góngora described the *carmen* as an " ornamental blend of water, plants and buildings".

Carmen de los Mártires. Behind wrought-iron grilles or walls, the *carmen* symbolises privacy.

Inspired by the Garden of Eden. The word *carmen* comes from the Arabic term *karm*, meaning "vineyard" and was a place of residence surrounded by orchards and vineyards, where grapevines did not only give fruit, but also shade and privacy. It was at a *carmen* like this where the musician Manuel de Falla composed some of his best works and the poet García Lorca, many of his verses.

Sacromonte. Above the *Albaicín*, is the area of cave-dwellings known as *Sacromonte* ("Holy Mount"), a hill which had primitively been called *Valparaíso* ("Valley of Paradise"). Today inhabited by gypsies, who settled here in the 17th century, the neighbourhood of *Sacromonte* is one of the most typical and original in Granada. Steep, narrow, winding streets and steps mix with caves and galleries, some natural and others dug out.

Towards the 17th century, *Sacromonte* was a Christian *Via Crucis* for those who venerated the relics of St. Cecil. The gypsies came here after it was proven that the Patron Saint of Granada's relics were, in fact, false. Muslims who did not wish to leave their land also found refuge here and, it is said, that *flamenco* was born from the mixture of both cultures.

The Albaicín

La Cartuja

Baroque Exaltation. In 1495, Gonzalo Fernández de Córdoba ("*El Gran Capitán*") paid for a monastery to be built on the outskirts of the city. Works began in 1516, but today only the courtyard corresponds to that period. Its definitive construction took place during the 17th century, resulting in a masterpiece of Spanish Baroque. The *Sanctum Sanctorum* of the church of *La Cartuja* is a fine example of aesthetics serving Christian faith.

La Cartuja Sacristy. Once the Muslim threat had been removed, by defeating them at Cephalonia, as well as the French at Cerignole and Garellano, and the kingdom of Naples had been handed over to the Castilian Crown, the *Gran Capitán* gave up part of his fortune to build a monastery in the city where he had chosen to stay. Architects and artists who took part in the definitive works include Luis de Arévalo, Luis Cabello, Francisco Hurtado, José Risueño and Antonio Palomino. The Sacristy represents the culmination of the Baroque, both in its way of dealing with space and its ornamental lavishness.

Baroque Art. The *Sanctum Sanctorum* dome, carried out by Antonio Palomino, and the Sacristy are identified with the spirit of the Counter Reformation that polarised European Christianism of the age. This spirit can also be observed in the Baroque paintings by Pedro Atanasio Bocanegra and Sánchez Cotán, who was a monk here, and in the sculptures carved by José de Mora.

La Cartuja